Mike Meyers' CompTIA Network+™ Guide to Managing and Troubleshooting Networks Lab Manual

Sixth Edition

(Exam N10-008)

About the Series Editor

Michael Meyers is the industry's leading authority on CompTIA Network+ certification. He is the president and founder of Total Seminars, LLC, a member of CompTIA and a major provider of IT fundamentals, PC and network repair, and computer security training and training materials for thousands of organizations throughout the world.

Mike has written numerous popular textbooks, including the best-selling *Mike Meyers' CompTIA A+™ Guide to Managing and Troubleshooting PCs*, *Mike Meyers' CompTIA Network+ Guide to Managing and Troubleshooting Networks*, and *Mike Meyers' CompTIA Security+™ Certification Guide*.

Mike has attained numerous industry certifications, including CompTIA A+, CompTIA Network+, CompTIA Security+, CompTIA Cybersecurity Analyst (CySA+), and Microsoft Certified Professional.

About the Author

Jonathan S. Weissman is a senior lecturer (Department of Computing Security) at Rochester Institute of Technology, where he was awarded the RIT Outstanding Teaching Award in 2014, the RIT GCCIS Outstanding Educator Award in 2018, and RIT Distinguished Teacher Recognition Program Honors in 2019. Weissman developed and teaches three courses for the edX RITx Cybersecurity MicroMasters program to more than 300,000 students worldwide.

Weissman is also a tenured associate professor and the Networking and Cybersecurity program coordinator (Department of Computing Sciences) at Finger Lakes Community College, where he was awarded the State University of New York Chancellor's Award for Excellence in Teaching in 2021.

All in all, Weissman is the recipient of eleven teaching honors and awards. Weissman began his teaching career in 2001 and has taught more than 50 graduate and undergraduate courses, which include networking, cybersecurity, systems administration, ethical hacking/pentesting, digital forensics, malware reverse engineering, cryptography, programming, scripting, Web design, database design, computer organization and architecture, operating system design, and many more. In addition to his two full-time teaching positions, Weissman teaches part-time at Syracuse University (Department of Electrical Engineering and Computer Science) and at Nazareth College (School of Business and Leadership).

In addition to the fourth and fifth editions of this book, Weissman is the author of *Principles of Computer Security: CompTIA Security+™ and Beyond Lab Manual* and *Mike Meyers' CompTIA Network+ Certification Passport* (fifth, sixth, and seventh editions). He also serves as technical editor for many industry textbooks, including this lab manual's corresponding textbook.

Furthermore, Weissman is a networking and cybersecurity consultant for local businesses and individuals. Weissman regularly appears on TV news and talk radio and in articles as a networking and cybersecurity expert. Additionally, he presents at conferences and in webinars, runs workshops, and appears in podcasts.

Weissman has a master's degree in computer science from Brooklyn College and holds 44 industry certifications, including CCNP Enterprise, Cisco Certified Specialist – Enterprise Core, Cisco Certified Specialist – Enterprise Advanced Infrastructure Implementation, CCNA Security, CCNA, CompTIA Security+, CompTIA Network+, CompTIA A+, CompTIA Linux+, CompTIA Server+, EC-Council Certified Ethical Hacker, EC-Council Computer Hacking Forensic Investigator, and IPv6 Forum Certified Network Engineer (Gold), among many others. He was inducted into the IPv6 Forum's New Internet IPv6 Hall of Fame as an IPv6 Evangelist in 2021.

Follow Jonathan S. Weissman on LinkedIn at https://linkedin.com/in/jonathan-s-weissman-058b649b/, Twitter at https://twitter.com/CSCPROF, and Instagram at https://instagram.com/cscprof/. Subscribe to his YouTube channel at https://youtube.com/Weissman52.

About the Technical Editor

Edward Tetz graduated in 1990 from Saint Lawrence College in Cornwall, Ontario, with a degree in business administration. Since that time, he has spent his career delivering certified technical training for a Microsoft Training Center and working as a service delivery professional in both Halifax, Nova Scotia, and Ottawa, Ontario. Over his career, Ed has supported Apple Macintosh, IBM OS/2, Linux, Novell NetWare, and all Microsoft operating systems from MS-DOS to Windows Server 2019, as well as hardware from most of the major manufacturers. Ed currently works for Microsoft in Customer Success in Ottawa, supporting enterprise and government customers.

When not working with technology, Ed spends time with his wife, Sharon, and his two daughters, Emily and Mackenzie.

Mike Meyers' CompTIA Network+™ Guide to Managing and Troubleshooting Networks Lab Manual

Sixth Edition
(Exam N10-008)

Mike Meyers, Series Editor
Jonathan S. Weissman

New York   Chicago   San Francisco
Athens   London   Madrid   Mexico City
Milan   New Delhi   Singapore   Sydney   Toronto

1 2 3 4 5 6 7 8 9   LOV   25 24 23 22

ISBN   978-1-264-27474-1
MHID   1-264-27474-2

Sponsoring Editor	**Technical Editor**	**Production Supervisor**
Tim Green	Edward Tetz	Thomas Somers
Editorial Supervisor	**Copy Editor**	**Composition**
Janet Walden	Lisa McCoy	KnowledgeWorks Global Ltd.
Project Manager	**Proofreader**	**Illustration**
Tasneem Kauser, KnowledgeWorks Global Ltd.	Rick Camp	KnowledgeWorks Global Ltd.
	Indexer	**Art Director, Cover**
Acquisitions Coordinator	Claire Splan	Jeff Weeks
Emily Walters		

To the three most important people in my life: my beautiful wife, Eva Ann, and our amazing sons, Noah Harrison and Jacob Meir. Thank you for being the best family a guy can have! I love you all so much!

—Jonathan S. Weissman

Contents at a Glance

Contents

Acknowledgments

Many great people worked together to make this book happen.

Our sponsoring editor at McGraw Hill, Tim Green, set the entire book in motion and provided valuable guiding hands. Thanks, Tim!

Our acquisitions coordinator, Emily Walters; our editorial supervisor, Janet Walden; and our project manager at KGL, Tasneem Kauser, helped us keep it all on track and did an outstanding job managing this book through the many phases of development.

At Total Seminars, CEO Dudley Lehmer was a great support, creating an environment for getting projects done. Scott Jernigan performed his usual magic as editor-in-chief. Shannon Murdoch, Dave Rush, and Michael Smyer assisted with photographs, illustrations, and as technical sounding boards.

Our technical editor, Ed Tetz, provided a helpful pair of eyes.

To the copy editor, Lisa McCoy; the proofreader, Rick Camp; and the indexer, Claire Splan—thank you for your excellent work!

Introduction

Many years ago, I fell in love with networking, and I still have the same passion for it today! Routers, switches, cables, packets, and more have always been fascinating to me. Enabling devices to communicate, with the many technologies and components involved, is one of the greatest feelings. With this book, I hope my passion for networking rubs off on you, and you become *connected* to this wonderful world!

Nerds 2.0.1: A Brief History of the Internet is an amazing three-part documentary series from 1998 that details, in a fun way, how networking and the Internet got started, decades earlier. The videos are publicly available via the Internet Archive, a nonprofit digital library with free universal access, at the following links:

- https://archive.org/details/Nerds_2.0.1_-_A_Brief_History_of_the_Internet_-_Part1

- https://archive.org/details/Nerds_2.0.1_-_A_Brief_History_of_the_Internet_-_Part2

- https://archive.org/details/Nerds_2.0.1_-_A_Brief_History_of_the_Internet_-_Part3

Watching those videos could get you excited for what awaits you in this book.

Ethernet and wireless. MAC addresses, IP addresses, and ports. ipconfig and netstat. ping, traceroute, and nslookup. ARP, IPv4, IPv6, ICMP, ICMPv6, TCP, and UDP. DNS, DHCP, HTTP, TLS, SSH, and FTP.VLANs, VPNs, and VMs. Wireshark, firewalls, and nmap. Windows and Linux. By the end of this book, you'll have a solid knowledge, understanding, and hands-on skills with all of these networking items and much more!

The lab exercises in this book can be performed imagining that you're in the field, working as a networking professional. You have to think and act like a professional to become one, so this is the perfect first step!

The lessons and lab exercises map to the CompTIA Network+ exam objectives, which will greatly help your chances of passing the exam. Furthermore, they also will give you the knowledge and hands-on skills to configure, manage, troubleshoot, and secure systems and networks. You'll become more marketable in your job search, and can even use this as a stepping stone for other certifications like the CompTIA Security+ certification.

The chapters have been designed to correspond in name and content to the chapters of the companion *Mike Meyers' CompTIA Network+ Guide to Managing and Troubleshooting Networks, Sixth Edition (Exam N10-008)* textbook (available separately), but can be done without the textbook and in any order.

This lab manual can be used for individual study for the CompTIA Network+ exam or as part of a college course. In fact, I'll be using this book for courses of mine at the multiple colleges where I teach. The chapters are varied in concepts, topics, and lab exercises.

This book includes two icons designed specifically for the use of this book in a college course with assigned lab exercises.

- Some steps require you to take a screenshot to prove that the step was done correctly, and this screenshot icon is a cue that you need to submit a screenshot for the specified steps. In most cases, one screenshot will suffice, but some steps might require more than one screenshot. Include only relevant parts of your screen in the screenshot. Crop the screenshot, if necessary, to remove unnecessary items such as the desktop.

  In Windows 10, you can use the Snip & Sketch utility to capture screenshots and even obfuscate personal information that you don't want shown. I recommend that you use Snip & Sketch on your Windows 10 host system to make screenshots of activities done in your VMs.

  To learn how to use Snip & Sketch, check out the following resources:

  - "Use Snip & Sketch to take a screenshot in Windows 10" (Windows Community video) https://youtu.be/T1p2kgd-Rsc

  - "How to take and annotate screenshots on Windows 10" with Snip & Sketch https://support.microsoft.com/en-us/windows/how-to-take-and-annotate-screenshots-onwindows-10-ca08e124-cc30-2579-3e55-6db63e36fbb9

- Some steps require you to type responses, and this keyboard icon is a cue that you need to submit typed answers for the specified steps.

For each assignment, submit a single document that contains your screenshots and typed answers. Your submission document should start with a header page that contains your name; course prefix, number, and title; and section number at the top. Include the chapter number and title and then the specific Lab Exercise number (for example, Lab Exercise 6.04). For the screenshots and typed answers, clearly label them with the associated step (for example, Step 1a).

Keep in mind that links, Web sites, programs, interfaces, and tools change. If you're seeing something different than what's described or shown in the book, welcome to the world of technology—a constant moving target. In fact, during the course of writing this book, various instances of the aforementioned items changed, ranging from minor to major issues, and I did my best to update the book before publication. By the time you're reading this, other things could have changed, too. Use Google searches and your own common sense to adapt. Feel free to contact me as well!

Many lessons and lab exercises are unique to this book, and they simply can't be found anywhere else. Some were part of my courses already and some are brand new. I'm excited to extend my classroom globally with this book. All chapters and lab exercises have thorough introductions, and they were written the way I present lectures to my students face-to-face.

Teaching is my absolute passion! Not only am I passionate about teaching, I also am extremely passionate about the subjects I teach. I am fortunate to live by the famous proverb, "Choose a job you love, and you will never have to work a day in your life."

My classes, like this book, consist of a mix of lecture and lab. In my opinion, you can't attempt any lab without having fundamental knowledge learned through the lecture. Furthermore, knowledge by itself is not enough. Being able to apply knowledge to hands-on lab scenarios, simulating real-world environments, offers your best chance at success!

As I say at the end of all my courses, "Once a student of mine, always a student of mine." Please get in touch and stay in touch with me. I'd love to hear how this book helped you!

—*Jonathan S. Weissman*

Additional Resources for Teachers

The answer keys to the lab manual activities in this book are provided along with resources for teachers using the *Mike Meyers' CompTIA Network+™ Guide to Managing and Troubleshooting Networks, Sixth Edition (Exam N10-008)* textbook (available separately). Instructors who have adopted these books for a course can access the materials identified next. Contact your McGraw Hill sales representative for details on how to access the materials.

Instructor Materials

A companion Web site provides resources for teachers in a format that follows the organization of the textbook. This site includes the following:

- Answer keys to the Mike Meyers' Lab Manual activities

- Answer keys to the end-of-chapter activities in the textbook

- Instructor's Manual that contains learning objectives, classroom preparation notes, instructor tips, and a lecture outline for each chapter

- Engaging PowerPoint slides on the lecture topics that include full-color artwork from the textbook

- Access to test bank files and software that allows you to generate a wide array of paper- or network-based tests and that feature automatic grading. The test bank includes hundreds of practice questions and a wide variety of question types and difficulty levels, enabling you to customize each test to maximize student progress.

Please contact your McGraw Hill sales representative for details.

Chapter 1
Network Models

Lab Exercises

Congratulations! You have decided to tackle the prestigious CompTIA Network+ certification. Whether you are a seasoned network engineer pursuing certification to further your career or a relative novice building your fundamental skills in networking, you're in the right place. The fact that you've got the *Mike Meyers' CompTIA Network+ Guide to Managing and Troubleshooting Networks* textbook and this Lab Manual in your hands shows that you're serious about earning that certification. That's a smart move!

As discussed in the textbook, the term *networking* describes a vast field of study, far too large for any single certification book, training course, or for that matter, lab manual to cover. However, armed with the textbook and this Lab Manual, you have the tools not only to pass the certification exam but also to exercise the skills you will need to develop and grow as a networking professional. Ask any veteran network tech, and they will tell you that the key to being a good tech is working through the installation, configuration, management, and troubleshooting of cabling, switches, routers, clients, servers, operating systems, protocols, applications, services, and more. That's where this Lab Manual is invaluable. It will take you through hands-on lab exercises with all of these!

Another skill required by network techs is the ability to find information regarding troubleshooting and interoperability, quickly and efficiently. Many times, when you run into problems, it's not necessarily a failure of one specific entity, but a combination of the configuration parameters and interaction between multiple entities. Many of the lab exercises will have you practice the art of researching information as if your job depended on it. You know what? It just might!

To help you grasp these networking concepts, the following scenario is used throughout this Lab Manual. You are a newly hired desktop support specialist in a mid-sized IT consulting firm, JSW. JSW has clients of all sizes scattered all over the country. Client networks can be as small as a single insurance office with 15 computers to a financial institution with many subnets, 1500 computers, and dozens of servers.

You are CompTIA A+ certified, but are immediately encouraged to pursue the CompTIA Network+ certification. Jonathan, your boss, offers to mentor you. He believes that achieving the CompTIA Network+ certification will strengthen your fundamental understanding of networking and will really help when communicating with both customers and coworkers. You respect his advice and dive right in to a CompTIA Network+ training course—this course!

So let's get going!

In 1983, ISO, the International Organization for Standardization (see the Note that follows) developed the Open Systems Interconnection (OSI) model. That's right, the ISO OSI model! This model provided a multiprotocol, prescriptive template for network hardware manufacturers and network software developers to use so that products from different manufacturers and developers would work together. This template, the OSI model, which consists of seven layers, is still in great use today. As you study to pass the CompTIA Network+ exam and work to be a better network tech, you should develop an understanding of the OSI model.

> **→ Note**
>
> ISO is often expanded as the International Standards Organization, but that's not correct. The International Organization for Standardization, founded in London in 1946, wanted to use three official languages. They didn't want different acronyms in different languages (IOS in English, OIN in French, and MOC in Russian), so the founders used ISO as the short form of the organization's name. According to their Web site, ISO is derived from the Greek word *isos*, meaning "equal," and is not an acronym. Standards bodies look to promote equality, which is why this organization chose to be known as ISO. However, this fact has been called into question, since the word "equal" never came up when the organization was founded. Read more at the following links:
>
> - https://fstoppers.com/originals/myths-iso-423056
> - https://www.iso.org/files/live/sites/isoorg/files/about%20ISO/docs/en/Friendship_among_equals.pdf
> - https://www.iso.org/about-us.html

Delivering data across a network is a process both elegant in its simplicity and mind-boggling in its complexity. For one thing, data doesn't move across the network intact. Instead, computers break any kind of data transfer into smaller chunks and then package, address, and send those chunks across the network. This applies to any kind of data, whether you browse the Web; copy files from a file server; or stream music, episodes of shows, or movies from the Internet. Computers on the receiving end reassemble all the pieces upon receipt. Every computer network—regardless of cabling, switches, routers, clients, servers, operating systems, protocols, applications, services, and more—works this way.

To appreciate and define the process using the OSI model, you have to understand a few important things. First, you should understand what kind of hardware and software a computer needs to connect to a network. You also need to know how a computer sends and retrieves data using a network. Finally, you need to understand the rules that govern the structure of networks and how data moves across these networks.

There's no time like the present to get started!

 **30 MINUTES**

Lab Exercise 1.01: Network Hardware and Software

In the OSI model, Layers 1 to 3, the Physical, Data Link, and Network layers, define the operation of network hardware. As you might imagine, hardware devices have related software components. Cables and wireless signals work at Layer 1, the Physical layer (hubs, long obsolete, operated at this layer too). The NIC (network interface card), a transceiver (transmitter and receiver) of network signals, is found at Layer 1 (as well as at Layer 2, to be explained next).

Layer 2, the Data Link layer, is where the physical address comes into play. The various devices that utilize the MAC address, such as NICs (where MAC addresses actually are burned into) and switches, devices that connect nodes of the same network together, function at Layer 2. *Ethernet* defines all Layer 1 and 2 aspects of wired networks, while 802.11 standards define all Layer 1 and 2 aspects of wireless networks.

Layer 3, the Network layer, handles IP addressing and routing. Routers, devices that connect different networks together, operate at Layer 3.

Network connectivity starts with the network connection—the physical link between the PC and the network media. A good network tech can quickly locate and identify the network cabling and network hardware installed on a PC and determine the PC's state of connectivity. The tech should also be able to identify the protocols used by the NIC to communicate on the network, as well as the PC's unique logical address and physical address. You're about to take a look at the steps to accomplish these goals.

Learning Objectives

In this lab exercise, you'll explore the hardware and software components of a networked PC. By the end of this lab exercise, you'll be able to

- Identify a NIC, cables, switches, and routers

- Determine which protocols the NIC uses

- Locate a PC's MAC address and IP address, as well as its default gateway's IP address

- Identify the manufacturer of your NIC

Lab Materials and Setup

The materials you'll need for this lab exercise are

- *Mike Meyers' CompTIA Network+ Guide to Managing and Troubleshooting Networks* textbook

- Windows 10 system with network access

Getting Down to Business

Your company, JSW, has three locations in New York: Rochester, Staten Island, and Brooklyn. All of the offices have multiple subnets with many computers, servers, and printers, all connected via the routers and switches in each office. The offices can communicate with each other and the outside world via the Internet.

When you speak with your boss, Jonathan, he recommends that you start your study by examining the network connections, devices, and addressing of the headquarters in Rochester, New York. He asks if you have learned about the OSI model yet and adds that you might want to define at which layers the various devices, protocols, and addresses belong.

Step 1 Locate the NIC of your computer. This interface will most likely be integrated onto the motherboard. Older machines may have a physical NIC installed in an expansion slot. Alternatively, an external NIC could be inserted into a USB port. What type of NIC does your machine have? At what layer(s) of the OSI model does the NIC operate? Take a picture of the visible part of your NIC.

Step 2 If your NIC is a wired NIC, identify the type of network cable and network connector that plugs into the NIC. At what layer of the OSI model do cables and connectors operate? Take a picture of the cable and connector going into your NIC. Skip this step if you are using a wireless NIC.

Step 3 Identify the network protocols installed for the NIC. On a Windows 10 system, click the Start button or in the search box, type **sharing**, and then select Manage Advanced Sharing Settings. In the title bar of the Advanced Sharing Settings window, click Network And Sharing Center. In the left pane, click Change Adapter Settings. A new Network Connections window will open. In that window, right-click the Ethernet icon (if you're using a wired Ethernet NIC) or Wi-Fi icon (if you're using a wireless NIC), and click the Properties menu item. You should see a window similar to Figure 1-1.

What items are listed in the This Connection Uses The Following Items: section?

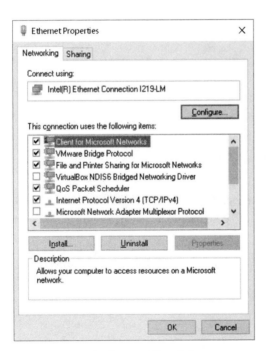

FIGURE 1-1 Windows 10 Local Area
Connections Properties window

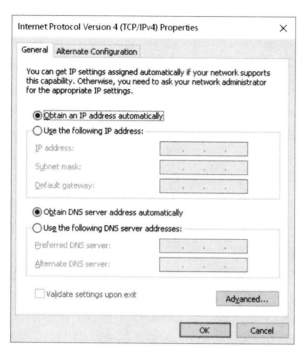

FIGURE 1-2 Windows 10 Internet Protocol Version 4
(TCP/IPv4) Properties window

Step 4   Highlight the Internet Protocol Version 4 (TCP/IPv4) item and click the Properties button.
See Figure 1-2.

How is the NIC configured to receive an address?

Step 5   If the NIC is configured to obtain an IP address automatically (which it most likely is), you will
need to determine the IP address elsewhere. Click the Start button or in the search box, type **cmd,** and
with Command Prompt selected, press the ENTER key. This will bring up a command prompt window.
Type `ipconfig /all` and press ENTER. Find your NIC's MAC address (listed as Physical Address) and
IPv4 address (listed as IPv4 Address). My system's information is shown in Figure 1-3.

```
Command Prompt                                                    —   □   ×

Wireless LAN adapter Wi-Fi:

   Connection-specific DNS Suffix  . :
   Description . . . . . . . . . . . : Intel(R) Dual Band Wireless-AC 8260
   Physical Address. . . . . . . . . : A0-AF-BD-BB-10-52
   DHCP Enabled. . . . . . . . . . . : Yes
   Autoconfiguration Enabled . . . . : Yes
   IPv6 Address. . . . . . . . . . . : 2605:9480:21a:fb70:9015:423d:a79e:9e95(Preferred)
   IPv6 Address. . . . . . . . . . . : fd93:1b7d:4b3d:9539::1(Preferred)
   Temporary IPv6 Address. . . . . . : 2605:9480:21a:fb70:905a:88fd:f051:dd71(Preferred)
   Link-local IPv6 Address . . . . . : fe80::9015:423d:a79e:9e95%26(Preferred)
   IPv4 Address. . . . . . . . . . . : 192.168.0.242(Preferred)
   Subnet Mask . . . . . . . . . . . : 255.255.255.0
   Lease Obtained. . . . . . . . . . : Saturday, September 18, 2021 8:00:45 PM
   Lease Expires . . . . . . . . . . : Sunday, September 19, 2021 12:52:18 AM
   Default Gateway . . . . . . . . . : fe80::1e3b:f3ff:fe78:7aa8%26
                                       192.168.0.1
   DHCP Server . . . . . . . . . . . : 192.168.0.1
   DHCPv6 IAID . . . . . . . . . . . : 681619389
   DHCPv6 Client DUID. . . . . . . . : 00-01-00-01-21-11-F7-C8-54-EE-75-D8-63-89
   DNS Servers . . . . . . . . . . . : 2001:4860:4860::8888
                                       2001:428::1
                                       192.168.0.1
   NetBIOS over Tcpip. . . . . . . . : Enabled
```

FIGURE 1-3 Partial results of running the `ipconfig /all` utility

✖ **Cross-Reference**

IP addressing will be covered fully in Chapter 6.

What layer of the OSI model is a MAC address associated with? What about an IP address?

Step 6   A MAC address consists of 12 hexadecimal digits. The first 6 represent the Organizationally Unique Identifier (OUI), also known as the Device ID, while the last 6 represent the Block ID, which is like a serial number for each NIC made by each vendor, manufacturer, or organization.

A MAC address is also known as a physical address and a hardware address (as well as a burned-in address), since the address is incorporated into the NIC when the NIC is manufactured.

✖ **Cross-Reference**

As you'll learn in Chapter 6, an IP address is also known as a logical address and a software address, in contrast to the terms used for a MAC address.

Each NIC vendor, manufacturer, and organization purchases an OUI from the Institute of Electrical and Electronics Engineers (IEEE), who won't give more than one vendor, manufacturer, or organization the same OUI.

In some cases, however, a NIC vendor, manufacturer, or organization can assign the same Device ID to more than one NIC, but in that case will ship NICs with the same address to various parts of the United States or the world, ensuring that two NICs with the same MAC address don't wind up on the same network.

✖ **Cross-Reference**

As you'll see in Chapter 6, MAC addresses are locally significant just to the network they're on.

Furthermore, a NIC can be configured with a locally administered address by an administrator or user. From the other side, MAC addresses can be spoofed by an attacker.

Enter the MAC address of your NIC into the Wireshark OUI Lookup tool here to see the organization that made your NIC: https://www.wireshark.org/tools/oui-lookup.html.

Step 7   Switches connect devices of the same network together, allowing the nodes on a network to communicate with each other. At what layer of the OSI model does a switch operate? If possible, take a picture of one side of the cable going into your NIC and the other side going into a switch or a wall jack that leads to a switch.

Step 8   Routers connect different networks together, allowing the nodes on a network to communicate with nodes on other networks. At what layer of the OSI model does a router operate? If possible, take a picture of your network's router(s).

In the output for `ipconfig /all`, locate the Default Gateway IP address. That's the IP address assigned to the interface of the router connecting to your LAN. The router will have another IP address on a different network for each interface, connecting it to either another router in your autonomous system or to your ISP (Internet service provider).

30 MINUTES

Lab Exercise 1.02: netstat, ping, and tracert

Three commonly used tools in the world of networking are netstat, ping, and tracert. Now, you'll be introduced to these utilities and gain a foundational understanding of what they are, how they work, and when they're used. All of these tools will return in future chapters for a more in-depth look.

Learning Objectives

In this lab exercise, you'll gain experience with important tools and utilities. By the end of this lab exercise, you'll be able to

- Generate network traffic for analysis
- Use the netstat utility
- Use the ping utility
- Use the tracert utility

Lab Materials and Setup

The materials you'll need for this lab exercise are

- *Mike Meyers' CompTIA Network+ Guide to Managing and Troubleshooting Networks* textbook
- Windows 10 system with network access

Getting Down to Business

You've examined your office and determined that most of the PCs and physical offices are fairly up to date. Most of the devices are connected through 1000Base-T interfaces over Cat 6A UTP cabling through Cisco 1000Base-T switches. Your boss, Jonathan, noticing that you have spent most of your lunch hour inspecting the office connections, asks you to provide a quick explanation of how data moves from one PC to another on the network.

Step 1   Jonathan is impressed with your work so far and introduces you to a utility that enables you to explore the connections between networked computers. To generate some network traffic, he has you launch your browser and access the CompTIA Web site at https://www.comptia.org/. He then has you bring up a command prompt and enter the following command:

```
netstat -a
```

The output should be similar to Figure 1-4.

```
 Command Prompt

C:\Users\jswics>netstat -a

Active Connections

   Proto  Local Address          Foreign Address        State
   TCP    0.0.0.0:21             jweissman:0            LISTENING
   TCP    0.0.0.0:135            jweissman:0            LISTENING
   TCP    0.0.0.0:445            jweissman:0            LISTENING
   TCP    0.0.0.0:5357           jweissman:0            LISTENING
   TCP    0.0.0.0:5985           jweissman:0            LISTENING
   TCP    0.0.0.0:47001          jweissman:0            LISTENING
   TCP    0.0.0.0:49664          jweissman:0            LISTENING
   TCP    0.0.0.0:49665          jweissman:0            LISTENING
   TCP    0.0.0.0:49666          jweissman:0            LISTENING
   TCP    0.0.0.0:49667          jweissman:0            LISTENING
   TCP    0.0.0.0:49673          jweissman:0            LISTENING
   TCP    0.0.0.0:49677          jweissman:0            LISTENING
   TCP    10.80.100.3:5040       jweissman:0            LISTENING
   TCP    10.80.100.3:49670      13.89.185.175:https    ESTABLISHED
   TCP    10.80.100.3:49712      13.89.188.5:https      ESTABLISHED
   TCP    10.80.100.3:49718      65.55.44.109:https     TIME_WAIT
   TCP    127.0.0.1:14147        jweissman:0            LISTENING
   TCP    127.0.0.1:49682        jweissman:4243         SYN_SENT
   TCP    127.0.0.1:49693        jweissman:62522        ESTABLISHED
   TCP    127.0.0.1:62522        jweissman:0            LISTENING
   TCP    127.0.0.1:62522        jweissman:49693        ESTABLISHED
   TCP    [::]:21                jweissman:0            LISTENING
   TCP    [::]:135               jweissman:0            LISTENING
   TCP    [::]:445               jweissman:0            LISTENING
   TCP    [::]:5357              jweissman:0            LISTENING
   TCP    [::]:5985              jweissman:0            LISTENING
   TCP    [::]:47001             jweissman:0            LISTENING
   TCP    [::]:49664             jweissman:0            LISTENING
   TCP    [::]:49665             jweissman:0            LISTENING
   TCP    [::]:49666             jweissman:0            LISTENING
   TCP    [::]:49667             jweissman:0            LISTENING
   TCP    [::]:49673             jweissman:0            LISTENING
   TCP    [::]:49677             jweissman:0            LISTENING
   TCP    [::1]:14147            jweissman:0            LISTENING
   UDP    0.0.0.0:500            *:*
   UDP    0.0.0.0:3702           *:*
   UDP    0.0.0.0:3702           *:*
   UDP    0.0.0.0:4500           *:*
   UDP    0.0.0.0:5050           *:*
   UDP    0.0.0.0:5353           *:*
   UDP    0.0.0.0:5355           *:*
   UDP    0.0.0.0:60633          *:*
```

FIGURE 1-4 Output of running the `netstat -a` command

Step 2   For now, don't worry about all of the information you see, but take notice of your computer name and the number of connections.

With which layer of the OSI model are these connections associated?

Step 3   Notice each connection is represented by a Local Address and Foreign Address. Sockets are endpoints of active communication links between two programs on separate machines, represented by a combination of IP address and port number, as well as the Layer 4 protocol, TCP (Transmission Control Protocol) or UDP (User Datagram Protocol), for both the source and destination. TCP sockets are actual connections between source and destination, whereas UDP sockets are connectionless. The Local Address is on the machine you're using, while the Foreign Address is on the machine you're connected to and communicating with.

Ports are endpoints of communication for specific programs or services and are represented by numbers, which, in turn, represent a way into and out of a program or service running on a machine.

✖ Cross-Reference

You'll learn a lot more about ports in Chapter 8.

For example, if you have an FTP (File Transfer Protocol) server and Web server running on the same machine, they both will be accessible by the same IP address. How does the traffic for the FTP server go to the FTP server and traffic for the Web server go to the Web server? Ports! FTP servers listen for control traffic on and send control traffic out of port 21, while Web servers listen for traffic on and send traffic out of port 80 (HTTP, Hypertext Transfer Protocol; unencrypted) or 443 (TLS, Transport Layer Security; encrypted).

➜ Note

Technically speaking, a server is a service (software) that responds to client service requests. The term server, though, is often used for the machines (hardware) on which server services run.

The NIC represents the way the 1s and 0s enter and exit a machine physically, while programs and services via ports are the way that data enters and exits a machine logically.

Source and destination MAC addresses are found in Layer 2 frames. Source and destination IP addresses are found in Layer 3 packets. Well, ports are one more form of addressing. Source and destination port numbers are found in Layer 4 TCP segments or UDP datagrams.

✖ Cross-Reference

TCP and UDP will be covered more in this chapter and deeper in Chapter 8.

Since you entered `netstat -a`, the output showed all connections and listening ports. Because you didn't add the `-n` option (`netstat -an`, `netstat -na`, `netstat -a -n`, and `netstat -n -a` would all work the same way) for the Foreign Address column, the output used computer names and FQDNs (fully qualified domain names) for IP addresses (the computer name instead of 127.0.0.1, for example) and protocol names for their corresponding port numbers (https instead of 443, for example) when possible.

→ **Note**

HTTPS (Hypertext Transfer Protocol Secure) is HTTP over TLS.

What are some ports that you observe in the netstat output from the Local Address column?

Step 4 Go to a few different Web sites and then execute `netstat -an`. What are some ports that you observe in the netstat output from the Foreign Address column?

Step 5 In the command prompt, execute `ping 8.8.8.8` to send a probe to one of the Google Public DNS servers. The ping command can be followed by either an IP address or an FQDN.

The ping utility uses ICMP (Internet Control Message Protocol), sending ICMP Echo requests, hoping to elicit ICMP Echo replies. By default, Windows sends four ICMP echo requests, so you should see four replies in the output.

✖ **Cross-Reference**

The ping utility is covered more in Chapter 6.

The ping utility is a commonly used test to see if you can communicate with another device. However, it's not perfect. Sometimes ICMP will be filtered by the destination machine itself or a router or firewall before the destination. If you get a "Request Timed Out" message instead of ICMP Echo replies, that doesn't necessarily mean you can't communicate with the destination machine. It could be that just these probes are being blocked for security (a weak form of hindering the ability of attackers to quickly and easily discover devices) or efficiency (taking devices away from what they're normally doing just to say "Yes, I'm here.").

Step 6 In the command prompt, execute `tracert google.com` (use `tracert -4 google.com` to force IPv4, if you're seeing IPv6 being used by default) to send probes to the Google Web server. The `tracert` command can be followed by either an IP address or an FQDN.

> ✖ **Cross-Reference**
>
> **IPv6 is covered in great detail in Chapter 12.**

The tracert (pronounced traceroute, which is also how the command appears in non-Microsoft OSes) utility, also uses ICMP underneath the hood, but very differently than the ping utility.

> ✖ **Cross-Reference**
>
> **The tracert utility is covered more in Chapter 6.**

The ping utility is a Boolean utility. You either get a response or you won't get a response. The tracert utility can be even more helpful. If a ping fails, with tracert, you'll be able to identify where it failed. The tracert will list all routers between you and the destination. The first column in the output lists the hop number. The second, third, and fourth columns represent the time in milliseconds it took to hear back from a router at that particular hop. Notice that there are three attempts sent for each hop. The fifth column shows either an IP address or FQDN and IP address (in square brackets) for each hop. A hop is a router/network that your packets pass through. The first hop in the list will always be your default gateway. The last "hop" in the list is the actual destination, so it isn't really a hop, even though the output makes it appear to be one. You can reach any destination machine in the world in usually 15 hops or less.

Step 7 Find three FQDNs in faraway countries and trace the route to those machines. Search Google for "Japanese ISPs" or something like that, and ping the FQDNs that end with the country codes, like. jp for Japan.

You'll still see that only around 15 hops or so are needed. Furthermore, most of those hops take place close to the destination machine itself. It's like you're taking a long trip, and you get on a highway, which leads to another, and others. The first 300 miles of your trip are the major highways, representing a few of the early steps in the driving directions. The last 50 miles could have many more steps for the local streets to get to your eventual destination. Turn left, turn right, turn right, turn left, and so on.

> ✖ **Cross-Reference**
>
> **Routing is covered more in Chapter 7.**

 **30 MINUTES**

Lab Exercise 1.03: The OSI Model

Given that the OSI model's functions are largely hidden from our eyes, it's sometimes difficult to appreciate how each discrete level performs a necessary step of the data delivery process. Nonetheless, it's important for you to understand just how the OSI model operates. Understanding the OSI model is one of the keys to understanding modern networking technology.

Think of the last time you were in an airport, waiting to board a flight. Finally, you hear, over the airport speakers, "Flight 260, now boarding." You get your boarding pass and carry-on luggage, then get in line. You're not flying. You're getting ready to fly. That's the Application layer. Contrary to how it sounds, applications do not exist at the Application layer (Layer 7). Applications actually exist above the OSI model. At the Application layer are APIs (application programming interfaces), which are shared libraries that allow programs on one machine to communicate with other programs on the same machine, the operating system, and even programs on other machines. Protocols like DNS, DHCP, FTP, and more exist at this layer as well. When you start the ball rolling for networking, API calls are made. You're not sending traffic across networks yet, but you're starting the process. That's just like boarding the flight. You're not flying (networking), but you're getting ready to! The data/payload that has just been formed at the Application layer is now passed to the layer below, the Presentation layer.

Think of the last time you got ready for a job interview. You got your clothes ready, your hair ready, and your face ready. That's the Presentation layer (Layer 6). Compression and decompression used to be done at this layer. Encryption and decryption, too. Formatting as well. Just about all of the old functions at this layer have been offloaded to other parts of the networking story, but this layer remains for backward compatibility. The data/payload generated at this layer is added to what came from the layer above and is sent to the layer below, the Session layer.

→ **Note**

> The terms data and payload are often used interchangeably. Technically speaking though, the payload is the actual transmitted data that is encapsulated inside a protocol of a layer below it. This data is the actual message, but it needs to be encapsulated in another protocol of a layer below it. The protocol at the layer below the payload puts a header in front of the data that serves as metadata for the data itself. As you're about to see, each layer has a protocol data unit (PDU), which is a single unit of information. The PDU for Layers 7, 6, and 5 is simply known as data. At Layer 4, the PDU could be either a segment or datagram. At Layer 3, the PDU is a packet. At Layer 2, the PDU is a frame. At Layer 1, the PDU is simply bits and bytes.

Back when I used dial-up, many years ago, I would be downloading a file, which often took a great amount of time. Suddenly, someone in the house picked up the phone! Oh no! The download stopped. I yelled, "You ruined my download," but in reality, it was the Session layer (Layer 5) that establishes, maintains, manages, and terminates connections between programs on different machines. Data/payload generated at this layer is added to what came from the two layers above and is sent to the layer below, the Transport layer.

At this point, the data/payload faces a pivotal moment. It will be encapsulated in a TCP segment or a UDP datagram at the Transport layer (Layer 4). For applications that require accuracy and integrity, TCP will be chosen. For applications that require speed, UDP will be chosen. If TCP is chosen, the data/payload, which could be quite large at this point, is chopped up into different parts (a process called segmentation) and is placed inside of multiple segments. If UDP is chosen, the data/payload will not be chopped up here, but rather at the Network layer. TCP segments and UDP datagrams vary greatly, but they do share an addressing component in common—ports. A source port and destination port will be added in each. Data/payload generated at this layer is added to what came from the three layers above and is sent to the layer below, the Network layer.

Everything that came from above is placed inside of an IP (Internet Protocol) packet at the Network layer (Layer 3). The IP header contains source IP address and destination IP address fields, among others. Routers operate at this layer. If the packet is too large (usually UDP at this point will be the culprit), the packet is fragmented into multiple packets. Data/payload generated at this layer is added to what came from the four layers above and is sent to the layer below, the Data Link layer.

Everything that came from above is placed inside of a frame—an Ethernet frame on a wired network or an 802.11 frame on a wireless network—at the Data Link layer (Layer 2). The frame contains destination MAC address and source MAC address fields, among others. Switches operate at this layer. NICs partially operate at this layer, since that's the device from where the MAC address comes from. Data/payload generated at this layer is added to what came from the five layers above and is sent to the layer below, the Physical layer.

The frame at this point is transmitted from the NIC out to the network medium, wired or wireless, in the form of bits and bytes, 1s and 0s, at the Physical layer (Layer 1). The traffic moves through switches and out of the local network through a router. After passing through multiple routers, the traffic reaches a switch on the destination's network and finds its way to the destination machine.

✖ Cross-Reference

Routing is covered in Chapter 7 and switching is covered in Chapter 11.

Unlike the other PDUs, frames also have a field that comes after the data/payload, a trailer. When the frame (frames are destroyed and recreated each hop, so this is not the original frame sent by the source if the destination is on a different network) gets to the destination, the destination checks the frame check sequence (FCS), the field in the trailer of the frame, implemented through a cyclic redundancy check (CRC). The purpose of this CRC is to detect accidental changes in the frame and its payload. A numeric value, based on the remainder of polynomial division of the contents, is placed in the trailer. The destination computes the same algorithm. If the computed value doesn't match the value in the trailer, the frame is discarded.

If the computed value matches the value in the trailer field, the frame has integrity. Then, the destination checks the destination MAC address field in the frame. If that address is not a broadcast, a multicast supported by this NIC, or the unicast address of this NIC, the frame is discarded. Otherwise, the frame is removed and the contents are analyzed. The Type field identifies what's inside the frame, which for data frames (not control frames) will either be ARP (Address Resolution Protocol) frames (which exist at Layer 2) or IP (Internet Protocol) packets (which exist at Layer 3). This happens each hop as the packet and its payload repeatably get encapsulated with new frames.

✖ Cross-Reference

ARP is covered greatly in Chapter 6.

➜ Note

The fields in an Ethernet frame header include Destination MAC Address, Source MAC Address, and Type. The header is followed by the actual data/payload. The data/payload is followed by the trailer. 802.11 frames have equivalents of all of these, as well as many other fields.

The destination IP address in the packet is scrutinized the same way. If it passes the check, the packet header is stripped off, and the OS looks at the destination port number in the TCP segment or UDP datagram. The Layer 4 header is stripped off at this point, and the actual data or payload is sent to the destination application or service. Any fragmented packets or segmented segments need to be reassembled before moving up the OSI model.

Learning Objectives

In this lab exercise, you'll examine the layers of the OSI model. By the end of this lab exercise, you'll be able to

- Identify and define the seven layers of the OSI model
- Recognize the functions of each layer in the OSI model

Lab Materials and Setup

The materials you'll need for this lab exercise are

- *Mike Meyers' CompTIA Network+ Guide to Managing and Troubleshooting Networks* textbook

Getting Down to Business

Using the *Mike Meyers' CompTIA Network+ Guide to Managing and Troubleshooting Networks* textbook and the previous lab exercises, work through the following steps to further examine the details of network data delivery using the OSI model.

Step 1 Place the various OSI model layers—Data Link, Application, Physical, Session, Presentation, Network, and Transport—in their proper order from top to bottom:

Layer 7	
Layer 6	
Layer 5	
Layer 4	
Layer 3	
Layer 2	
Layer 1	

✔ **Hint**

Remember that the OSI model is diagrammed with Layer 7 at the top and Layer 1 at the bottom. As noted in the textbook, many students will develop mnemonics to remember the layers and their order.

2a–2g

Step 2 Read the following descriptions and specify the appropriate OSI model layer.

a. At this topmost layer, programs access network services using APIs (application programming interfaces).

b. This layer enables computers to establish, maintain, manage, and terminate connections.

c. This layer includes either TCP segments or UDP datagrams and port numbers.

d. This layer has featured compression and decompression, encryption and decryption, and formatting, but almost all of the old functions at this layer have been offloaded elsewhere.

e. This layer is where frames are created.

f. This layer is responsible for transmitting and receiving signals.

g. This layer adds IP addresses and encapsulates segments or datagrams in packets.

 **60 MINUTES**

Lab Exercise 1.04: OSI Model Presentation

Sometimes the network tech's role as installer and administrator takes a back seat to the tech's role as educator. There is a second benefit to the latter role. One of the best ways to learn the concepts of networking is to teach those concepts to others. This helps you review the concepts and reinforce them in your memory. Jonathan knows that you have just finished learning about the OSI model and asks you to prepare a brief presentation for the other desktop support technicians.

You should plan on preparing enough material for a 15- to 20-minute presentation and leave about 10 minutes for a question-and-answer session. If things keep going this well at work, you may have that new pay grade in conjunction with your CompTIA Network+ certification.

Learning Objectives

In this lab exercise, you'll research the OSI model and develop a presentation to teach the concepts and layers of the OSI model. Finally, you will teach this information to your peers. By the end of this lab exercise, you'll be able to

- Introduce the OSI model

- Define the layers of the OSI model

- Teach the concepts and functions of networking based on the OSI model

- Prepare and deliver a professional presentation

Lab Materials and Setup

The materials you'll need for this lab exercise are

- *Mike Meyers' CompTIA Network+ Guide to Managing and Troubleshooting Networks* textbook

- Microsoft PowerPoint or Google Slides

- Optionally, a projector or large display to deliver the presentation

Getting Down to Business

A good presentation begins with an introduction of what you plan to present. The body of the presentation will cover the actual material—in this case, the OSI model. For a strong finish, the conclusion to the presentation should include a review of what you just presented. The following steps will walk you through setting up an informative presentation on the OSI model.

> **Note**
>
> If you are in an instructor-led class, you may be assigned to a group and instructed to focus on only one or two of the layers for your presentation. Given this situation, work with your team members to develop a comprehensive introduction and concise summary review of the entire OSI model. You may then spend the remaining time developing the details of your assigned layers.

Step 1   Using the textbook and prior lab exercises, review the OSI model.

Step 2   Using Microsoft PowerPoint or Google Slides, begin your presentation by developing an outline of the number of slides and subject of each slide. Two slides per layer is fine, so plan on your presentation being around 16 to 18 slides, including an introduction and conclusion.

Step 3   Develop an introduction based on the overview of the OSI model.

Step 4   For each of the layers, include details on the slides regarding the function, protocols, addressing, and, where applicable, the hardware associated with the layer. Building the model from either the bottom up or the top down is acceptable as long as you remain consistent. You may want to integrate a block diagram of the model as it unfolds.

Step 5   Conclude the presentation with a summary review of the OSI model.

Step 6   Deliver the presentation to an audience of your peers.

 **60 MINUTES**

Lab Exercise 1.05: Networking (in Another Sense) and Staying Current with Industry

As we put a wrap on Chapter 1, I'd like to invite you to follow me on social media:

- **LinkedIn**   https://www.linkedin.com/in/jonathan-s-weissman-058b649b/

- **Twitter**   https://twitter.com/CSCPROF

- **Instagram**   https://www.instagram.com/cscprof/

You can also subscribe to my YouTube channel: https://www.youtube.com/user/Weissman52

Here's my Amazon Author Page: https://amazon.com/author/jonathansweissman

I respond to every single message, so feel free to contact me about this book, networking, or anything else.

In my opinion, creating and maintaining a LinkedIn profile is one of the best decisions you can make, because it will bring numerous benefits to your career.

Learning Objectives

In this lab exercise, you'll explore reasons for creating a LinkedIn profile and becoming an active member on that platform. By the end of this lab exercise, you'll be able to

- Understand why LinkedIn is important for all professionals, especially networking professionals

- Publish your own professional profile on LinkedIn

- Actively use LinkedIn to both give and get professional benefits

Lab Materials and Setup

The materials you'll need for this lab exercise are

- A Web browser with an Internet connection

Getting Down to Business

On LinkedIn, you can

- Meet and network with professionals in any industry, sector, or field

- Find someone who can be a mentor to you

- Serve as a mentor to others

- Get discovered by hiring managers and recruiters

- Stay in contact with other professionals and share career milestones

- Brand and promote yourself with a profile that professionals will see

- Get validated by professionals in terms of your knowledge and expertise

- Share your creative content and use it as a way to connect with others

- View content from others and use it as a way to connect to them

- Learn about companies, track companies for future job opportunities, and engage with companies

But the biggest reason, in my opinion, to join LinkedIn is to

- Stay current with events and happenings in your industry, sector, or field

1a–1c

Step 1   Most days I post dozens of articles on technology, networking, systems administration, cybersecurity, hacking, pentesting, forensics, malware, cryptography, programming, and more. Reading, posting, and discussing these articles on LinkedIn with fellow professionals and students (I have over 30,000 connections) are some of the many ways I stay up to date on everything.

a.   Follow me on LinkedIn (see Figure 1-5), and join in on the fun! https://linkedin.com/in/jonathan-s-weissman-058b649b/

b.   Read the latest article I posted on LinkedIn.

c.   Reply to my post with your thoughts on the article.

If someone reacts to, comments on, or shares your posts, their connections (two-way relationships) and followers (those who see your posts, articles, and shares) will see it—and you! When you react to or comment on my posts, my connections and followers will see you! These are great ways to grow your own network.

→ **Note**

When you are connected to someone, you are following them and they are following you by default.

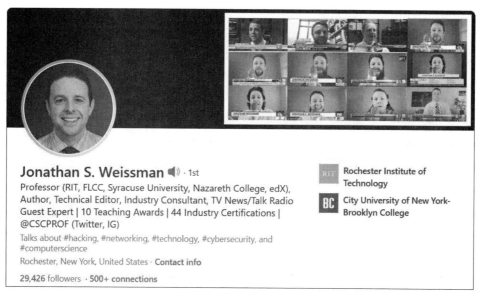

FIGURE 1-5 Jonathan S. Weissman on LinkedIn

Certifications are another way that I stay current. I stress the importance of industry certifications to my students. In that same vein, I model myself for them. Having achieved 44 high-level industry certifications, I am never *not* studying for a certification exam. The first thing I do upon earning a new certification is pick my next target. This shows my students that the learning process never ends, and, especially in this industry, if you stand still in terms of your knowledge or skills for even a short amount of time, you could be obsolete and undesirable rather quickly. By studying for the CompTIA Network+ certification, you're following me on that path as well!

→ **Note**

> **Other ways I stay current include consulting, appearing on TV news and talk radio as a networking/cybersecurity expert, writing and being quoted in articles and blogs, presenting at conferences and webinars, running workshops, appearing in podcasts, tech editing industry books, and writing industry books like this one. Some or all of these could be good future goals for you!**

 2a

 2b

Step 2 A good link to check out is https://www.linkedin.com/learning/learning-linkedin-for-students-2021, which features lots of resources that illustrate why all students should absolutely have a LinkedIn profile.

    a. Find what you determine to be the most valuable resource at the link.

    b. Explain why you think it is the most valuable resource.

Lab Analysis

    1. Jonathan wants to see if you know why the function of the NIC can be said to exist in both the Data Link layer and the Physical layer of the OSI model. How would you explain it to him?

    2. Eva keeps hearing the term "frames" when discussing networking with fellow techs. What is a frame, and what does a frame encapsulate?

    3. Nina wants to know what information can be seen from the output of `ipconfig /all`. What can you tell her?

    4. Jacob would like you to explain how encapsulation works in the OSI model. Can you help him out?

Key Term Quiz

Use the terms in this list to complete the sentences that follow.

datagrams	packets
frames	ping
IP	ports
`ipconfig /all`	router
MAC	segments
`netstat`	switch
NIC	tracert

1. Running the _____ command on a Windows computer will display the MAC and IP addresses.

2. The _____ utility will show you information about endpoints in network communications.

3. The _____ utility shows you the hops between your machine and a destination.

4. The _____ utility allows you to see if your machine can communicate with a destination (the filtering of ICMP notwithstanding).

5. Found at the Data Link layer, _____ contain source and destination _____ addresses.

6. Found at the Network layer, _____ contain source and destination _____ addresses.

7. Found at the Transport layer, _____ and _____ contain source and destination _____.

8. A computer's physical connection to a network is through a _____.

9. A _____ connects devices of the same network together.

10. A _____ connects different networks together.

Chapter 2
Cabling and Topology

Lab Exercises

Most of JSW's clients' users never give a moment's thought to the mechanics of how their particular workstation ties into their corporate network. They just want to know that their data gets where it's supposed to go when they click the Send button in their e-mail client or that they can get to important sites on the Internet. As a network technician, you're the one who has to make sure that your network users' data can get from here to there, and vice versa. You've already learned about the concepts and models that serve as a basis for modern networks. Now it's time to look at the base hardware that makes a network a network.

First, you will explore the network's physical and logical layout—the topology. Next, you'll examine the needs of a new building project and recommend the different types of physical network media, or cabling. Then, you'll explore a number of the governing bodies that handle the management and configuration of the networking standards. You have already met the ISO organization; now you'll learn more about them and also meet and learn more about ANSI, TIA, and the IEEE.

 10 MINUTES

Lab Exercise 2.01: Network Topologies

A network's physical topology defines the physical layout of network cabling, switches, routers, patch panels, and other hardware that carries the network's data.

If you're setting up a network from scratch, start with your topology design. You won't always have this luxury, of course. If you're walking into a situation where a network is already in place, for example, evaluating the topology design is a top priority. Identifying the current network topology is the key to determining the type of network cabling and hardware or wireless communication technology that you'll be using.

Good network techs document everything about their network, listing the location of every network cable (usually called a *cable run* or *drop*) and all wireless access points (WAPs). They make sure to describe the type of cabling used and give details about the associated network hardware (brand and model of each network switch, router, etc.). Unfortunately, not all network techs take the time to create this documentation or update it when they make changes, so you may wind up having to gather this information on your own. This is where your knowledge of the different network topologies, network cabling, and network hardware will pay off.

✖ Cross-Reference

When network techs or, more importantly, professional cable installers plan a new network installation or upgrade existing network installations, they will utilize much more formal techniques to organize and document the install. These techniques include a formal site survey in which the installer will identify and document the location of demarcs (demarcation points), MDFs (main distribution frames), IDFs (intermediate distribution frames), and punchdown blocks. You will further explore these components in Chapter 5 of the *Mike Meyers' CompTIA Network+ Guide to Managing and Troubleshooting Networks* textbook, as well as the lab exercises in Chapter 5 of this Lab Manual.

Learning Objectives

In this lab exercise, you'll examine several network topologies. By the end of this lab exercise, you'll be able to

- Identify and describe different topologies
- Identify the advantages and disadvantages of the topologies

Lab Materials and Setup

The materials you'll need for this lab exercise are

- *Mike Meyers' CompTIA Network+ Guide to Managing and Troubleshooting Networks* textbook
- Internet access

Getting Down to Business

You are studying network topologies at the end of the day, when your boss, Jonathan, stops by. You explain to him that you have a handle on the obsolete network topologies like bus and ring, but you are trying to better understand the current network topologies, star and mesh. Making a little bit of time in his busy schedule, Jonathan offers to help.

✖ Cross-Reference

To review the various network topologies, refer to the "Network Topologies" section of Chapter 2 of the *Mike Meyers' CompTIA Network+ Guide to Managing and Troubleshooting Networks* textbook.

Step 1   Jonathan recommends that you take a look at the network installation in your own office. You begin by examining the computer in your cubicle. A Cat 6A unshielded twisted pair (UTP) cable runs from the back of your computer to a wall jack. It appears to use RJ45 connectors. You then walk down the hall to the wiring closet, observing a mass of cables (also UTP) terminating in a number of patch panels. Patch cables are then connected from the patch panel to gigabit switches that are all connected together in a hierarchy. What physical topology does this depict? Why is this specific physical topology advantageous over older, obsolete physical topologies?

➜ **Note**

> The term RJ45 is actually a misnomer. Read more here: https://www.arrow.com/en/research-and-events/articles/rj45-connectors.

Step 2   Now, Jonathan wants you to look into mesh topologies. What do they involve? How are they different than star topologies? What are the advantages and disadvantages of mesh topologies? Where are they deployed?

Using the following links as a reference, formulate a response in your own words.

- https://en.wikipedia.org/wiki/Mesh_networking
- https://internetofthingsagenda.techtarget.com/definition/mesh-network-topology-mesh-network
- https://support.google.com/wifi/answer/7182746?hl=en
- https://www.linksys.com/us/r/resource-center/whole-home-mesh-wifi/
- https://www.zdnet.com/article/mesh-vs-standard-wi-fi-what-is-best-for-your-home-office/
- https://behrtech.com/blog/mesh-vs-star-topology/
- https://www.geeksforgeeks.org/advantage-and-disadvantage-of-mesh-topology/
- https://www.pcmag.com/picks/the-best-wi-fi-mesh-network-systems

 **30 MINUTES**

Lab Exercise 2.02: Cabling Requirements

One of JSW's larger clients, the Department of Transportation, is building a new regional Department of Motor Vehicles (DMV) complex consisting of two physical buildings. One building will house all of the administrative departments (licensing, title, tags, and registration). The other building, located approximately 900 feet away from the administrative building, will be a large garage-like structure, where the physical inspection of the automobiles will be conducted. Along with designing the overall network infrastructure, JSW has been asked to make recommendations regarding the physical cabling for the two buildings, as well as the connection between the two buildings. You have been invited to work with the team to make these cabling recommendations. Professional installers will be hired, so you may even get to review some of the proposals.

You have two choices when it comes to network cabling: glass-cored fiber-optic cables or good old-fashioned copper wire. UTP copper cable is currently used in most network installations, from small to gigantic. UTP cabling is differentiated by characteristics such as cost, bandwidth, and fire ratings. Fiber-optic cable provides high speed, the ability to travel long distances, and a high degree of security, but is considerably more expensive than UTP cable. To make informed decisions about what kind of network cabling best suits a given network installation, you have to examine the features, functions, and limitations of different network cabling media as applied to various networking applications.

Learning Objectives

In this lab exercise, you'll practice researching the characteristics, typical application, and overall cost of network cables. By the end of this lab exercise, you'll be able to

- Identify the various network cabling options

- Compare the function, speed, and maximum data transfer distance of each cable

- Recommend specific cabling based on application

- Recommend the cabling solutions with the best price/performance ratio

Lab Materials and Setup

The materials you'll need for this lab exercise are

- *Mike Meyers' CompTIA Network+ Guide to Managing and Troubleshooting Networks* textbook

- Internet access

Getting Down to Business

When you're designing a new building plan, one of the major expenses can be the network infrastructure, and a portion of that is the physical cabling. It is imperative that the design implemented meet a price/performance balance along with future-proofing for technological improvements. The cabling installation can be broken down into two distinct applications. Cabling will need to be purchased for the two buildings—the main administrative building and the inspection garage—and the backbone between the two buildings.

  1a–1b

Step 1   You'll start the cabling layout with the administrative building and the inspection garage. The team determines that approximately 11,500 feet of cabling will be required. The cabling will have to meet the strict fire codes for office buildings and should meet the specifications allowing for future technology improvements.

    a.   What grade of cable would you recommend to meet the city's building codes?

    b.   What category cable would you recommend to future-proof this cable installation?

Step 2   Now, launch your browser and navigate to https://www.primuscable.com/. Search for the bulk cost of 1000 feet of the following two categories and grades of cable:

- Category 6A, Riser

- Category 6A, Plenum

Based on your recommendations, what are the final specifications and total cost for the 11,500 feet of internal cabling for the two buildings?

Step 3   The run between the two buildings, as stated previously, is approximately 900 feet. You'll want to select cabling that will handle the distance in one run, require the least amount of maintenance, and provide for future technological improvements. It will probably be buried, so it will be very difficult and expensive to upgrade in the future.

What type of cable would you recommend for the run between the two buildings?

  4a–4d

Step 4   Fire up your browser again and visit https://www.l-com.com/ (That's a lowercase "L," not the digit "1."). Search for bulk cable, and use the information from this site or, alternatively, Google to answer the following questions.

Here are a couple of links to get you started if you just want to see the numbers and not actual cables for sale (as shown in the previous link):

- https://www.flukenetworks.com/knowledge-base/copper-testing/om1-om2-om3-om4-om5-and-os1-os2-fiber

- https://www.foa.org/tech/Linkspec.htm

a. What are the differences between the five levels of Optical Multimode (OM): OM1, OM2, OM3, OM4, and OM5? Which one would you recommend for this project?

b. What's the difference between breakout and distribution cables? Which one would you recommend for this project?

c. List a pro and con for using single-mode fiber for this project instead of multimode fiber.

d. Based on your recommendations, what are the final specifications and total cost of the cabling for the run between the two buildings? Remember, you want the cable to provide for improvements for years to come, so you'll want to select the highest-performance cable you can purchase today.

Step 5   After working with the team on the prior cabling project, Jonathan informs you that a number of the remote offices of the Department of Transportation are scheduled for network upgrades. The offices are currently using Cat 5e UTP, and the office space is roughly 2000 square feet. There are approximately 15 computers and two servers at each office.

Based on this information, he asks what type of network cabling you would recommend for this network upgrade. Give your recommendation and list your reasons.

20 MINUTES

Lab Exercise 2.03: Standards Organizations

One of the amazing aspects of networking in general is that thousands of hardware manufacturers and software developers can create devices and applications that allow computers to communicate with each other, and it all works! Part of the reason that it works is that there are standards organizations, which are established organizations that set the standards for development and manufacturing of these components and devices. These organizations define the international standards so that when you try to access a Web site in Malaysia from a computer in the United States, it works.

You have already encountered the International Organization for Standardization (ISO) in Chapter 1, but other organizations are also valuable to the world of networking, including ones that work with cabling, devices, and technologies like Ethernet.

Learning Objectives

In this lab exercise, you'll explore various organizations that are responsible for the development and management of international standards. By the end of this lab exercise, you'll be able to

- Describe the purpose of selected standards organizations, the organizations that define the standards for networking

- Detail some of the features of the standards organizations

Lab Materials and Setup

The materials you'll need for this lab exercise are

- *Mike Meyers' CompTIA Network+ Guide to Managing and Troubleshooting Networks* textbook

- Internet access

Getting Down to Business

If you've Zoomed with people from all over the world, have you ever thought about the fact that their computer is connected to some switch in some distant country, yet here they are virtually, sitting next to you? Thank goodness for standards!

Step 1   You're going to start with the granddaddy of all the organizations, the International Organization for Standardization (ISO). Launch your Web browser and enter this URL: https://www.iso.org/about-us.html. Take a few notes on who ISO is, where it's located, how long it's been around, and its general purpose.

Step 2   Navigate to this Web site, https://www.ansi.org/about/introduction, to learn about the American National Standards Institute (ANSI), which is both the official U.S. representative of ISO and a major international player. Review the page and capture the same information as you did in Step 1.

Step 3   ANSI has the responsibility of checking the standards and accrediting other groups, such as the Telecommunications Industry Association (TIA). A related organization that was also accredited by ANSI, the Electronics Industries Alliance (EIA), ceased operations on February 28, 2011.

Read about TIA at https://tiaonline.org/about/ and https://tiaonline.org/about/history/ (as well as other pages from the site). What are their credentials?

▦ **4a–4d**

Step 4 Finally, check out the Institute of Electrical and Electronics Engineers (IEEE), often pronounced as "I-triple-E," at https://www.ieee.org/about/index.html.

  a. What pertinent information can you find about the IEEE? Check out this link: https://standards .ieee.org/products-services/regauth/index.html.

  b. What specific item from Chapter 1 is the IEEE in charge of?

  c. What is IEEE 802 (as described here: https://standards.ieee.org/featured/802/index.html)?

  d. Which working group deals with Ethernet, and which working group deals with wireless LANs?

Lab Analysis

  1. Which physical topology is used today, and which ones were used in the past?

  2. When designing a cable installation, what is the primary grade of cabling that should be used for horizontal runs in the ceilings and walls? Why?

  3. What are the most common categories and speeds of UTP cabling?

  4. Why are standards organizations important?

Key Term Quiz

Use the terms in this list to complete the sentences that follow.

ANSI	IEEE
Cat 6	mesh
Cat 6A	star

  1. When you're planning a new local area network infrastructure, the most common type of network cable implemented would be either _____ or _____ cable.

  2. A topology in which nodes connect to a central device is a _____.

  3. A common topology for IoT devices in smaller coverage areas in smart homes is a _____.

  4. The standards organization, _____, is responsible for accrediting other groups.

  5. The standards organization, _____, handles MAC address registration.

Chapter 3
Ethernet Basics

Lab Exercises

Ethernet is the infrastructure used by all wired LANs. For this reason, it's important for network techs to understand Ethernet's functions and features as defined by the IEEE 802.3 standards. These include such things as how Ethernet network nodes build data frames, how they access the network media, and how they send and receive data.

Even though Ethernet speeds have increased exponentially over the years—primarily by increasing the bandwidth of the media (cables) and hardware (NICs and switches)—the core technology remains the same. Network nodes identify each other by MAC address, and data is transferred between machines using Ethernet frames. The basics you explore here still apply to the higher-speed implementations, which you will explore in the next chapter.

 20 MINUTES

Lab Exercise 3.01: IEEE 802.3

In the early 1970s, researchers at Xerox PARC (Palo Alto Research Center) developed a set of standards to facilitate the exchange of data between computers. These standards, known as Ethernet, have gone on to become the dominant industry standard. Over the years, the control of these standards has changed hands a few times. In 1979, Xerox joined forces with Digital Equipment Corporation (DEC) and Intel to develop the original standard, which was published in 1980. Version 2.0, known as Ethernet II, was published in 1982 (http://decnet.ipv7.net/docs/dundas/aa-k759b-tk.pdf). Today, the Institute of Electrical and Electronics Engineers (IEEE) has the responsibility of controlling and updating the Ethernet standards. The IEEE formed a special 802.3 working group to manage these standards. Their IEEE 802.3 formal standardization was published in 1983. Incredibly enough, the Ethernet II frame format, which uses a Type field, is used for data frames today, while the IEEE 802.3 frame format, which replaced the Type field with a Length field, is only used for special types of control traffic.

✖ Cross-Reference

You'll see the Ethernet frame in great detail in Chapter 6.

As a competent network technician, you should have a basic understanding of how Ethernet operates.

Learning Objectives

In this lab exercise, you'll explore Ethernet. By the end of this lab exercise, you'll be able to

- Understand key components of the Ethernet standard

Lab Materials and Setup

The materials you'll need for this lab exercise are

- *Mike Meyers' CompTIA Network+ Guide to Managing and Troubleshooting Networks* textbook
- Internet access

Getting Down to Business

According to their Web site (https://www.ieee802.org/), "The IEEE 802 LAN/MAN Standards Committee develops and maintains networking standards and recommended practices for local, metropolitan, and other area networks, using an open and accredited process, and advocates them on a global basis. The most widely used standards are for Ethernet, Bridging and Virtual Bridged LANs, Wireless LAN, Wireless PAN, Wireless MAN, Wireless Coexistence, Media Independent Handover Services, and Wireless RAN. An individual Working Group provides the focus for each area." The IEEE 802.3 working group specifically manages the standards for Ethernet. At Jonathan's suggestion to learn more about Ethernet, you're going to visit the IEEE Web site, download an official Ethernet standard, and then answer some questions based on the information contained within these documents.

Step 1   Open a browser and navigate over to https://www.ieee802.org. What are the listed IEEE 802 Working Groups and Study Groups?

Step 2   Now, head to https://ieeexplore.ieee.org/document/8457469. At the time of writing (July 2021), 802.3-2018 – IEEE Standard for Ethernet is the current version. By the time you're reading this, you could see the words "Superseded by" followed by a hyperlink to an updated version.

Click the orange PDF button at the top. In the popup that opens, click the Purchase tab. You'll see "Access PDF/HTML at no charge through the IEEE GET Program™." Sign in with your IEEE account to access. Click the Sign In hyperlink, which will bring you to the Sign In tab. Click the Create Account hyperlink. Fill out the required information, put a check in the "I have read and accept IEEE privacy policy" box, and click the blue Create Account button at the bottom. In the "Your account has been created!" popup, click the blue Continue button at the bottom.

You'll be brought back to the original page. Click the orange PDF button again. In the Sign In tab, fill out the required information, put a check in the Accept Terms Of Use checkbox (optionally, remove the check in the "Yes, I would like to receive communications." checkbox), and click the blue View Document button at the bottom right, which will be active when all the required information is provided.

Once again, you'll be brought back to the original page. Third time's a charm! Now, click that orange PDF button for the third time, and you'll finally see the PDF open in the browser. Save the PDF to your hard drive. At the bottom of each page you'll see "Authorized licensed use limited to:" followed by your name and the date and time, with a disclaimer.

➜ **Note**

> **Due to the dynamic nature of the content available on the Internet, Web sites, Web pages, and hyperlinks change often. If one or more of the sites, pages, or links referenced in the steps of any lab exercise in this book are no longer available, with a little help from Google, you should be able to find what you're looking for.**

 3a–3b

Step 3   Within the introduction, scroll down to the paragraphs defining the contents of each section (page 22).

➜ **Note**

> **The page numbers given in this chapter for the PDF are for the 2018 version. If you're using a later version, the page numbers might vary.**

a.   What are some of the key points covered in Section One?

b.   Which section contains general information on 1000 Mb/s (Gigabit) Ethernet?

Step 4   Locate Section One's Clause 3.1.1, "Packet format" (page 118). Note the diagram of the Ethernet frame. List and explain the purpose of each of the fields of an Ethernet frame. A full explanation of the fields follows and goes through page 122.

 **20 MINUTES**

Lab Exercise 3.02: CSMA/CD—Past and Present

Originally, with half-duplex Ethernet, where nodes could transmit and receive—but not at the same time—just a single node could access any given network segment at a time. When two or more PCs tried to send data on the network at the same time, the frames collided, causing the frames to become corrupted.

Therefore, the designers of Ethernet had to devise a method for the network nodes to access the network media without stepping on each other's frames. This network access method was called *carrier sense multiple access/collision detection*, or CSMA/CD. The CSMA part of CSMA/CD defined the method by which multiple network nodes monitored the network media to determine if any other nodes were currently transmitting data. The CD part defined how the network nodes dealt with collisions when they occurred. CSMA/CD went from always used on earlier networks to never used on modern networks.

Learning Objectives

In this lab exercise, you'll review the carrier sense multiple access/collision detection function of Ethernet. By the end of this lab exercise, you'll be able to

- Explain why half-duplex used CSMA/CD

- Explain why full-duplex doesn't use CSMA/CD

Lab Materials and Setup

The materials you'll need for this lab exercise are

- *Mike Meyers' CompTIA Network+ Guide to Managing and Troubleshooting Networks* textbook

- Internet access

Getting Down to Business

Jonathan remembers the first CompTIA Network+ exam he passed many years ago. He tells you that at that time, CSMA/CD was still a thing! Then he asks you to explain why half-duplex communications always used CSMA/CD, while full-duplex communications don't use it at all.

Step 1　In the PDF you downloaded in the previous exercise, read Clause 1.1.2.1 Half duplex operation (page 56). In your own words, explain why half-duplex communications always used CSMA/CD.

Step 2   In the PDF you downloaded in the previous exercise, read Clause 1.1.2.2 Full duplex operation (page 56). In your own words, explain why full-duplex communications never use CSMA/CD.

Lab Exercise 3.03: Origins of Ethernet

Now that you've had a chance to examine actual Ethernet standards, it's time for you to learn how it all began. It's a rather interesting story!

Learning Objectives

In this lab exercise, you'll learn about the origins of Ethernet. By the end of this lab exercise, you'll be able to

- Explain the story of how Ethernet began

Lab Materials and Setup

The materials you'll need for this lab exercise are

- Internet access

Getting Down to Business

Read the following Web pages. You'll answer questions about what you read in this lab exercise.

- https://www.parc.com/about-parc/parc-history/

- https://www.techspot.com/guides/477-xerox-parc-tech-contributions/

- https://www.hpe.com/us/en/insights/articles/the-birth-and-rise-of-ethernet-a-history-1706.html

- https://youtu.be/g5MezxMcRmk (a video linked to in the previous link)

- https://www.arnnet.com.au/slideshow/462393/pictures-20-milestones-ethernet-first-40-years/

- https://personal.utdallas.edu/~zhoud/ee6375-2004/lecture_2_introduction_to_VLSI_design/The%20History%20of%20Ethernet%20-%20Robert%20Metcalfe.htm

- https://blog.telegeography.com/luminiferous-ether-how-ethernet-got-its-name-local-access-pricing-service

- http://www.fundinguniverse.com/company-histories/3com-corporation-history/
- https://ethernethistory.typepad.com/my_weblog/2007/08/genesis-of-3com.html
- https://www.versatek.com/the-non-linear-evolution-of-standards/
- https://ifnetwork.biz/resources/blog/12-important-moments-evolution-ethernet-metro-ethernet

Step 1   In what year was Ethernet invented?

Step 2   At which company was Ethernet invented?

Step 3   Why was that company formed?

Step 4   Which person is credited as the main inventor of Ethernet?

Step 5   What were the motivations for creating Ethernet?

Step 6   What earlier network was used as a template for Ethernet, and how was it fundamentally different?

Step 7   Why was the network called Ethernet?

Step 8   What was the original speed of Ethernet?

Step 9   What was the topology used originally for Ethernet?

Step 10   What type of cable was used for the original Ethernet?

Step 11   Which company did the main creator of Ethernet start to commercialize Ethernet products?

Step 12   What were their first products?

Step 13   Which companies standardized Ethernet?

Step 14   What types of networks and companies that created them competed with Ethernet, but ultimately went away?

Lab Analysis

1. What's the difference between half-duplex and full duplex?
2. What is the basic function of the FCS (frame check sequence) in an Ethernet frame? What algorithm is used for the FCS?
3. Which addresses are found in Ethernet frames?

Key Term Quiz

Use the terms in this list to complete the sentences that follow.

CSMA/CD   half-duplex

full-duplex

1. When devices are operating in _____ mode, _____ is active.
2. Switches and NICs today operate in _____ mode.

Chapter 4

Ethernet Standards

Lab Exercise

Ethernet has gone through a number of evolutionary changes to bring us to where we are today. Modern Ethernet networks are based on the same technologies and standards that you learned about in the previous chapter. The newer versions continue to improve the bandwidth, but they use the same frame types, access methods, and more. Even the connectors, NICs, and switches have relatively the same form factor. Modern Ethernet enables network techs to build larger, faster, more reliable networks!

 **30 MINUTES**

Lab Exercise 4.01: Gigabit Ethernet Standards and NICs

Ethernet networks have evolved over the last four decades, from the early 10 Mbps implementations to today's standards of 100 Mbps, 1 Gbps, 10 Gbps, 40 Gbps, 100 Gbps, 200 Gbps, 400 Gbps, and now 800 Gbps! It's even looking like 1.6 Tbps (terabits per second!) will be standardized between 2023 and 2025. Wired networks utilize either copper wire or fiber-optic cabling to physically transmit the Ethernet frames in the form of 1s and 0s from device to device.

100Base-TX (copper wire) and 100Base-FX (fiber-optic) Ethernet provide 100 Mbps performance. Both technologies have a large installed base. You'll still need to familiarize yourself with their characteristics to provide quality network support for existing installations. However, the current trend when installing or upgrading wired networks is 1000Base-T utilizing Cat 6A UTP cabling and Gigabit Ethernet NICs and switches. Cat 5e was the first standard to support Gigabit Ethernet. In addition, many backbones are implementing either 1000Base-SX multimode fiber or 1000Base-LX single-mode fiber, depending on distance.

At Jonathan's recommendation, you're going to spend some time exploring the characteristics of Gigabit Ethernet and gather some information on Gigabit Ethernet NICs. In the next lab exercise, you will examine Gigabit Ethernet switches.

Learning Objectives

In this lab exercise, you'll examine the standards and technology of 1000Base-T, 1000Base-SX, and 1000Base-LX Ethernet. By the end of this lab exercise, you'll be able to

- Define the 1000Base-T, 1000Base-SX, and 1000Base-LX Ethernet specifications, requirements, and limitations
- Recommend Gigabit Ethernet NICs
- Determine appropriate use of fiber-optic Ethernet based on application

Lab Materials and Setup

The materials you'll need for this lab exercise are

- *Mike Meyers' CompTIA Network+ Guide to Managing and Troubleshooting Networks* textbook
- Internet access

Getting Down to Business

Recalling the cabling scenario from Chapter 2, your client, the Department of Transportation, is building a new regional Department of Motor Vehicles (DMV) complex consisting of two physical buildings. One building will house all of the administrative departments (licensing, title, tags, and registration). The other building, located approximately 900 feet away from the administrative building, will be a large, garage-like structure, where the physical inspection of the automobiles will be conducted. The professional installers have submitted a proposal that has been accepted, outlining the following parameters:

- The proposed cabling for the internal office space of the administrative building is Cat 6A UTP. The administrative network will need to support 75 to 100 devices (computers and printers).
- The proposed cabling for the internal area of the inspection building is Cat 6A UTP. The network in the inspection building will need to support 25 to 40 devices (computers and printers).
- For the backbone between the two buildings, the proposal is single-mode fiber-optic cabling.

Using this general information, follow Steps 1 through 7 to develop an implementation plan for the new site. The design should take advantage of Gigabit Ethernet technology.

Step 1 Utilizing the textbook and online resources, research and document the following information for 1000Base-T Ethernet:

Distance:	
Cabling:	
Connectors:	

Step 2 Utilizing the textbook and online resources, research and document the following information for 1000Base-LX Ethernet:

Distance:	
Cabling:	
Connectors:	

Step 3   Utilizing the textbook and online resources, research and document the following information for 1000Base-SX Ethernet:

Distance:	
Cabling:	
Connectors:	

Step 4   As discussed in the scenario, the new facility will have approximately 100 to 140 network devices (computers and printers). In order to implement Gigabit Ethernet throughout the organization, each device will need a Gigabit Ethernet NIC. Launch your browser and research the current pricing for Gigabit Ethernet NICs. Document your findings.

→ **Note**

Commercial computer vendors provide Gigabit Ethernet NICs on the motherboards of new machines. For the purposes of this lab exercise step, assume that you are purchasing NICs for 100 new computers not coming from a commercial computer vendor. Also, keep in mind that the NICs will be listed as 10/100/1000, which means they are backward compatible to Fast Ethernet (100 Mbps) and Ethernet (10 Mbps) in the event that they connect to a switch port not operating at 1000 Mbps.

Step 5   Ethernet networks using 1000Base-SX and 1000Base-LX fiber-optic hardware and cabling share most of the qualities of 1000Base-T networks, but they are considerably more expensive to implement. What are the circumstances under which 1000Base-SX or 1000Base-LX would be preferable to 1000Base-T?

Step 6   Which technology would you recommend for the 900-foot backbone run between the administrative building and the inspection building?

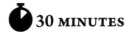 **30 MINUTES**

Lab Exercise 4.02: Gigabit Ethernet Switches

Continuing with the installation of the Department of Transportation regional DMV complex, the professional cable installers will calculate the horizontal runs and cable drops needed from the telecommunications rooms to each node.

Jonathan wants you to research Gigabit Ethernet switching technologies, to provide recommendations regarding make and model, quantity, and specific solutions based on application.

Learning Objectives

In this lab exercise, you'll explore Ethernet switch technology. By the end of this lab exercise, you'll be able to

- Research and recommend Ethernet switches to meet specific applications

- Define solutions to implement a high-speed backbone

- Design a network using Gigabit Ethernet switches

Lab Materials and Setup

The materials you'll need for this lab exercise are

- *Mike Meyers' CompTIA Network+ Guide to Managing and Troubleshooting Networks* textbook

- Internet access

Getting Down to Business

The physical layout of the buildings and proposed location of telecommunications rooms, cubicles, computers, and printers is complete. The cable installers have provided 100 drops in the correct locations throughout the administrative building and 40 drops in the inspection garage. The design of the network will have to meet the following criteria:

- A total of 82 devices will be installed in Phase 1 of the administrative building.

- A total of 30 devices will be installed during Phase 1 of the inspection garage.

- In the administrative building, there are two areas where clusters of computers will outnumber the wall jacks in close physical proximity. It has been recommended that desktop switches be employed in these two areas.

- The cable installers have qualified the single-mode fiber-optic backbone and have terminated a pair of the cables with LC connectors on each end. Each termination is fed into the telecommunications room of both the administrative building and the inspection garage.

In the following steps, you will research and select the switches to meet the design specifications of the campus and define the quantity and location(s) of each switch. You'll also explore some of the modular interface options to connect LAN and WAN backbones.

 1a–1b

Step 1   With the current layout of the facilities and total number of network nodes (devices), you will need to provide anywhere from 100 to 140 network connections throughout the two physical buildings. Each NIC ultimately connects to a port on a switch.

Depending on the application of the switch, you may have to make some decisions, such as whether to install economical desktop switches or enterprise fully managed switches and whether you will provide power to downstream devices through the Ethernet cabling known as Power over Ethernet (PoE). You'll also want to plan on having one switch in each physical building that will provide fiber-optic ports to tie in the backbone between the two buildings.

> **✖ Cross-Reference**
>
> **You will study and perform other exercises with Ethernet switches in Chapter 5 and Chapter 11. If you would like to familiarize yourself with managed and unmanaged switches or multilayer switches, you can jump ahead and read the sections "Virtual LANs" and "Multilayer Switches" in Chapter 11 of the textbook. You do not need detailed understanding of these switching technologies to complete this lab exercise step, but you will want to understand these technologies before taking the CompTIA Network+ Certification Exam.**

Using Google, explore the various Gigabit Ethernet available today, and price out a configuration to meet the needs of this project. You should document the following varieties at various price points:

a.   Economical desktop switches

b.   Managed switches supporting PoE

Step 2   To implement the fiber-optic backbone, you can use almost any mid- to high-end switch that offers some type of small form-factor pluggable (SFP) port. Most manufacturers are offering a modular design with either SFP or gigabit interface converter (GBIC) transceivers to support multiple technologies and connections without replacing the switch. Explore the offerings for 1000Base-LX SFP transceivers to enable these switches for the single-mode fiber-optic backbone connection between the buildings and document some possibilities.

✔ **Hint**

You can learn a lot about switches and switching technology from the manufacturers' product descriptions. Take some time while you are researching to explore the various applications and options presented in the online documentation. You will also find that you may have to visit multiple Web sites of manufacturers and resellers to uncover aspects of specifications, options, and pricing.

Here are some keywords to help you in your search: Gigabit Ethernet switch, Cisco, Juniper, Extreme, D-Link, Netgear, Linksys, Belkin, SFP LC, GBIC, and 1000Base-LX SFP.

 **3a–3c**

Step 3   Now it is time to configure the telecommunications rooms and workgroups to enable the network. Using the information you have gathered in Step 1, describe the switch configuration you will be using to support the regional DMV.

a.   The administrative building will initially implement 82 of the 100 cable drops available throughout the building. Remember that you will need to configure the interface for the fiber-optic connection between the two buildings. What quantity and configuration of switches do you recommend to meet the requirements of the network design?

b.   Two workgroups will be located in areas that will not support the total number of network devices that the workgroups will be using (only one or two drops in these areas). What is your recommendation to accommodate the additional network devices?

c.   The inspection garage will initially implement 30 of the 40 cable drops available throughout the building. Remember that you will need to configure the interface for the fiber-optic connection between the two buildings. What quantity and configuration of switches do you recommend to meet the requirements of the network design?

⏱ **60 MINUTES**

Lab Exercise 4.03: Beyond Gigabit Ethernet

Gigabit Ethernet is the standard for new installs right to the desktop. As you learned in previous lab exercises, many Gigabit Ethernet NICs and switches are available to complement the design of modern organizational networks.

10 Gigabit Ethernet (10 GbE), providing 10 gigabits of data per second over copper or fiber-optic connections, is still comparatively pricey and therefore relegated to high-demand, high-speed applications: high-demand servers, campus backbones, and WAN communications.

Learning Objectives

In this lab exercise, you will examine 10 GbE options for modern network environments. By the end of this lab exercise, you'll be able to

- Describe the 10GBase-T, 10GBase-SR/SW, 10GBase-LR/LW, and 10GBase-ER/EW Ethernet specifications, requirements, and limitations

- Examine 10 GbE NICs

- Determine appropriate switching interfaces to implement 10 GbE backbones

- Explore Ethernet standards that offer speeds beyond 10 Gbps

- Understand the differences between Metro Ethernet and Carrier Ethernet

Lab Materials and Setup

The materials you'll need for this lab exercise are

- *Mike Meyers' CompTIA Network+ Guide to Managing and Troubleshooting Networks* textbook

- Internet access

Getting Down to Business

One of the benefits of the network design the team has implemented for the regional DMV is known as *future-proofing*. Throughout the design and install, the highest-performance cabling has been used (Cat 6A UTP), and switches in the telecommunications room utilize modular SFP interfaces that can be upgraded as well. Running 10 GbE to the desktop is still cost-prohibitive, but implementing 10 GbE for the communication on the high-traffic servers and the backbone between the administrative building and the inspection garage may be feasible.

Jonathan asks you to research 10 GbE solutions and to prepare a presentation of your findings, including interfaces and pricing, for the network design team. Then, he has you see what lies beyond 10 GbE!

 1a–1d

Step 1   Using various resources such as the textbook and the Internet, research and document the following implementations of 10 GbE:

a.   10GBase-T

Cabling:	
Cable Details:	
Connectors:	
Length:	

b. 10GBase-SR/SW

Cabling:	
Cable Details:	
Connectors:	
Length:	

c. 10GBase-LR/LW

Cabling:	
Cable Details:	
Connectors:	
Length:	

d. 10GBase-ER/EW

Cabling:	
Cable Details:	
Connectors:	
Length:	

 2a–2b

Step 2

    a. The high-traffic servers are located in the telecommunications room, so copper or fiber-optic solutions are feasible. Research the current availability of NICs supporting 10 GbE technology. Document some of the makes, models, characteristics, and pricing.

    b. What implementation do you recommend for 10 GbE? Why?

Step 3 Using online manufacturers' and resellers' Web sites, explore the various SFP 10 GbE interfaces available. Document the make, model, characteristics, and pricing as if you are shopping for the modular transceivers for the switches to implement the link between the administrative building and the inspection garage.

→ **Note**

In keeping with the scenario presented, the fiber-optic cabling you choose between the administrative building and the inspection garage may be specified to support 10 Gigabit Ethernet multimode fiber (MMF) (10GBase-SR). However, the total distance recommended for 10GBase-SR is only 26 to 300 meters (about 85 to 984 feet), so the distance of 900 feet could push the specifications for 10 GbE performance. In this case, higher-performance single-mode cable would be the better choice to implement 10 GbE. For the purposes of this lab exercise, provide the results of both 10GBase-SR and 10GBase-LR.

You will also have to be careful when physically implementing 10 GbE transceivers due to the various form factors of both the modular interfaces and the cable interfaces. Currently SFP+, XENPAK, X2, and XFP modules are available, utilizing SC, LC, and various other fiber-optic cable connectors.

 4a–4b

Step 4   Before you start dreaming about a 40, 100, 200, 400, or 800 Gbps NIC for your computer, you need to understand that the standard isn't concerned with local area networks (LANs). When a speed limit from a highway is raised, it has nothing to do with the speed limits on the local streets. Furthermore, certain types of vehicles on the road, like police cars, fire trucks, and ambulances, are authorized to move quicker than the general public. Think of the highway as a wide area network (WAN) and think of special vehicles as servers as you answer the following questions, using Google:

    a.   What was the motivation for 40 Gbps and 100 Gbps Ethernet?

    b.   What is IEEE P802.3ba, and what were its objectives?

Step 5   On December 6, 2017, Terabit Ethernet (Ethernet with speeds over 100 Gbps, including 200 Gigabit Ethernet and 400 Gigabit Ethernet) was standardized. Read about it at https://www.ieee802.org/3/bs/ and https://en.wikipedia.org/wiki/Terabit_Ethernet.

Who are these technologies for? What are some reasons these technologies are needed?

Step 6   On April 6, 2020, a new 800 Gigabit Ethernet standard was released. Read about it at the following links:

- https://ethernettechnologyconsortium.org/press-room/press-releases/25-gigabit-ethernet-consortium-rebrands-to-ethernet-technology-consortium-announces-800-gigabit-ethernet-gbe-specification-152/

- https://www.hpcwire.com/2020/04/07/ethernet-technology-consortium-launches-800-gigabit-ethernet-specification/

- https://screenrant.com/800-gigabit-ethernet-new-announcement-explained/

- https://www.tomshardware.com/news/800-gigabit-ethernet-gbe-spec-standard

Who are these technologies for? What are some reasons these technologies are needed?

Step 7   Using these links, https://ifnetwork.biz/resources/blog/12-important-moments-evolution-ethernet-metro-ethernet and https://business.sparklight.com/the-wire/tech-talk/business-internet/metro-ethernet-vs-carrier-ethernet, what are Metro Ethernet and Carrier Ethernet?

Lab Analysis

1. Dave has decided to install Cat 6A UTP cabling in a small office so that they may upgrade to 10GBase-T in the future without having to "pull" cable again. Are there any concerns you would voice to Dave before he installs the Cat 6A cable?

2. Julia is going to implement Gigabit Ethernet for a small office/home office (SOHO) environment. What kind of network cabling is necessary to implement Gigabit Ethernet?

3. Aaron and Carrie are studying fiber-optic technology. They ask what the major differences are between 10GBase-SR and 10GBase-LR. Can you explain the differences to them?

4. Will understands that high throughput speeds and longer throughput distances are two advantages of fiber-optic cabling over copper cabling. He doesn't understand why the cable installers are recommending the use of fiber-optic cable for the machine shop of a local high school. Can you describe two other advantages that fiber-optic cabling offers over copper wire that would help him understand?

Key Term Quiz

Use the terms in this list to complete the sentences that follow.

1000Base-LX	GBIC (gigabit interface converter)
1000Base-SX	modular transceivers
1000Base-T	SFP (small form-factor pluggable)
800	

1. The latest standard of Ethernet is _____ Gbps.

2. To implement _____, Cat 5e or higher, UTP cabling must be installed, although new installs should use Cat 6A.

3. _____ uses multimode fiber.

4. _____ uses single-mode fiber.

5. Many Gigabit Ethernet switches support _____ to allow support of the ever-increasing speeds. The two dominant forms of these devices are _____ and _____ .

Chapter 5
Installing a Physical Network

Lab Exercises

Now that you're familiar with the major network types, topologies, and technologies that network techs have at their disposal, it's time to dive into the physical aspects of network implementation. These include installing the network media and network hardware that tie your network together, installing the switches that form the central communication point of the physical network, configuring the NICs that connect your network nodes (clients, servers, printers, etc.) to the network, testing network connections, and troubleshooting any ensuing network errors.

As discussed in the textbook and as defined in the CompTIA Network+ Certification Exam Objectives, you are not expected to be as knowledgeable as a professional network designer or cable installer when it comes to the actual implementation of the physical network. However, you will need to be familiar with the concepts. Working with the cable, hardware, devices, installation tools, and troubleshooting tools is a great way to learn the concepts, so this is a good place to start practicing!

One quick note—in this chapter, instead of actual screenshots, submit actual pictures (taken with your phone's camera) of your hands-on work.

 **20 MINUTES**

Lab Exercise 5.01: Structured Network Cabling

One of the proposals that your client received for the installation of the Department of Motor Vehicles (DMV) complex was from an inexperienced firm. The professional cable installers calculated the horizontal runs and cable drops needed from the telecommunications room to each node, the methods to install the cable runs in the inspection garage, the type of UTP cabling to implement, and the outfitting of the telecommunications room. Jonathan asks for your assistance to double-check the proposal.

Learning Objectives

In this lab exercise, you'll examine the principles that lead to a successful structured network cabling installation. By the end of this lab exercise, you'll be able to

- Understand the proper planning issues that go into a network deployment

- Make informed recommendations for a network installation

Lab Materials and Setup

The materials you'll need for this lab exercise are

- *Mike Meyers' CompTIA Network+ Guide to Managing and Troubleshooting Networks* textbook

- Small length of Cat 6A plenum-grade, solid-core cable

- Small length of Cat 6A stranded copper patch cable

Getting Down to Business

When planning a building project these days, almost all designs will consider the design of the network infrastructure. The professional network designers will work hand in hand with the architects to include one or more telecommunications rooms right from the initial design. If it is a new build, as the DMV project is, network cable will be strung along with electrical and telephone cabling during the building process, saving the cable installers from the tedious task of "pulling cable" after the building is in place.

Examine the following steps as if they were components of the proposal from the professional cable installers and network infrastructure design team.

> ✖ **Cross-Reference**
>
> **You may want to review the "Understanding Structured Cabling" section of Chapter 5 in the *Mike Meyers' CompTIA Network+ Guide to Managing and Troubleshooting Networks* textbook.**

Step 1 The administration building will have 100 cable runs. You are examining the network cabling installation proposal that was submitted by the inexperienced professional cable installers. The following is a sample of some of the runs, shortest to longest, that the proposal calls out:

Location	Distance
MDF Telecommunications Room Patch Panel to Network Node A	48 meters (158 feet)
MDF Telecommunications Room Patch Panel to Network Node B	55 meters (181 feet)
MDF Telecommunications Room Patch Panel to Network Node C	60 meters (197 feet)
MDF Telecommunications Room Patch Panel to Network Node D	68 meters (224 feet)
MDF Telecommunications Room Patch Panel to Network Node E	75 meters (247 feet)
MDF Telecommunications Room Patch Panel to Network Node F	84 meters (276 feet)
MDF Telecommunications Room Patch Panel to Network Node G	91 meters (299 feet)
MDF Telecommunications Room Patch Panel to Network Node H	102 meters (335 feet)
MDF Telecommunications Room Patch Panel to Network Node I	113 meters (371 feet)
MDF Telecommunications Room Patch Panel to Network Node J	122 meters (401 feet)
MDF Telecommunications Room Patch Panel to Network Node K	125 meters (411 feet)

The proposal calls for using Cat 6A UTP network cabling. Which, if any, of the network cabling runs are outside the limits for that type of cabling? Does your answer change if you are running 10 GbE equipment? What solutions can you offer to overcome any limit violations?

Step 2   Many of the runs in the inspection garage will be terminated at inspection stations right on the garage floor. These stations will be unfinished areas of the garage with no office walls or cubicles. The walls of this area are concrete. What is the best way to install the network cable drops in this area?

Step 3   As you have learned, the horizontal cable runs will most likely be snaking through walls and ceilings of public offices. Because of this, the proper type of cabling should be used for the horizontal runs. Closely examine a small length of UTP cable recommended for horizontal use. Look for information printed right on the outer insulation of the cable and then strip a length off one end and examine the copper wires. Document some of the features of the cable.

Step 4   There will also be patch cables between the wall jack and the network devices, as well as the patch panels and switches. Closely examine a small length of UTP patch cable. Look for information printed right on the outer insulation of the cable and then strip a length off one end and examine the copper wires. Document some of the features of the cable.

Step 5   List at least four requirements for the telecommunications room(s) that will house rack-mounted patch panels, a stack of switches, and at least one file server.

1 HOUR

Lab Exercise 5.02: Small Network Infrastructure

Installing the cabling that carries data frames from one network node to another (affectionately called "pulling cable") is the most physically demanding task in a network installation and is typically left to professional cable installers. Believe me, once you've got your network cabling installed, you don't want to have to go back into the walls and pull it out again! Tasks include planning the installation, pulling the cabling, connecting network access jacks, and, finally, testing the connections to ensure that your installation is successful.

Though full-blown corporate cable installs are left to the professionals, many network techs have been called upon to wire a room, upgrade a floor, or punch down a new patch panel. You'll want to be familiar with the basic skills of pulling cable through a ceiling, punching down a patch panel, and connecting the wall jack (also known as a *keystone*). This will not only help you in the field; it will also clarify key concepts you will see on the CompTIA Network+ exam.

Learning Objectives

In this lab exercise, you'll practice the art of installing network cabling, hardware, and devices. By the end of this lab exercise, you'll be able to

- Pull a length of cable through a ceiling (or raceway)

- Use a punchdown tool and terminate UTP cabling into a rack-mounted patch panel

- Drop a cable through a wall and terminate the cable drop with an RJ45 keystone

- Mount a wall plate

- Verify the run using a cable tester

Lab Materials and Setup

The materials you'll need for this lab exercise are

- Bulk UTP cabling (Cat 6A)

- Nylon pull rope

- 24- to 48-port rack-mounted patch panel

- RJ45 wall jack keystone (quantity: two to four)

- Low-voltage mounting bracket and faceplate (quantity: two to four)

- Drywall saw

- Wire snips

- 110-punchdown tool

- Cable tester

- Label maker

➜ **Note**

It would really help to have an actual wall and equipment rack to perform this lab exercise. Commercial practice walls are sold just for this purpose. However, over the years I have actually built my own practice wall with a handful of drywall screws, a number of 2 × 4 studs, and a couple of sheets of drywall (see Figure 5-1). It doesn't have to be pretty, just functional. You can even get some cable trays to form a false ceiling for the cables to run over. Worst case, just get the cable, hardware, and devices and complete all of the punchdowns on a lab bench. You should still be able to demonstrate connectivity.

FIGURE 5-1   Do-it-yourself wall

Getting Down to Business

Installing structured network cabling begins with planning. You should physically survey the site and examine the site's floor plan for any hazards that you may not be able to spot visually. Then you can examine the logistics of your planned installation, such as the methods that you will use to deploy and install the horizontal cabling, network outlet drop locations, and so on. You also need to select the most appropriate type of cabling for the job, making sure to comply with any applicable codes and regulations. Then you should document your plans and note any discrepancies during installation. Remember to label your runs and outlets while you're at it. Finally, you need to test your network cabling for continuity and troubleshoot any problems that arise. These are the basic steps that apply to any network cabling installation, from the small office/home office (SOHO) environment with only a few workstations to the large enterprise with thousands of clients.

➜ **Note**

> **Slab-to-slab concrete walls can quickly hamper an installation. Slab-to-slab drywall walls are only an inconvenience. Buildings that have asbestos insulation prevent you from accessing the ceiling space without special procedures and gear, which would pose a major challenge for a cable installation!**

In the following steps, you will "pull cable," drop it through a small practice wall, punch down one end to a rack-mounted patch panel, punch down the other end to an RJ45 keystone, and then fix the RJ45 keystone into a wall-mounted faceplate. You will repeat this a second time, providing two cable drops. Later, in Lab Exercise 5.03, you will install and verify the configuration of a couple of NICs, add a switch, connect the two computers, and then, voilà, you will have a small network! You have a lot of work to do, so let's get going!

FIGURE 5-2 Cutting a hole

Step 1 Start with the placement of the wall jack. Using a pencil and tape measure, choose the location along the wall for the wall jack and mark the wall 18 inches off the floor. Depending on the style of low-voltage mounting bracket you are using, use the drywall saw to cut an appropriate-size hole to mount the bracket. See Figures 5-2 and 5-3 for an example of cutting the drywall and mounting a bracket, respectively.

✖ Cross-Reference

Consult the "Installing Structured Cabling" section of Chapter 5 in the *Mike Meyers' CompTIA Network+ Guide to Managing and Troubleshooting Networks* textbook.

Step 2 Using the tape measure, measure the lateral distance between the proposed cable drop and the telecommunications room. This will be the basis for the length of cable you will need for this run. Remember, you will typically be "pulling" this cable through the drop ceiling and using either cable hangers or trays to keep it suspended off the ceiling tiles. Be sure to include in the total length of cable that you will cut the distance for the height of the ceiling and the cable hangers or trays to the wall outlet and the patch panel.

FIGURE 5-3 Installing a low-voltage mounting bracket

→ Note

Professional cable installers typically pull one or more cables at a time from the telecommunications room through the walls and ceilings to the cable drop location. They leave the cable on the spool as they pull it through the ceiling and walls, rolling out the amount needed plus some slack before snipping the cable from the spool. Since you are most likely using a smaller practice wall, you may not follow this exact technique.

What is the total length of cable that you have calculated?

Step 3   Starting at the telecommunications room (where you have located your equipment rack and patch panel), attach a nylon pull rope to the UTP cable and begin to pull the cable through the cable hangers or cable trays until you reach the cable drop location. Be careful to ease the cable through any snags or twists—you do not want to break the internal wires, rendering the run useless.

At the point of the cable drop, fasten a small weight to the end of the nylon pull rope and, using some finesse, drop the pull rope through the wall to the hole created for the wall jack (see Figure 5-4). The cable should be long enough that you have 6 to 12 inches of spare cable at each end. One end will be terminated to the patch panel; the other will be terminated to the RJ45 keystone.

FIGURE 5-4 Dropping the cable

Step 4   While located at the equipment rack, strip approximately 1 inch of the outer insulation from the UTP cable and slightly untwist the four pairs. Following the labeling or color-code guide on the patch panel, use the 110-punchdown tool to fasten the cables to the block for port 1 of the patch panel (see Figure 5-5).

Step 5   While you're at the wall jack, feed the cable through the low-voltage mounting bracket and fasten the bracket to the wall. Strip approximately 1 inch of the outer insulation from the UTP cable and slightly untwist the four pairs. Following the labeling or color-code guide on the RJ45 keystone, use the 110-punchdown tool to fasten the cables to the block (see Figure 5-6).

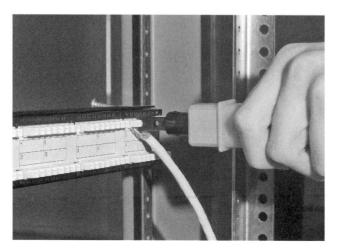

FIGURE 5-5 Punching down the patch panel

→ **Note**

RJ45 keystones come in many styles, incorporating different methods to connect the wires to the pins of the RJ45 jack. Most use a small 110-punchdown block to facilitate this connection. Follow the instructions for the style of RJ45 keystone you are working with.

FIGURE 5-6 Punching down the RJ45 keystone

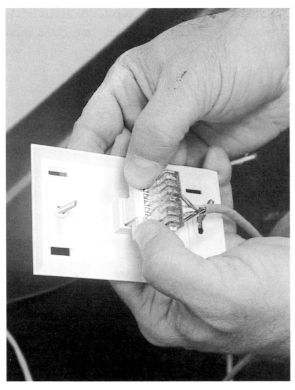

FIGURE 5-7 Fitting the keystone into the faceplate

Step 6 Insert the keystone into the faceplate, and fasten the faceplate to the low-voltage mounting bracket (see Figure 5-7).

Step 7 Verify the cable run using a commercial cable tester.

> **➜ Note**
>
> **Professional cable installers will use much more complex, and expensive, cable certifiers to verify not only connectivity but also attenuation, near-end crosstalk (NEXT), and far-end crosstalk (FEXT) of the cable run. For the purposes of this lab exercise, only the connectivity of the cable run will be verified. If you have access to a high-end cable certifier, by all means, examine the attenuation, NEXT, and FEXT.**

Most testers come with a remote end and a master module. Using a known-good patch cable, connect the master module to port 1 of the patch panel. Using a second known-good patch cable, connect the remote end to the RJ45 connector in the wall jack. Following the directions provided with the cable tester, verify the connectivity of the cable run. Record your result in the following table:

ANSI/TIA-568 Pair	Connection	Result (Good/Bad)
Wire Pair 1	Pin 5 to Pin 5	
	Pin 4 to Pin 4	
Wire Pair 2	Pin 1 to Pin 1	
	Pin 2 to Pin 2	
Wire Pair 3	Pin 3 to Pin 3	
	Pin 6 to Pin 6	
Wire Pair 4	Pin 7 to Pin 7	
	Pin 8 to Pin 8	

Step 8   Don't forget to label both the patch panel and the wall jack (see Figures 5-8 and 5-9). After all of the runs are in place, you will save hours of troubleshooting time with properly labeled patch panels and wall jacks!

FIGURE 5-8 A labeled patch panel

FIGURE 5-9 Properly labeled wall jack

Step 9   Create a second run and drop, following Steps 1 through 8. In Step 4, use the second port of the patch panel.

 30 MINUTES

Lab Exercise 5.03: Switches, NICs, and PCs

In the prior lab exercise, you completed the installation of the physical wiring of the network and verified that you had connectivity from the patch panel to the wall jack. Now you are going to explore and install the devices that allow PCs to use that physical network to communicate: Ethernet switches and network interface cards (NICs).

Switches form the central meeting point for all of the cable runs and provide smooth communication between all of the devices attached to those cable runs. The telecommunications room is the gathering place for patch panels and switches. Each run that is terminated at the patch panel will be "patched" into the switch to provide connectivity to all the other devices on the network.

Your PC's physical link to the network is the NIC. You're probably used to hearing this piece of equipment referred to as a network interface card (NIC), because originally, this device was only available as an add-on peripheral card. With the worldwide application of networking, most notably the Internet, PC manufacturers have adopted the practice of integrating the NIC (electronics and connector) right on the motherboard.

> **→ Note**
>
> Often, an older machine can be upgraded with higher-speed copper, fiber-optic, or wireless adapters. Sometimes USB adapters are used to facilitate connectivity (especially for wireless and Bluetooth). For many years now, laptop manufactures have incorporated wired and wireless interfaces into the onboard electronics. Installing and configuring switches, NICs, and PCs is a task that many network techs do so often it becomes second nature. In later chapters you will study more complex configuration components and practices for both switches and network interfaces. Currently, I want you to focus on the physical aspects of the installation and configuration; that is, connecting and communicating from one PC to another over your physical installation.

Learning Objectives

In this lab exercise, you'll begin by installing and patching the Ethernet switch into the rack. You will then install and/or configure a NIC. This may include an integrated NIC or an add-on component, such as an internal NIC or USB NIC, on your PC. You'll finish up by verifying proper operation through the device and configuration tools included with the operating system and establishing connectivity between two machines. By the end of this lab exercise, you'll be able to

- Install a rack-mount switch and correctly cable it to a patch panel

- Properly install and configure a NIC

- Verify connectivity between two PCs

Lab Materials and Setup

The materials you'll need for this lab exercise are

- Rack-mount Ethernet switch

- Minimum of four Cat 6A straight-through patch cables

- Two PCs with either integrated NICs or expansion card NICs (PCIe)

- Windows 10 operating system installed

- Phillips screwdriver

Getting Down to Business

With the fine art of pulling cable, terminating connections, and verifying continuity of the structured cabling complete, it's time to get the telecommunications room and the work area up to par. This is where the network tech is responsible for the connectivity! The network tech must be able to connect and verify switches, servers, and wide area network devices in the telecommunications room and guarantee that all of the PCs can communicate with the servers and the outside world.

Using the mock wall from the previous exercise, you are now going to install a rack-mount switch and two PCs (with NICs) to complete a small working office network.

Step 1 Starting in the telecommunications room (the equipment rack between your two mock walls), mount the Ethernet switch.

Step 2 Using two of the straight-through patch cables, connect ports 1 and 2 of the patch panel to two of the open ports on the switch.

Step 3 Now moving to the work area (the two PCs you are going to use near the two wall jacks), examine the physical PCs and determine if there are integrated network interfaces. If the systems are equipped with onboard interfaces, you may skip to Step 8. If a NIC needs to be installed in either of the machines, use the following guidelines (Steps 4 through 7) to install the NIC.

Step 4 To install a NIC in a Windows 10 system, turn the PC off. Once the PC is completely powered down, unplug all cables, including the power cable, from the power supply.

→ Note

As recommended by CompTIA A+ certified techs the world over, be sure to follow all proper antistatic procedures when working inside your PC case. Use an antistatic mat and antistatic wrist strap if you have them. If you lack these components, the next best thing is to discharge any static electricity in your body by touching a grounded metal component on the PC case (such as the power supply casing). Before you start poking around inside the PC case, remove any rings, bracelets, watches, or any other items that may snag on exposed components.

Step 5 Place the PC case on an antistatic mat and attach your antistatic wrist strap (aka nerd bracelet), and then remove the PC case cover to expose the interior.

Step 6   Locate an available expansion bus slot for your PCIe NIC. Remove the slot cover, and then insert the NIC into the slot. Be sure to handle the NIC only by its edges, and firmly press the card straight down into the slot. Once the NIC is properly seated in the slot, make sure it is secure by applying whichever locking mechanism the expansion card uses.

Step 7   Replace the PC case cover and reattach all cables to the PC, including the power cable, then start the PC and log on when the desktop appears. Windows 10 has built-in support for many NICs. Plug and play will kick in, detect the card, install Windows 10's built-in drivers, and alert you that the NIC is ready to use. In most cases, the Windows 10–supplied NIC driver works fine, but it's usually a good idea to use the latest driver provided by the NIC manufacturer.

Step 8   Click in the search bar, type **Device Manager**, and click Device Manager to open the Windows Device Manager. Expand the Network Adapters section, and double-click the NIC's icon to open its Properties window. Record the make and model of the NIC. Is the NIC functional? What are the details of the driver that is installed?

Step 9   Once the systems have been verified to have working network interfaces, place each system in proximity of each wall jack. Using the patch cables, connect each machine to the respective wall jack.

✔ **Hint**

At this point in your studies, you are not expected to perform the configuration of the operating system and protocols. The next two steps will go much more smoothly if the computers have been preconfigured for network connectivity. If any of the results seem incorrect, troubleshoot and diagnose the connectivity issues.

Step 10   Power up the Ethernet switch and the two PCs. With a little effort, you should be able to determine if the network has basic connectivity. Are there any visual indicators that the systems are connected to the switch?

Step 11 Sign in to the systems and experiment with Windows Explorer to see if you can see each system from the other. Can you share or copy files from machine to machine? Are there any additional visual clues that the systems are communicating over the network?

 30 MINUTES

Lab Exercise 5.04: Diagnostics and Troubleshooting

Network connectivity issues come in many shapes and sizes. Just like networks themselves, these issues can range from the simple to the complex. In this exercise, you'll walk through some simple diagnostic and troubleshooting steps to ensure that the physical network is in tip-top shape. NIC hardware is fairly foolproof, assuming that it has been installed and configured correctly. A couple of quick tests confirm whether a lack of network connectivity lies with the NIC hardware or somewhere else.

Once installed, network cabling doesn't suffer from a lot of wear and tear—after all, there are no moving parts, and the voltage carried is very low. Nonetheless, network cabling is subject to physical damage and interference, so it's important for you to be able to diagnose and repair this type of failure. Locating breaks in the cable is particularly frustrating, so having a time domain reflectometer (TDR) really comes in handy.

Even well-meaning, organized network techs can have a telecommunications room become a nightmare of snaked, unlabeled patch cables and runs. A toner is invaluable in this situation and will allow the network tech to get organized!

Basic Ethernet switches are fairly robust and normally provide for auto-sensing multispeed communications. It is not uncommon to have legacy devices on a gigabit network operating at 100 Mbps (and maybe even 10 Mbps). It is important that you be able to quickly verify that the switch is indeed communicating with legacy devices.

Learning Objectives

In this lab exercise, you'll go through some basic network connectivity troubleshooting scenarios. By the end of this lab exercise, you'll be able to

- Troubleshoot simple, physical network connectivity issues

Lab Materials and Setup

The materials you'll need for this lab exercise are

- The two networked Windows PCs from the previous exercise

- Length of patch cable that can be cut in half

- 10/100/1000 Ethernet switch

- Time domain reflectometer (TDR)

- Toner unit

- Access to the telecommunications room and patch panel from the previous exercise

Getting Down to Business

The first symptom of a network connectivity issue usually manifests itself as a loud screeching noise! Oddly enough, the noise is not coming from the network hardware or fancy test equipment, but from the frustrated user. Typically, this noise will be accompanied by a vocal error message, such as "I can't get on the Internet!" or "I can't get my e-mail!" "Great, the network is down!" is also pretty common. In most cases, network connectivity problems are simple in nature. Accordingly, you should begin your diagnosis and troubleshooting with simple solutions.

Assume for a moment that one of your network users is unable to access network resources. In the following steps, you'll go through a simple diagnostic and troubleshooting scenario.

✖ **Cross-Reference**

Additional information may be found in the "Testing the Cable Runs," "Link Lights," and "Diagnostics and Repair of Physical Cabling" sections of Chapter 5 in the *Mike Meyers' CompTIA Network+ Guide to Managing and Troubleshooting Networks* textbook.

Step 1   Your first step is to determine whether or not the PC has a network connection and then determine the state of the connection. The obvious place to start is with the physical connection. Locate the PC's NIC. Is the RJ45 connector of the Ethernet cable plugged into the NIC?

If so, check the status lights. What is the result?

Step 2   If you have physical connectivity, your next step is to determine if the operating system recognizes the connection.

On a Windows 10 system, in the search box on the taskbar at the bottom, type **sharing**, and then select Manage Advanced Sharing Settings. In the title bar of the Advanced Sharing Settings window, click Network And Sharing Center. In the left pane, click Change Adapter Settings. A new Network Connections window will open. In that window, double-click the Ethernet icon (if you're using a wired Ethernet NIC) or the Wi-Fi icon (if you're using a wireless NIC).

Fill in the following information:

IPv4 Connectivity:	
IPv6 Connectivity:	
Media State:	
Duration:	
Speed:	

Step 3 An alternative path to the Status window in Windows 10 is as follows:

Click the Start button, select Settings (two up from the bottom on the left), select Network & Internet, and click Change Adapter Options.

Right-click the appropriate icon and select Status to bring up the network connection's status dialog box. Are the reported results for IPv4 Connectivity, IPv6 Connectivity, Media State, Duration, and Speed the same as in the previous step?

Step 4 Disconnect the PC's network cable from the NIC. What do you see from both a hardware and software perspective as a result?

Step 5 Using a loose patch cable, possibly with a partial slice or a missing RJ45 connector, connect the cable to a TDR. What are the results?

Step 6 Using the mock wall with the equipment rack and the patch panel, attach the tone generator unit from a network toner to an active network drop wall outlet. Then go to the patch panel and use the tone probe unit to locate the patch panel cable that corresponds to the network outlet. What are the results?

Step 7 Most gigabit switches support auto-sensing, multispeed performance enabling 10-Mbps, 100-Mbps, and 1000-Mbps devices to connect and communicate through the same switch. Often, these switches will even have status lights (LEDs) that indicate the operating speed of the attached device.

Using a 10/100/1000 Ethernet switch, configure a small network with devices using a mixture of 100Base-T NICs and 1000Base-T NICs. Include a device with a 10Base-T NIC, if one is available, just to see what happens. Document the results of the status lights on the switch. Can all of the devices communicate with each other?

→ **Note**

A simple five-port or eight-port 10/100/1000 Ethernet switch will work fine for this exercise. Different switches may or may not support status indicator lights for multispeed operation, so the only confirmation of the operation of the switch with different speed NICs will be successful communication. You may also need to work with the network configuration of the devices (computers or printers) to implement network communication.

 OPEN

Lab Exercise 5.05: Field Trip: A Visit with the IT Department

You have thus far spent some time studying the physical components of computer networking. Classroom exercises involving topologies, technologies, the OSI model, Ethernet, and devices have strengthened your understanding of these components. Now it is time to go see these components in a real-world environment!

Just about every organization has some collection of information technology, and often, the IT department is more than happy to show off their implementation of the technology to meet their users' needs. If you are attending a CompTIA Network+ course or a college networking course, the facility or the college where you are taking the course is a great place to get a tour of the IT department and the telecommunications room(s). Your instructor should be able to make a few inquiries and set up a visit with the IT department of an organization in your community. If you are self-studying for the exam, see if your own inquiries can get you a tour.

Learning Objectives

In this lab exercise, you'll be going on a field trip! By the end of this lab exercise, you'll be able to

- Explore the real-world implementation of the physical network
- Establish communication with local IT department personnel

Lab Materials and Setup

The materials you'll need for this lab exercise are

- Invitation to tour an organization's facilities and telecommunications room(s)

Getting Down to Business

It is important to establish a rapport with the personnel that you will be spending time with. Obviously, it is not their primary responsibility to be ushering students around through their facilities and discussing their physical network with you. However, you will find that if you are courteous, many network techs enjoy talking about their network infrastructure solutions.

If you are in an instructor-led class, you will most likely be invited to visit a location of the instructor's choosing. This can be very informative, as the instructor usually will have established a rapport with the techs prior to your visit, which means they will probably be very agreeable to entertaining your questions. If you have arranged a tour on your own, likely just for yourself, great job! In either case, plan on asking a bunch of questions!

⌨ 1a–1d

Step 1   When visiting a physical location, it would be beneficial if you could examine a copy of the floor plans. However, with the need for heightened security at every level, viewing the floor plans will probably not be an option. Work through the following scenario even if your answers do not pertain to an actual physical location. The steps will still reinforce your understanding of the physical layout of a network.

The blueprints will offer a visual indication of all of the important areas of the facility, including the main distribution frame (MDF), any intermediate distribution frames (IDFs), the demarc, and all of the cable drops to wall outlets. Study the floor plan and prepare a detailed description of the facility, including the following points:

   a.   Identify and note the approximate location of the MDF.

   b.   Identify the IDF(s). How many are implemented in this facility? What is the approximate location of each compared to the MDF?

   c.   Is the demarc identified in the floor plans? Is it located in the MDF, or is it located in a completely isolated part of the building?

   d.   What is the approximate total number of drops (wall outlets) for this facility? The network administrator may be able to help you with this one, as opposed to your counting all of the cable drops in the floor plan!

⌨ 2a–2f

Step 2   Ask if it is possible to get a tour of the facilities. One area of interest would be the MDF telecommunications room. Most likely this is where the foundation of the network infrastructure has been established. You might use some of the following questions as openers for further discussion about the facilities:

   a.   Are there any special conditions that have been set up in the telecommunications room like air conditioning or electrical services?

   b.   Is most of the equipment (UPSs, switches, patch panels, and servers) rack-mounted? What are the approximate quantities of equipment (racks, patch panels, switches, servers, etc.)?

    c.   Note the labeling technique. Are most of the important components and runs labeled?

    d.   What category of cable is used throughout the facility?

    e.   What are the common speeds of switches and NICs?

    f.   What fiber-optic technologies are implemented in the facility?

Step 3   What complement of test equipment (cable testers, TDRs, cable certifiers, toners, etc.) do the network techs employ to verify the connectivity of the network?

Lab Analysis

1. Garret complains that he cannot get on your corporate network. You discover that he moved his desk and PC to another part of his office, and in doing so forcibly pulled the Cat 6A patch cable out of its wall outlet. A quick visual inspection doesn't reveal any obvious damage to the patch cable. How do you determine if the patch cable is damaged?

2. Michael has been asked to patch in a new install. What specialized equipment will he use to connect the endpoint of a cable run to a patch panel?

3. The cable installers have been working all day and have now completed the internal wiring for 48 wall outlets. Natalie asks if she can use the leftover cabling to create the patch cables for some of the workstations. You explain to Natalie that this would not be a good idea. What do you tell her?

4. Shannon was talking with Jonathan. She asked why you would always defer to professional cable installers to guarantee cable runs and why the higher-bandwidth cabling and connections needed more precise placement and termination when installed. How do you think Jonathan responded to these questions?

5. Maria has upgraded a small 25-node network with cabling and switches to operate at 1000Base-T. She has a few old printers with 100Base-T NICs. She is concerned that they will have to be upgraded as well. What do you recommend?

Key Term Quiz

Use the terms in this list to complete the sentences that follow.

auto-sensing	time domain reflectometer (TDR)
demarc	tone generator
link light	tone probe
multispeed	

1. Once you determine that a connectivity problem is between the patch panel and the wall outlet, you'd use a(n) _____ to pinpoint the exact location of the cable break.

2. Use a(n) _____ and _____ to trace network cabling between a wall outlet and a patch panel.

3. In a facility, the point where responsibility of the physical cabling shifts from the ISP to the organization is known as the _____.

4. Practically all modern Ethernet switches and NICs are _____ and _____.

5. The simplest test of network connectivity is to check the NIC's _____.

Chapter 6

TCP/IP Basics

Lab Exercises

The first four network nodes—the University of California, Los Angeles (UCLA); Stanford Research Institute (SRI); the University of California, Santa Barbara (UCSB); and the University of Utah—were connected to the Advanced Research Projects Agency Network (ARPANET) in 1969. In 1970, with the number of ARPANET nodes and host computers growing, Network Control Program (NCP) was implemented, allowing for connections as well as flow control, forming the middle layers of the ARPANET computers' protocol stack.

NCP wasn't able to scale with the growth of more and more network traffic, however. Described in RFC 675 (https://datatracker.ietf.org/doc/html/rfc675), the first TCP (Transmission Control Program; not to be confused with Transmission Control Protocol) was implemented and provided for more robust end-to-end communication. Routers, known back then as gateways (which were renamed routers so they wouldn't be confused with other types of gateways), were dealing with this end-to-end protocol, and it seemed too much for them to deal with. That belief eventually led to the development of IP (Internet Protocol), which was the routing part, removed from the end-to-end communication part. In fact, that is the reason the TCP/IP protocol suite is called the TCP/IP protocol suite—originally it was one protocol, TCP (Transmission Control Program), but the suite consists of many protocols performing specific functions.

Designed in the 1970s by Vint Cerf (often referred to as the "Father of the Internet") and Bob Kahn, the TCP/IP protocol suite, with the new Transmission Control Protocol and Internet Protocol, was officially "launched" on January 1, 1983. On this historical flag day, NCP was turned off and TCP/IP was turned on.

While other networking protocols and suites (like Novell's IPX/SPX, Digital Equipment Corporation's DECnet, and Apple's AppleTalk) have come and gone, TCP/IP has stood the test of time and is the only protocol suite used on the Internet today. If you send or receive an e-mail, research information, or Zoom with people from around the world, you're using the TCP/IP protocol suite to communicate. Many factors have contributed to this popularity. The TCP/IP protocol suite was placed in the public domain, ensuring that companies could design network software using it. All of the major operating systems—Windows, Linux, Unix, and macOS—provide network communications and services via TCP/IP. Another important contribution to TCP/IP's popularity is that it is built on a set of numbered publications containing specifications, methods, behaviors, research and more, that are constantly modified and updated through publications known as Request for Comments (RFC). RFCs ensure that TCP/IP is relevant to the networking technologies and methodologies now and in the future. You may peruse the thousands of RFCs at https://www.ietf.org/standards/rfcs/.

Historical RFCs about IP and TCP themselves can be found at the following links:

- https://datatracker.ietf.org/doc/html/rfc791 (Internet Protocol)
- https://datatracker.ietf.org/doc/html/rfc793 (Transmission Control Protocol)

As you develop the skill sets required of a network technician and study to pass the CompTIA Network+ certification exam, it is imperative that you comprehend the finer details of the TCP/IP protocol suite. There is a lot to cover in this chapter, and at times it will be pretty intense, but I know you have what it takes to see it through.

 45 MINUTES

Lab Exercise 6.01: IP Address and Subnet Mask

There are two key components to all IP addressing: the IP address itself and the IP address's corresponding subnet mask. IP addresses follow defined rules that specify whether they are valid IP addresses, which network they belong to, and their unique host ID on that network. The subnet mask is used to identify which part of the IP address is the network ID, shared by all hosts on the network, and which portion of the IP address is the host ID, unique to each network host.

An IP address is also known as a logical address and a software address, in contrast to the terms used for a MAC address.

✖ Cross-Reference

As you learned in Chapter 1, a MAC address is also known as a physical address and a hardware address (as well as a burned-in address), since the address is incorporated into the NIC when the NIC is manufactured.

A network host's IP address and subnet mask, both displayed in dotted decimal notation (four base 10 numbers separated by three dots), are simply numeric representations of the binary values. It's these binary values that identify each node on a TCP/IP network. There were defined IP address classes originally, with each of those classes containing its own default subnet mask.

Valid IP addresses must follow a specific format. Knowing the rules for valid IP addresses is particularly important when you must manually configure a network node's IP address. Configuring an IP address incorrectly means that your PC won't communicate on the network.

There's a famous joke that reads, "There are only ten types of people in the world: those who understand binary, and those who don't." It's good for a laugh for anyone who understands the basics of IP addressing. As a network tech, you should be able to perform simple decimal-to-binary and binary-to-decimal conversions.

Learning Objectives

In this lab exercise, you'll review the basic rules of IP addressing. By the end of this lab exercise, you'll be able to

- Convert IP addresses and subnet masks from dotted decimal notation (base 10) to binary values (base 2)

- Identify IP address class ranges (no longer implemented today, but still important to know in order to understand how today's classless addressing works) and their purposes

- Locate your system's IP address and subnet mask

- Define the function of a subnet mask

- Identify default subnet masks for classes

- Identify classes of given IP addresses

- Identify the number of networks and number of hosts per network for the different classes of IP addresses

Lab Materials and Setup

The materials you'll need for this lab exercise are

- *Mike Meyers' CompTIA Network+ Guide to Managing and Troubleshooting Networks* textbook

- Windows 10 system with Internet connectivity

- Pencil and paper

Getting Down to Business

Jonathan has appropriated some funds to set up a small Networking Lab in one of the spare offices at JSW. It will consist of six Windows 10 systems, two Linux systems (Ubuntu and Kali Linux), and a system running Windows Server 2019. For the time being, he has provided a couple of simple eight-port switches and a wireless router.

Jonathan recommends that you head up the group to assemble and configure the network. Before working with the hardware, you'll work through the basic configuration of IP addressing. Follow these steps to strengthen your prowess in IP addressing.

Step 1 Jonathan explains that every TCP/IP network must have a valid network ID and that each device (host) on the network must have a unique host ID on that network. He starts you off with the following IP address and subnet mask.

IP address	192.	168.	5.	1
Subnet mask	255.	255.	255.	0

You'll start this exercise by converting the network ID and subnet mask to their binary equivalents. The built-in Windows calculator is an invaluable tool for configuring and converting network IDs, IP addresses, and subnet masks into their rudimentary binary format.

In Windows 10, type **calc** in the Windows search box and select Calculator. Once the Calculator program is up and running, select the Open Navigation icon (three horizontal lines) from the menu bar at the top left, and click Programmer to change the view to programmer mode.

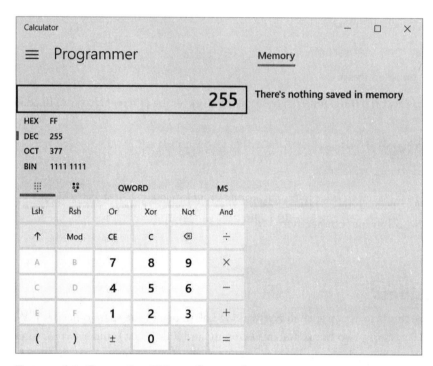

FIGURE 6-1 Converting 255 to other number systems

By default, the decimal numeral system (base 10) is selected. To convert a value from decimal, simply enter the value in decimal, and notice that the number is automatically listed in HEX (hexadecimal, base 16), DEC (decimal, base 10), OCT (octal, base 8), and BIN (binary, base 2), as shown in Figure 6-1.

✔ **Hint**

For accurate results, convert each decimal value one octet at a time rather than entering the entire string of the IP address's digits all at once. Note, when using Calculator, also that decimal values under 15 will generate four rather than eight digits when converted to binary. This is simply Calculator leaving off the leading zeroes of the binary octet. When this happens, simply pad the binary value with enough leading zeroes to bring the total number of digits to eight. For example, the decimal value 13 converted to binary in Calculator displays a four-digit binary value of 1101. To bring this value "up to code," add four zeroes at the beginning for a result of 00001101.

IP Address	Dotted Decimal Notation	192.	168.	5.	1
	Binary Equivalent				
Subnet Mask	Dotted Decimal Notation	255.	255.	255.	0
	Binary Equivalent				

Step 2   Now close Calculator, and use the following chart to convert the IP addresses and subnet masks into binary values the "old-fashioned" way.

Consider this mapping of powers of 2:

2^7	2^6	2^5	2^4	2^3	2^2	2^1	2^0
128	64	32	16	8	4	2	1

✔ **Hint**

The binary numeral system, also referred to as the base 2 numeral system, is based on powers of 2, just as the decimal system is based on powers of 10. Each digit in this conversion table can be turned "on," represented by a value of 1, or "off," represented by a value of 0, to complete the eight digits contained in a binary octet, also known as a byte (8 bits).

To convert a decimal value to binary using this table, start with the 128s column and work your way to the right, marking a 1 in each position where your decimal value "fits" and subtracting that value from the decimal total. Then move to the next position, and the next position, until you arrive at 0. For example, take the decimal value 155 and match it to the chart. Can 128 fit into 155? Yes, so mark a 1 in that position. That leaves 27. Can 64 fit into 27? No, it cannot, so mark a 0 in that position. Same for 32—it does not fit into 27, so mark a 0 in that position. Since 16 fits into 27, mark a 1 in that position. This leaves 11, and 8 fits into 11, so mark a 1 in that position. You now have a 3 left. The 4s position gets a 0 since it's too large to fit into 3. However, 2 does fit into 3, so mark a 1 in that position. This leaves you with 1, which can be subtracted from 1. This finalizes the conversion with a 1 in the last position and a remainder of 0.

Here's the binary representation of 155:

128	64	32	16	8	4	2	1
1	0	0	1	1	0	1	1

Now, it's your turn. Try the following four conversions (two IP addresses and two subnet masks):

IP Address	Dotted Decimal Notation	10.	1.	52.	7
	Binary Equivalent				
Subnet Mask	Dotted Decimal Notation	255.	0.	0.	0
	Binary Equivalent				
IP Address	Dotted Decimal Notation	172.	16.	213.	111
	Binary Equivalent				
Subnet Mask	Dotted Decimal Notation	255.	255.	0.	0
	Binary Equivalent				

⌨ **3a–3b**

Step 3   Jonathan wants you to understand how classless addressing works today. Classless addressing, introduced in 1993, replaced the classful addressing that was in place for the previous ten years, from when the networking world switched to TCP/IP. Jonathan explains that in order to understand how classless addressing works today, you must first understand how classful addressing worked.

Using Google, research the IP address ranges and purpose for each of the address classes. In the following table, fill in the appropriate IP address ranges and purpose for each IP address class.

✖ **Cross-Reference**

Additional information may be found in the "IP Addresses" and "Class IDs" sections of Chapter 6 in the *Mike Meyers' CompTIA Network+ Guide to Managing and Troubleshooting Networks* textbook.

IP Address Class	IP Address Range	Purpose
Class A		
Class B		
Class C		
Class D		
Class E		

Step 4   There are ranges of private addresses for Class A, Class B, and Class C, explained in RFC 1918: https://datatracker.ietf.org/doc/html/rfc1918

What are the ranges and why are they used?

> ✖ **Cross Reference**
>
> You'll learn more about these ranges in the next chapter.

> → **Note**
>
> There are quite a few reserved IP ranges in addition to the ones described in RFC 1918. Check them out here: https://en.wikipedia.org/wiki/Reserved_IP_addresses

Step 5   The IP address classes skip the entire 127.0.0.0–127.255.255.255 range. This is a special range reserved for testing the configuration of TCP/IP on the local machine. 127.0.0.1 is referred to as the loopback address. Open a command prompt, type `ping 127.0.0.1` (pinging any IP address that starts with 127 will resolve into 127.0.0.1), and press ENTER.

What's the purpose of this address?

Step 6   Before closing the command prompt, type `ipconfig /all` and press ENTER. What are your PC's IP address and subnet mask?

Step 7   Define the function of a subnet mask.

Step 8   In the following table, fill in the default subnet mask for each IP address class used for hosts (back in the days of classful addressing):

IP Address Class	Default Subnet Mask
Class A	
Class B	
Class C	

Step 9   In the default subnet masks from the previous step, a 255 in an octet means that the corresponding octet in the IP address is a network octet, shared by all hosts on the network, and a 0 in an octet means that the corresponding octet in the IP address is a host octet, unique in totality to each host.

Based on the default subnet masks for the preceding classes, identify the IP address class, network ID (the first one, two, or three octets with the dots), and host ID (the last three, two, or one octets with the dots) for the following IP addresses For network IDs, set all host octets to 0. For host IDs, set all network octets to 0. The first row is filled in as an example.

IP Address	IP Address Class	Network ID	Host ID
192.168.1.1	C	192.168.1.0	0.0.0.1
131.194.192.3			
45.200.49.201			
194.39.110.183			
208.154.191.9			
126.9.54.172			

Step 10   Classful addressing created networks of different sizes: small, medium, and large.

The default Class A subnet mask is 255.0.0.0, which means the first octet is a network octet (shared by all hosts on the network) and the last three octets are host octets (unique in totality to each host).

Since all Class A networks need to have a first octet value of 1 to 126, the first octet, in binary, must start with a 0 in binary (the 128 column): 0xxxxxxx. If the other 7 bits in the octet are 0s, that's the value of 0, which is not valid. If the other 7 bits in the octet are 1s, that's 127, which, as mentioned earlier, is reserved. Therefore, we can say that if there are 8 bits in a Class A address that are network bits but the first one is locked in as a 0, there are 7 bits that can vary. The formula for determining how many Class A networks there are is $2^7 = 128$. After throwing away the two invalid numbers (0 and 127), we get 126, which is how many Class A networks there are. On a related note, you won't have to "throw away" any invalid values for Class B or Class C networks.

To figure out how many hosts there can be on a Class A network, we have to raise 2 to the power of the number of host bits. In this case, it would be $2^{24} = 16,777,216$. Then we throw away two of these addresses, because they can't all be 0s (an IP address where all host bits are 0s is the network ID), and they can't all be 1s (an IP address where all host bits are 1s is the broadcast address), leaving us with 16,777,214. You wouldn't dream of putting anything close to that number of hosts on a network, but this massive number allows for more flexibility when subnetting (covered later).

Fill in the rest of the chart for the corresponding information for Class B and Class C networks.

IP Address Class	Number of Networks	Number of Hosts per Network
Class A	126	16,777,214
Class B		
Class C		

 **45 MINUTES**

Lab Exercise 6.02: Subnetting and CIDR

As you learned in Lab Exercise 6.01, when it comes to IP addressing, the IP address is only half of the story. The other component is the subnet mask. Network hosts need both an IP address and a corresponding subnet mask in order to communicate on a network.

Up to now, you have only explored IP addresses and default subnet masks that conform to standard configurations for each major IP address class. There were problems with classful addressing, though, that came to light almost immediately, in 1984. Subnetting provides great benefits, as well. Network speed and overall performance will go up, since instead of one large broadcast domain, you'll have multiple subnets separated by routers. Routers never forward broadcasts. This is why college courses are taught in their own individual rooms, as opposed to many classes taught in a single lecture hall. I don't want my students to hear the broadcast traffic from other professors while I teach, just mine!

Other benefits of subnetting include the following:

- Subnetting cuts down on network congestion, because the traffic in each subnet goes down.

- You could filter traffic at Layer 3 with router ACLs (access control lists) and more.

- You could control how the network grows by using custom subnet masks.

- Administration is easier in terms of keeping track of devices and troubleshooting, since with multiple networks it won't be like looking for a needle in a haystack, but rather smaller sections.

However, there were three more problems on the way. Classless Inter-Domain Routing (CIDR) solved two of them, while a new form of addressing solved the other.

Learning Objectives

In this lab exercise, you'll explore subnetting and CIDR. By the end of this lab exercise, you'll be able to

- Understand the reasons for and benefits of subnetting

- Determine the number of hosts supported by a subnet

- Determine the number of subnets created

- Determine custom subnet masks

- Calculate custom subnet masks and the total number of network IDs and host IDs they define for each IP address class

- Understand the reasons for and benefits of CIDR

- Understand VLSM

- Understand CIDR notation

- Determine if IP addresses are valid for hosts on a particular subnet

- Subnet a network ID given the requirements of number of subnets and number of hosts per subnet

Lab Materials and Setup

The materials you'll need for this lab exercise are

- *Mike Meyers' CompTIA Network+ Guide to Managing and Troubleshooting Networks* textbook

- Pencil and paper

Getting Down to Business

While working on the configuration of the lab systems in the previous exercise, you may have noticed that all of the addresses are on the same network. You know that in the near future, you would like to expand to additional networks, separated by routers, but Jonathan has provided only the Class C network ID of 192.168.5.0 with a subnet mask of 255.255.255.0.

Jonathan would like you to explore using subnetting to create multiple networks from the one Class C network address, dividing the lab network into several subnets (logical divisions of an initial network).

Step 1   To determine the number of hosts supported by a subnet, convert the 32-bit subnet mask into binary. Count the number of bits in the 0 ("off") position of the subnet mask. Then use the formula $2^x - 2$, with x being the number of bits with a value of 0 (which means the corresponding bits in the IP address,

if you line the 32 bits of the IP address over the 32 bits of the subnet mask, are host bits). Using a default Class C subnet mask as an example, note that there are 8 bits with a value of 0 in the subnet mask, so $2^8 - 2 = 254$ possible hosts. We always subtract 2 when calculating the number of hosts, because, as mentioned in the previous lab exercise, all host bits (no matter how many you have) can't be 0, as that represents the Network ID, and all host bits (no matter how many you have) can't be 1, as that represents a broadcast address for that subnet.

To get you started with some calculations, Jonathan presents you with the network ID of 165.1.0.0 and a subnet mask of 255.255.0.0. How many hosts can this network support?

2a–2c

Step 2   Subnetting involves "borrowing" bits (although it should be called stealing, because you never give them back). The process starts by taking host bits (0s) in the subnet mask and turning them into network bits (1s).

To determine the number of subnets that you have, use the formula 2^y = number of subnets, where y represents the number of bits that you borrowed. For example, with a network ID of 165.1.0.0 and a subnet mask of 255.255.0.0, we didn't borrow any bits yet, so y has a value of 0. Using the formula, we have $2^0 = 1$ (anything raised to the power of 0 is 1). That means we have one network, as we should, since we haven't done any subnetting yet!

To calculate the number of bits you will have to turn from 0 to 1 in the subnet mask, you'll need the number of subnets required. For example, to define 12 subnets for a Class C network using the default subnet mask of 255.255.255.0, convert the subnet mask to binary: 11111111.11111111.11111111.00000000. Now calculate the number of bits to borrow. Using the formula 2^y, plug in successive numbers of bits to borrow for the y value, until you arrive at the number that is the number of subnets you need (12 in this case) or more.

$2^1 = 1$

$2^2 = 2$

$2^3 = 8$

$2^4 = 16$

Using 2^4, you will arrive at 16 subnets. Yes, I know we were asked for 12 subnets, but you'll always get a power of 2 for the number of subnets. Having extra subnets for scalability/future growth is a good thing!

Subnet masks follow just one binary pattern: a string of 1s followed by a string of 0s. A 1 bit in a subnet mask means that the corresponding bit in the IP address (when you line the 32 bits of the IP address up in one row and line the 32 bits of the subnet mask directly underneath those 32 bits of the IP address) is a network bit. A 0 bit in a subnet mask means that the corresponding bit in the IP address is a host bit. For example, let's use the network ID of 165.1.0.0 and a subnet mask of 255.255.0.0.

In binary, we have:

10100101.00000001.00000000.00000000 (165.1.0.0)

11111111.11111111.00000000.00000000 (255.255.0.0)

The 1 bits in the subnet mask identify the corresponding bits in the IP address as network bits (the first 16), and the 0 bits in the subnet mask identify the corresponding bits in the IP address as host bits (the last 16).

When we borrow bits in the subnet mask, we start at the very first 0 from the left, right after the string of 1s. Since we just concluded that we need to borrow 4 bits, the subnet mask now looks like this (with the borrowed bits in bold):

11111111.11111111.**1111**0000.00000000

To determine the decimal value of the subnet mask, add together the numeric value of each borrowed binary bit. With the first four bits of the host portion of the subnet mask borrowed, add 128 + 64 + 32 + 16 for a decimal value of 240.

Using the same address of 165.1.0.0 and subnet mask of 255.255.0.0, if you needed at least 50 subnets:

a. How many bits would you need to borrow?

b. What will the new custom subnet mask be?

c. How many hosts will each subnet support?

Step 3   Using the techniques practiced in the preceding steps, create a table of the custom subnet masks. Include the appropriate values for both the binary and decimal representations; the number of subnets; and the number of Class A, Class B, and Class C hosts for each subnet mask. The first two subnets have been calculated already as examples.

Subnet Mask Host Portion	Decimal and Binary Value of Subnet	# of Subnets	# of Class A Hosts	# of Class B Hosts	# of Class C Hosts
No bits borrowed	.0 (00000000)	1(2^0)	16,777,214 ($2^{24} - 2$)	65,534 ($2^{16} - 2$)	254 ($2^8 - 2$)
One bit borrowed	.128 (10000000)	2 (2^1)	8,388,606 ($2^{23} - 2$)	32,766 ($2^{15} - 2$)	126 ($2^7 - 2$)
Two bits borrowed					
Three bits borrowed					
Four bits borrowed					
Five bits borrowed					
Six bits borrowed					
Seven bits borrowed					
Eight bits borrowed					

Step 4 CIDR was introduced in 1993 to solve the following three problems, as listed in RFC 1338 (https://datatracker.ietf.org/doc/html/rfc1338) and RFC 1519 (https://datatracker.ietf.org/doc/html/rfc1519):

> As the Internet has evolved and grown over in recent years, it has become evident that it is soon to face several serious scaling problems. These include:
>
> **1.** Exhaustion of the class B network address space. One fundamental cause of this problem is the lack of a network class of a size which is appropriate for mid-sized organization; class C, with a maximum of 254 host addresses, is too small, while class B, which allows up to 65534 addresses, is too large for most organizations.
>
> **2.** Growth of routing tables in Internet routers beyond the ability of current software, hardware, and people to effectively manage.
>
> **3.** Eventual exhaustion of the 32-bit IP address space.

There are five RIRs (Regional Internet Registries) around the world that assign IP address blocks, in their geographical locations, to ISPs (Internet service providers) and large organizations.

The first problem was solved by *subnetting* at the RIR and ISP level, using *variable-length subnet masking (VLSM),* a component of CIDR that allows arbitrary-length prefixes instead of the fixed-length ones of classful addressing. Since these prefixes don't fit nicely into the classful addressing scheme, they are called classless. This made it possible to create subnets with different host sizes and not use the wasteful Class A, Class B, and Class C fixed host lengths.

✖ Cross Reference

You'll learn more about RIRs in Chapter 12.

Underneath the hood, VLSM is the process of subnetting a subnet. For example, instead of one organization getting a single Class B network, consisting of a possible 65,534 hosts (which would be subnetted, of course), an RIR could subnet that Class B network, and then subnet the subnets differently, creating networks of many different sizes. Now, networks of appropriate sizes can be assigned to organizations, proportional to their sizes and actual host requirements.

Furthermore, VLSM can be done internally by an organization, based on their needs. Traditional subnetting creates subnets of the same size. VLSM allows a company to create subnets of variable lengths. For example, a subnet can be further subnetted to allow for just two hosts on a network, and networks of those sizes could be assigned to router interfaces that are directly connected together. There's no need for more than two host IP addresses on those networks consisting of just two router interfaces. Other subnets of an organization can be subnetted to allow for different host sizes, like 14, 62, or 126.

The second problem was solved with a concept known as *supernetting*, summarizing multiple network IDs in the router routing tables when possible to cut down on the number of entries. For example, if all North American IP addresses start with 198.0.0.0 (using the subnet mask of 255.0.0.0), all routers from South America could have one entry pointing to routers in North America for all addresses that start with 198.0.0.0 (regardless of the values of other octets). Then, all North American routers will have more specific routes for each ISP. For example, one ISP could be in control of all 198.133.0.0 (using the subnet mask of 255.255.0.0) addresses, and another ISP could be in control of all 198.134.0.0 (using the subnet mask of 255.255.0.0) addresses. Then, each ISP will have more specific routes for each customer company of theirs. For example, the first ISP could have customers with IP addresses starting with 198.133.1.0 (using the subnet mask of 255.255.255.0), 198.133.2.0 (using the subnet mask of 255.255.255.0), etc.

✖ **Cross-Reference**

Routing is covered in the next chapter.

The third problem was solved with a new protocol known as *IPv6*.

✖ **Cross-Reference**

IPv6 is covered deeply in Chapter 12.

Why do you think CIDR was needed so soon after classful addressing was implemented?

Step 5   With CIDR, came CIDR notation. In CIDR notation, the IP address is followed by the subnet mask, represented with a / (forward slash) followed by a number that corresponds to the number of network bits in the IP address (which also represents the number of 1s in the subnet mask in binary). For example, 192.168.5.0/24 means there are 24 network bits. /24 is a lot easier to say and write than 255.255.255.0.

Now that you have explored IP addresses and subnet masks, Jonathan asks you to take a look at some of the network IDs someone has suggested for the lab network.

The network ID is 192.168.5.0/24. Jonathan asks you to determine if they are valid host addresses to be assigned to hosts on the 192.168.5.0/24 network and, if not, to explain why.

IP Address	Valid/Invalid
192.168.6.10/24	
192.168.5.10/24	
192.168.5.10/24 (to another PC)	
192.168.5.11/26	
192.168.7.12/24	
192.168.5.13/24	
192.168.5.255/24	
172.16.5.15/16	
10.168.5.16/8	
192.168.5.0/24	

⌨ **6a–6d**

Step 6 Let's say you were asked to subnet 192.168.5.0/24 with the following two requirements: three subnets and at least 50 hosts on each subnet. Let's say one subnet needed 20 hosts, another needed 30, and another needed 50. When you subnet, you always create the exact number of hosts on each subnet, so if one needs at least 50, they all need at least 50.

Using 2^y, you conclude that you need to borrow at least 2 bits, because $2^2 = 4$ (which is 3 or more). Since 2 represents the number of bits that you borrowed, using $2^x - 2$, you conclude that this would give you 62 hosts per subnet, because $2^6 - 2 = 64$ and 6 represents the number of host bits left after you borrowed 2 bits.

Could you have done it differently? If you borrowed another bit, $2^3 = 8$ (which is also 3 or more). Now you have 8 subnets. What's the story with the host bits? Now, since you borrowed 3 bits, you only have 5 host bits left: $2^5 - 2 = 30$ and 30 is less than the required 50 hosts per subnet, so the only way to satisfy both requirements is to borrow 3 bits. However, if the requirement was 3 subnets and 20 hosts per subnet, you'd have to decide if you'd need more subnets in the future or more hosts per subnet. That decision will let you know whether to borrow 2 bits or 3 bits.

Let's say you had to subnet 192.168.5.0/24 with the following two requirements: 10 subnets and 10 hosts per subnet.

    a.   How many bits would you need to borrow?

    b.   How many subnets would that create?

    c.   How many hosts would be on each subnet?

    d.   What would the custom subnet mask be?

Step 7   To define the network ID, host address range, and broadcast address for each subnet, you first must determine a value known as all of these terms: multiplier, spacing, and magic number. It's just the column of the furthermost right one bit. It's also the same value of base 2 raised to the power of the number of host bits. This defines the spacing between each subnet. Using 192.168.5.0/24 with 2 borrowed bits, the subnet mask in binary looks like this:

Dotted Decimal Notation	255.	255.	255.	192
Binary Equivalent	11111111.	11111111.	11111111.	11000000

Now identify the furthermost right one bit and convert it to its decimal equivalent, in this case, 64 (the second column from the left in the fourth octet is the 64s column). This is the number you will use to increment each network. Computing base 2 raised to the power of 6 (the number of host bits) will also give you the number 64.

The first subnet ID will always be the same as the network ID you started with, so in this case, it's 192.168.5.0. Now, increment the octet where the borrowing stopped. In this example, the borrowing stopped in the fourth octet. The borrowing also started in the fourth octet, but that's not taken into consideration. Keep incrementing that octet by the multiplier, 64 in this case, until you get the number 256. You can't make the number 256 with 8 bits, so that's a good check to know that you're done making your subnet IDs. Back up the 256, and the row before that is the last row.

The first host address on each subnet is the number that comes sequentially after that subnet's subnet ID. For example, one after 192.168.5.0 is 192.168.5.1.

Each subnet's broadcast address is the number that comes before the next subnet's subnet ID. For example, one before 192.168.5.64 (the second subnet ID) is 192.168.5.63 (the first subnet's broadcast address).

The last host address on each subnet is the number that comes sequentially before that subnet's broadcast address. For example, one before 192.168.5.63 (the first subnet's broadcast address) is 192.168.6.62 (the first subnet's last host address).

The last subnet's broadcast address is always going to be the same as the original network's broadcast address.

Each column's fourth octet values also increment by the multiplier, 64 in this case.

This produces the following four subnets:

Subnet ID	First Host Address	Last Host Address	Broadcast Address
192.168.5.0/26	192.168.5.1	192.168.5.62	192.168.5.63
192.168.5.64/26	192.168.5.65	192.168.5.126	192.168.5.127
192.168.5.128/26	192.168.5.129	192.168.5.190	192.168.5.191
192.168.5.192/26	192.168.5.193	192.168.5.254	192.168.5.255

Now it's your turn. Take the original network ID of 192.168.5.0/24 and calculate the custom subnet mask to produce at least five subnets for the lab network.

Document the total number of "masked" bits for the network ID and record the subnet mask for this custom subnet mask.

Using the method just described, define the subnet, host address range, and broadcast address of each subnet created (including the ones for scalability/future growth) and record it in the following table:

Subnet ID	First Host Address	Last Host Address	Broadcast Address

→ **Note**

There are online subnet calculators out there, as well as a great tool put out by SolarWinds: https://www.solarwinds.com/free-tools/advanced-subnet-calculator.

Use these to check your work, not to do the problems, because when it comes time to subnet on a certification exam, job interview, or other situations where you'll be without a tool, you'll be lost and will fail the task at hand. Also, you'll be considered a "script kiddie."

 45 MINUTES

Lab Exercise 6.03: Local Communication vs. Remote Communication

Now it is time to expand your horizons, so to speak, and facilitate communication beyond the LAN. Wise network techs, after plowing through the "bits" and pieces of configuring IP addresses and subnet masks, inevitably ask themselves, "Why am I doing this again?" It's a valid question, because when your brain is overheating from converting decimal to binary and calculating subnet network IDs and host IDs, it's easy to lose sight of the real purpose behind all of these mathematical gymnastics. The answer is deceptively simple: to distinguish between local and remote network communication!

That's right. The whole point of all the previous number crunching and decimal-to-binary flip-flopping is to tell the network host how to distinguish between packets meant for the LAN and those meant to go beyond the LAN.

Learning Objectives

In this lab exercise, you'll examine how computers determine if communication is meant for another device on the same LAN or a device on a different LAN and what they do in each case. By the end of this lab exercise, you'll be able to

- Define how a network host distinguishes between local communication and remote communication with the logical AND operation

- Identify traffic as local or remote with given source and destination IP addresses

- Understand how the traffic flows for local and remote communication

Lab Materials and Setup

The materials you'll need for this lab exercise are

- *Mike Meyers' CompTIA Network+ Guide to Managing and Troubleshooting Networks* textbook

- Pencil and paper

Getting Down to Business

Local communication flows from a source to a destination through one or more switches. The traffic never reaches a router or leaves the LAN. Remote communication flows from a source to a destination through at least one switch, but will always find its way to that LAN's default gateway, a router interface that takes traffic off the LAN destined for other networks and brings traffic from other networks into the LAN. You're about to see how the source of traffic determines whether network traffic is local or remote.

Step 1   To determine if a destination IP address is local or remote, the source performs a logical AND between the source IP address and source subnet mask. The result is the network ID of the source.

Then, the source takes the destination IP address and the source subnet mask and does a second logical AND. Yes, the source uses the source subnet mask again in the second logical AND. Why? First off, the source doesn't have the destination subnet mask, nor is it able to even get it. Second, if the source and destination are on the same network, they're going to have the same subnet mask anyway!

If the two computed network IDs match, the source concludes that the destination is on the same network and it's local communication. If the two computed network IDs don't match, the source concludes that the destination is on a different network and it's remote communication.

→ **Note**

There is actually a more complex process involving ANDing the destination host's IP address against entries in the source's workstation routing table (seen with the `route print` command). This example is a simplified method for educational purposes.

In the logical AND operation, a 1 bit is produced on the output only if both the first and the second input bits are 1s:

0 AND 0 = 0

1 AND 0 = 0

0 AND 1 = 0

1 AND 1 = 1

For example:

Source IP Address (192.168.5.1)	11000000.10101000.00000101.00000001
Source Subnet Mask (255.255.255.0)	11111111.11111111.11111111.00000000
ANDed Result/Network ID (192.168.5.0)	11000000.10101000.00000101.00000000

Destination IP Address (192.168.5.2)	11000000.10101000.00000101.00000010
Source Subnet Mask (255.255.255.0)	11111111.11111111.11111111.00000000
ANDed Result/Network ID (192.168.5.0)	11000000.10101000.00000101.00000000

Source ANDed Result (192.168.5.0)	11000000.10101000.00000101.00000000
Destination ANDed Result (192.168.5.0)	11000000.10101000.00000101.00000000
Result	The network IDs match, local communication

Source IP Address (192.168.5.1)	11000000.10101000.00000101.00000001
Source Subnet Mask (255.255.255.0)	11111111.11111111.11111111.00000000
ANDed Result/Network ID (192.168.5.0)	11000000.10101000.00000101.00000000

Destination IP Address (192.168.6.1)	11000000.10101000.00000110.00000001
Source Subnet Mask (255.255.255.0)	11111111.11111111.11111111.00000000
ANDed Result/Network ID (192.168.6.0)	11000000.10101000.00000110.00000000

Source ANDed Result (192.168.5.0)	11000000.10101000.00000101.00000000
Destination ANDed Result (192.168.6.0)	11000000.10101000.00000110.00000000
Result	The network IDs don't match, remote communication

Now try this one:

- Source IP address 188.254.200.13/20

- Destination IP address 188.254.157.9/20

Is it local or remote communication?

Step 2   Compare the following IP addresses and determine whether communication is local or remote:

Source IP Address	Source Subnet Mask	Destination IP Address	Local or Remote?
210.145.149.123	255.255.255.0	210.145.253.199	
192.168.4.189	255.255.255.224	192.168.1.107	
10.154.187.89	255.192.0.0	10.152.179.88	
132.100.45.5	255.255.252.0	132.100.45.45	
151.251.100.101	255.255.0.0	166.200.110.10	

Step 3   When a network host determines that a packet is intended for a remote network, who does it realize it has to send the traffic to?

60 MINUTES

Lab Exercise 6.04: Packet Sniffing

Has anyone ever caught a professor sniffing a whiteboard marker? Well, I confess there's something that I love to sniff, more than anything else in the whole world—packets!

Of course, IP packets, which exist at Layer 3 of the OSI model, are encapsulated inside of Layer 2 frames. On wired LANs, they are Ethernet frames. On wireless LANs, they are 802.11 frames. In the context of capturing and analyzing network traffic, though, even though the lowest unit to capture and analyze is the frame, it's still called packet sniffing.

Wouldn't it be nice if we knew about every single detail about every little thing that entered and exited our body? Every liquid, solid, or gas. Every molecule. Every atom. Well, in the wonderful world of digital networking, we can do the equivalent! Every single bit, all the 1s and 0s that go in and out of a network interface card (NIC), can be seen and analyzed. There is an option to see them in true binary, even hexadecimal, but as humans, we prefer a format that is more intuitive. A packet sniffer (also known as a packet analyzer and protocol analyzer), implemented in software or hardware, will not only intercept and log all the 1s and 0s moving in and out of a NIC but show it to us humans in a human-readable format in addition to binary and hexadecimal. All of the fields of every single frame, packet, segment, datagram, and upper-layer data will be shown with their names, along with their corresponding data values. For example, in the IP packet, you'll see the source IP address with a value like 192.168.1.113 and the destination IP address with a value like 192.168.1.107. You'll see the content as it's listed in the RFC or other specifications.

Packet sniffers can provide so much insight into network traffic. This impressive list of functions of packet sniffers can be found in Wikipedia's "Packet analyzer" entry, https://en.wikipedia.org/wiki/Packet_analyzer:

- Analyze network problems

- Detect network intrusion attempts

- Detect network misuse by internal and external users

- Document regulatory compliance through logging all perimeter and endpoint traffic

- Gain information for effecting a network intrusion

- Aid in gathering information to isolate exploited systems

- Monitor WAN bandwidth utilization

- Monitor network usage (including internal and external users and systems)

- Monitor data in transit

- Monitor WAN and endpoint security status

- Gather and report network statistics

- Identify suspect content in network traffic

- Troubleshoot performance problems by monitoring network data from an application

- Serve as the primary data source for day-to-day network monitoring and management

- Spy on other network users and collect sensitive information such as login details or user cookies (depending on any content encryption methods that may be in use)

- Reverse engineer proprietary protocols used over the network

- Debug client/server communications

- Debug network protocol implementations

- Verify adds, moves, and changes

- Verify internal control system effectiveness (firewalls, access control, Web filter, spam filter, proxy)

While there are a few dozen packet sniffers, some with specialized purposes, there is one that stands above the rest. From Wireshark's Web site (https://www.wireshark.org/):

> Wireshark is the world's foremost and widely-used network protocol analyzer. It lets you see what's happening on your network at a microscopic level and is the de facto (and often de jure) standard across many commercial and non-profit enterprises, government agencies, and educational institutions. Wireshark development thrives thanks to the volunteer contributions of networking experts around the globe and is the continuation of a project started by Gerald Combs in 1998.

I agree!

✔ Tech Tip

The terms *frame* and *packet* are often used interchangeably. However, this is incorrect. Frames are found at Layer 2 and encapsulate packets, while packets are found at Layer 3 and encapsulate ICMP packets, TCP segments, UDP datagrams, and more. You should use the proper terms!

Learning Objectives

In this lab exercise, you'll install and run the Wireshark packet sniffer application, use it to capture data from your network, and examine the captured data. By the end of this lab exercise, you'll be able to

- Perform a live capture of network traffic by sniffing and filtering with Wireshark

- Examine the captured data to understand components of Ethernet frames, ARP frames, IP packets, and ICMP packets

- Examine the captured data to understand what happens in local communication and remote communication, and how they differ

Lab Materials and Setup

The materials you'll need for this lab exercise are

- A Windows 10 system with Internet connectivity

- Another device on the same network as the Windows 10 system (PC, phone, tablet, etc.)

Getting Down to Business

Recently, a new family, the Smiths, moved into a house on our street. My wife, Eva, made them a welcome package with assorted goodies, and asked me to deliver it to them. A few new houses on the block were sold recently, and I wasn't exactly sure which house the Smiths moved into. Late one night, from my front porch I shouted, "Hey, Bob Smith, which house did you guys move into?" In the process, I woke up the whole neighborhood, including our two kids, Noah and Jacob. However, I did in fact get Bob's attention and he very discreetly walked to my front porch and said, "Hey Jonathan, it's 123 Main Street." Then, he walked home. Later that night, I brought the package over to the Smiths.

Also, recently, our kids made art projects at school for their grandparents—my parents, who live in Staten Island, New York, and my in-laws, who live in Huntingdon Valley, Pennsylvania. I didn't want to drive around six hours to either of those locations from Rochester, New York, just to deliver the works of art, so I Googled for the nearest UPS store to our house. I brought the packages of art there, paid for them, and went home.

The magical world of networking uses the same logic. Computing devices directly deliver messages for other devices on the same network through switches. Switches connect devices of the same network together. However, computing devices rely on a router to communicate with devices on different networks. We'll see exactly how routing and switching work in future chapters, but for now, all you need to know is that switches connect devices of the same network together and routers connect different networks together.

The source of traffic knows its own MAC address and IP address, but before any traffic can be sent, that host needs to have a destination MAC address and a destination IP address to send traffic to. The host will know the destination's IP address. It will either just have that IP address or Domain Name System (DNS), coming up in Chapter 9, will resolve a fully qualified domain name (FQDN) into its corresponding IP address. Getting the destination MAC address, though, is a different story, made possible by a protocol called Address Resolution Protocol (ARP). In fact, the process differs for local communication (meant for a device on the same network) and remote communication (meant for a device on a different network).

Get ready to explore the mechanics of ARP and ICMP (Internet Control Message Protocol) and dissect network traffic to fully understand the differences between local communication and remote communication, as well as understand the relationship between IP addresses and MAC addresses.

To perform a detailed analysis of network traffic, you must install Wireshark on one of the networked PCs.

Step 1   Follow these steps to download and install Wireshark:

a.   Go to https://www.wireshark.org and click on the Download Get Started Now button.

b.   On the Download Wireshark page, click the link for the 64-bit Windows Installer.

c.   Download the Wireshark executable installation file (the current version at the time of this writing is 3.4.9) to your Downloads folder.

d.   Double-click the Wireshark installation file to start the installation wizard, and follow the prompts, accepting all defaults, to complete the installation.

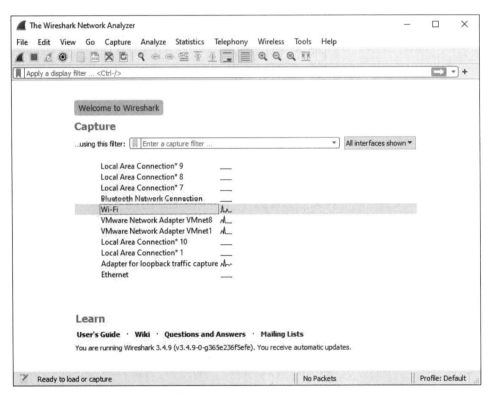

FIGURE 6-2 Welcome to Wireshark!

Step 2 Start the Wireshark packet sniffer by typing Wireshark into the Windows search box and clicking on Wireshark. All you have to do to start sniffing is to double-click the NIC you want to capture traffic from, as shown in Figure 6-2.

Step 3 Notice the Wireshark window is divided into three panes, as shown in Figure 6-3. The top section is the Packet List pane, which lists a summary of each frame captured. The middle section is the Packet Details pane, which displays details of each captured frame. The bottom section is the Packet Bytes pane, which shows hexadecimal values of captured data. The right side of the bottom section will show the ASCII/Unicode values for the hex values, even if the hex values are not meant to be translated into ASCII/Unicode. When you see a dot, it means that there is no ASCII/Unicode equivalent. Other times you'll see ASCII/Unicode translations that make no sense because they weren't meant to be translated, but coincidentally can be interpreted as an ASCII/Unicode character. When you click a row

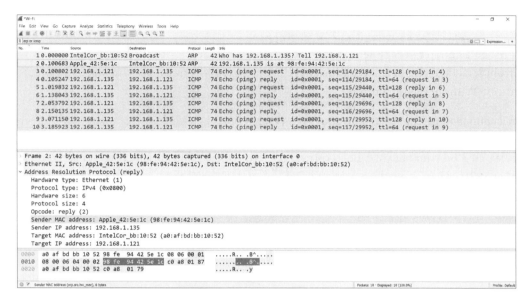

FIGURE 6-3 ARPs and ICMPs in Wireshark

in the Packet List pane, the Packet Details pane changes to fields and values for all protocols involved in the row you selected in the Packet List pane. When you click a field/value in the Packet Details pane, the Packet Bytes pane will highlight the corresponding hex digits and ASCII/Unicode representation. You can even turn that hex into binary by right-clicking in the Packet Bytes pane and selecting ... As Bits.

Step 4 Computers and devices generate a large amount of network traffic just establishing communications. To clear away some of these packets from the view of your capture, you are going to apply a filter. In the display filter on the toolbar, enter the string **arp || icmp**, which can also be entered as **arp or icmp** (this is case-sensitive, so use only lowercase letters), and press ENTER (or click the Apply button, the arrow at the far right of the bar). This will filter out all other traffic except ARP frames (ARP exists at Layer 2) or ICMP packets (ICMP exists at Layer 3) from the displayed traffic, although Wireshark will continue to capture everything.

→ **Note**

Display filters can be added before, during, or after a capture. Everything is always captured, but the display filter limits what is seen to make searching and focusing on certain packets easier. You can also perform a capture filter, which only captures packets that meet certain criteria. While display filters use an easy syntax of Boolean operators and intuitive syntax, capture filters use a different, less intuitive, cryptic, and obscure syntax.

Step 5   Now to see a concrete example of a capture, stop the running capture by clicking the red square (second icon from left), and then click the blue shark fin (first icon from the left) to start a new capture. Click the Continue Without Saving button.

Now, open a command prompt by typing **cmd** in the search box, right-clicking Command Prompt and selecting Run As Administrator. Type ping, followed by a space and then the IP address of another device (PC, phone, tablet, etc.) on your network. Press ENTER to execute the command. The ping command can be followed by either an IP address, a hostname, or an FQDN. You don't need to run the command prompt as an administrator to send pings or view your ARP cache (coming up), but you do need to run it as an administrator to clear your ARP cache (coming up as well).

Step 6   Close the command prompt window by typing exit at the prompt and pressing ENTER. In Wireshark, click the Stop button (the red square, second from the left on the toolbar) to stop the capture. Now it's time to analyze the captured traffic for the ping operation you just ran.

➜ **Note**

> After you stop a capture, you can click File from the menu bar, then click Save, then give the file a name (the extension will be .pcapng—PCAP Next Generation, a derivative of .pcap that allows for captures from multiple interfaces and more extras, as explained here: https://www.qacafe.com/ resources/5-reasons-to-move-to-pcapng/), and then select a location. Now you have a saved capture file! When you open it up (Wireshark will default as the application it opens in, of course), it will look exactly the same, with all panes, fields, and values. Start a packet capture library that you can learn from, review with, and reference in the future. I've got hundreds of saved packet captures organized in folders by various categories.

Step 7   Packet sniffers can capture hundreds of frames in just a matter of seconds, especially if left in promiscuous mode, so applying filters like the one we did here should help you to more easily identify the traffic you want to analyze. The important information you are interested in for this lab exercise are the frames containing ARP or ICMP. There should be two lines of ARP frames (an ARP request, which is a broadcast, looking for the MAC address of the destination, and an ARP reply, which is a unicast, answering the ARP request with the MAC address of the destination) followed by eight lines of ICMP packets (four ICMP Echo requests and four ICMP Echo replies). Refer back to Figure 6-3, which has the answer to the question ("What's your MAC address?") highlighted.

You may see other ARP requests as well as some other ICMP traffic, but you can disregard anything (other traffic going in and out of your NIC meeting the filter) not dealing with this current lab exercise.

If, when you display the capture information, no ARP frames are displayed, it may be caused by one of two situations. First, if you have been communicating with the target system prior to the capture, there may be entries in the ARP cache. Open a command prompt and run the following command to see all entries in the ARP cache (-a stands for all):

```
C:\>arp -a
```

If the following information (or similar with the IP address of your target system) is displayed, you have an entry in the ARP cache:

```
Interface: 192.168.5.12 --- 0x3
Internet Address        Physical Address
192.168.5.12            00-0e-28-92-ac-b7
```

Once two systems have communicated, they will place entries into the ARP cache to avoid generating more broadcast traffic. The entries remain in the cache in widely varying amounts of time depending on the operating system. Since these steps require you to create ARP broadcast traffic to capture, you'll want to delete the entries in the ARP cache. To clear the ARP cache entries, use the following command (-d stands for delete):

```
arp -d
```

To verify the ARP cache is cleared, type arp -a and press ENTER once again. Your results should match the following output:

```
C:\>arp -a
No ARP Entries Found
```

The second situation could be an incorrectly entered filter setting in Wireshark. Open Wireshark and examine both the Capture and Display filters. Confirm that the **arp || icmp** (or using the word *or* instead of the ||) filter has been selected in the display filter and that there is no Capture filter set (from the menu bar choose Capture | Capture Filters...).

Step 8   For the following steps up to Step 12, you will be recording information in the Local Communication column in the tables. Then, when you get to Step 13, you will go back and perform Steps 5 to 12 a second time with a remote destination, this time filling in the Remote Communication column in the same tables. The remote destination could be www.google.com (which will be resolved into its IP address by DNS, coming up in Chapter 9), for example. If your ISP is giving you native IP connectivity, you'll see IPv6 addresses in the replies for Web sites that are configured to use IPv6 addresses. If so, use ping -4 (followed by an FQDN) to force IPv4. IPv6 doesn't use ARP. IPv6 actually uses a completely different IP header, as well as ICMPv6 (ICMP for IPv6), not ICMP. See Figure 6-4.

✖ Cross-Reference

IPv6 is covered deeply in Chapter 12

Also, ICMP can be filtered in multiple places, so if you see results like the ones shown for a ping to www .flcc.edu (which does filter ICMP) in Figure 6-5, pick another Web site.

```
Administrator: Command Prompt                                    —  □  ×

Microsoft Windows [Version 10.0.19042.1110]
(c) Microsoft Corporation. All rights reserved.

C:\WINDOWS\system32>ping www.google.com

Pinging www.google.com [2607:f8b0:4006:81c::2004] with 32 bytes of data:
Reply from 2607:f8b0:4006:81c::2004: time=24ms
Reply from 2607:f8b0:4006:81c::2004: time=23ms
Reply from 2607:f8b0:4006:81c::2004: time=23ms
Reply from 2607:f8b0:4006:81c::2004: time=26ms

Ping statistics for 2607:f8b0:4006:81c::2004:
    Packets: Sent = 4, Received = 4, Lost = 0 (0% loss),
Approximate round trip times in milli-seconds:
    Minimum = 23ms, Maximum = 26ms, Average = 24ms

C:\WINDOWS\system32>ping -4 www.google.com

Pinging www.google.com [142.250.80.36] with 32 bytes of data:
Reply from 142.250.80.36: bytes=32 time=14ms TTL=116
Reply from 142.250.80.36: bytes=32 time=12ms TTL=116
Reply from 142.250.80.36: bytes=32 time=13ms TTL=116
Reply from 142.250.80.36: bytes=32 time=13ms TTL=116

Ping statistics for 142.250.80.36:
    Packets: Sent = 4, Received = 4, Lost = 0 (0% loss),
Approximate round trip times in milli-seconds:
    Minimum = 12ms, Maximum = 14ms, Average = 13ms

C:\WINDOWS\system32>
```

FIGURE 6-4 IPv6 and IPv4 results from a ping to www.google.com

```
Administrator: Command Prompt                          —  □  ×

C:\WINDOWS\system32>ping www.flcc.edu

Pinging www.flcc.edu [192.156.234.2] with 32 bytes of data:
Request timed out.
Request timed out.
Request timed out.
Request timed out.

Ping statistics for 192.156.234.2:
    Packets: Sent = 4, Received = 0, Lost = 4 (100% loss),

C:\WINDOWS\system32>
```

FIGURE 6-5 www.flcc.edu is filtering ICMP.

In the Packet List pane, select the first ARP frame listed and fill in the information displayed in the following column fields:

Packet List Column	Local Communication	Remote Communication
No. (Number)		
Time		
Source		
Destination		
Protocol		
Length		
Info		

Step 9 In the Packet Details pane, you'll see a wealth of information, including the Ethernet frame that contains some of the information that you viewed in Step 8 in the Packet List pane. Clicking the > symbol at the beginning of each line expands the line into related fields, and the symbol will change to a down arrow. Expand the Frame (summary information from Wireshark), Ethernet II (the actual Ethernet frame), and Address Resolution Protocol (request) tree listings (ARP is encapsulated inside the Ethernet frame at Layer 2).

Look at the fields in the Address Resolution Protocol (request) section. The Hardware type is Ethernet. This might strike you as odd if you captured on a wireless device, especially when you notice in the capture that the ARP frame is encapsulated inside of an Ethernet frame. This is explained on the Wireshark Wiki page:

> 802.11 adapters often transform 802.11 data packets into fake Ethernet packets before supplying them to the host, and, even if they don't, the drivers for the adapters often do so before supplying the packets to the operating system's networking stack and packet capture mechanism.

> This means that if you capture on an 802.11 network, the packets will look like Ethernet packets, and you won't be able to see all the fields in the 802.11 header. (Wireshark Wiki, "Packet Types," https:// wiki.wireshark.org/CaptureSetup/WLAN#Packet_Types)

- The Protocol type field lists IPv4.

- Hardware size (6) and Protocol size (4) list how long MAC addresses (hardware) and IP addresses (protocol) are in bytes.

- The Opcode for a request is 1, while the Opcode for a reply is 2.

Using the other fields in the ARP frame, fill in the following information:

ARP Row Field	Local Communication	Remote Communication
Sender MAC address		
Sender IP address		
Target MAC address		
Target IP address		

Remember, when you click a field/value in the Packet Details pane, the Packet Bytes pane will highlight the corresponding hex digits and ASCII/Unicode representation, as shown in Figure 6-4.

Now look just above the Address Resolution Protocol (request) section, and you'll notice the Ethernet II section. This is the actual Ethernet frame. Fill in the information displayed in the following row fields:

Ethernet II Row Field	Local Communication	Remote Communication
Destination		
Source		
Type		

What's the difference between Destination in the Ethernet header and Target MAC address in the ARP frame? Why is this so?

Step 10   In the Packet List pane, select the very next ARP frame listed (which should be an ARP reply to the ARP request; if it isn't, find it someplace below) and fill in the information displayed in the following column fields:

Packet List Column	Local Communication	Remote Communication
No. (Number)		
Time		
Source		
Destination		
Protocol		
Length		
Info		

Step 11   In the Packet Details pane, expand the Frame (summary information from Wireshark), Ethernet II (the actual Ethernet frame), and Address Resolution Protocol (reply) sections (ARP is encapsulated inside the Ethernet frame at Layer 2).

Look at the fields in the Address Resolution Protocol (reply) section, and fill in the information displayed in the following row fields:

ARP Row Field	Local Communication	Remote Communication
Sender MAC address		
Sender IP address		
Target MAC address		
Target IP address		

Now look just above the Address Resolution Protocol (reply) section, and you'll notice the Ethernet II section. This is the actual Ethernet frame. Fill in the information displayed in the following row fields:

Ethernet II Row Field	Local Communication	Remote Communication
Destination		
Source		
Type		

How do the Destination in the Ethernet header and the Target MAC address in the ARP frame compare, now? Why is this so?

Step 12   In the Packet List section, directly underneath the ARP request and ARP reply, you should see the four sets of ICMP Echo requests and ICMP Echo replies. In the Info column they are listed as Echo (ping) request and Echo (ping) reply.

In the Packet Details section, you'll notice that, unlike before (with the ARPs), there is now an IP header inside of the Ethernet frame. Inside the IP header is the ICMP header and the ICMP data.

For now, just look at the gray section headers, without expanding the > signs. If you expanded them and they are now down arrow signs, you can click the down arrow signs to collapse them back, or just view the gray section headers with the fields and values expanded.

The purpose of ARP (and of this exercise up until now) is to find the MAC address for the IP address that the source of traffic wanted to contact. ICMP is used for informational and error reporting, providing connection-related information to IP. ICMP Echo requests and ICMP Echo replies are used under the hood by the ping utility.

Now, while the ICMP Echo request is selected, using the information in the Ethernet II frame header and the Internet Protocol Version 4 header, fill in the following information:

Ethernet II	Local Communication	Remote Communication
Destination		
Source		
Type		

Internet Protocol Version 4	Local Communication	Remote Communication
Source		
Destination		

Step 13   Now you are going to repeat Steps 3 through 12. However, this time you will use the address of a computer on a remote network. Fill in the previous tables again, but this time use the Remote Communication column. Review the instructions for this next part in Step 8.

To make sure you see the ARPs, this time, make sure to start the capture first, then execute `arp -d` (you must run the command prompt as an administrator to execute `arp -d` by right-clicking the Command Prompt icon and selecting Run As Administrator), and immediately after execute `ping www.google.com` (or `ping -4 www.google.com`). This is necessary because some routers are configured to send gratuitous ARPs every two seconds (to prevent an attack called ARP spoofing and ARP cache poisoning). If that ARP gets to your system after you clear your ARP cache but before you send the ping to the remote host, your system will not send an ARP, because it will already have the gateway's MAC address from the gratuitous ARP. Another way to do this would be to make a batch file by typing `notepad pinger.bat` at the command prompt. When Notepad opens up, add the following two lines:

```
arp -d
ping -4 www.google.com
```

Save the file and exit Notepad.

Now, from the command prompt, type `pinger` (with or without the .bat extension, it makes no difference) and press ENTER. This is a guaranteed way to capture the relevant ARPs!

⌨ **14a–14m**

Step 14 Using your results from this lab exercise, compare local communication and remote communication with these questions. Record your answers in the table that follows after these instructions.

a. Who is the ARP request sent to?

b. Whose MAC address is being looked for in the ARP request?

c. Who is the ARP reply sent to?

d. Who's MAC address is contained in the ARP reply as an answer to the ARP request?

e. For the outgoing ICMP Echo requests, which device's source MAC is used?

f. For the outgoing ICMP Echo requests, which device's source IP address is used?

g. For the outgoing ICMP Echo requests, which device's destination MAC is used?

h. For the outgoing ICMP Echo requests, which device's destination IP is used?

i. For the incoming ICMP Echo replies, which device's source MAC address is used?

j. For the incoming ICMP Echo replies, which device's source IP address is used?

k. For the incoming ICMP Echo replies, which device's destination MAC is used?

l. For the incoming ICMP Echo replies, which device's destination IP is used?

m. What is the use of the router?

For rows a–l in the table, only use the following to fill in the blank cells:

Source of the ping

Destination of the ping

Default gateway

Keep in mind that the source of the ping will be the destination of certain traffic and that the destination of the ping will be the source of certain traffic. In these cases, refer to them by the same references, source of the ping and destination of the ping.

For row m, provide your own answers.

	Local Communication	Remote Communication
a		
b		
c		
d		
e		
f		
g		
h		
i		
j		
k		
l		
m		

Step 15   Write multiple paragraphs clearly explaining how local communication is different than remote communication, based on your answers from Step 14. You must include an explanation on how ARP, ICMP, source and destination MAC addresses, and source and destination IP addresses are used in both local communication and remote communication. Also include a correlation between each component in the two stories (the Smiths and the art projects) in the "Getting Down to Business" section and the lab exercise you just performed.

 **30 MINUTES**

Lab Exercise 6.05: Static IP Address Configuration

MAC addresses alone wouldn't be enough for network communications. They are not hierarchical, but rather flat addresses. You can buy a NIC on the Web right after someone in another state or country from the same Web site. Even with the NICs being ordered from different countries, the MAC addresses of those NICs could very well be sequential.

IP addresses alone wouldn't be enough for network communications either. These logical addresses that identify both the network and the host itself are either configured statically or leased to client devices on a dynamic basis. In many cases, they're even geographical, and can represent different parts of the world. How do we tie those geographical, logical addresses to the devices that are using them?

That's why the NICs and their MAC addresses are so very important. The logical IP addresses can now be bound to and associated with a device's MAC address for an indefinite amount of time with a static address or a certain duration of time with a dynamic address. That's how we keep track of which device is using an IP address of a network at any point in time.

Think of a restaurant. At one point in a given day, a certain couple might be sitting at table number 5. Later, a group of friends will be sitting there. Table number 5 will be associated with different reservations at different points in time. Think of the table number as the host ID portion of the IP address. The restaurant's street address would be the network ID portion of the IP address. All tables in the restaurant, after all, are found at that location. Table number 6 would be a different host ID but it will still have the same street address as table number 5. How do we know who is using that table at any given point in time? The reservation name. How do we know which device is using a given IP address at any point in time? The MAC address.

Having now spent some time working through the concepts of IP addressing and subnet masks, it is time to build and configure the lab network. The addressing scheme will vary from one network administrator to another, but all will have some logic to the class range and assignment that they use. Jonathan has already provided the network ID and subnet mask of 192.168.5.0/24. Now it is up to you to choose how to assign individual host addresses. You will work through planning the address scheme, connecting the hardware, and then configuring each system's TCP/IP properties to communicate on the network.

Learning Objectives

In this lab exercise, you'll configure the IP addresses and subnet masks for a small lab network. By the end of this lab exercise, you'll be able to

- Assemble the hardware (computers, cabling, and switch) in a small network environment

- Determine an addressing scheme for the 192.168.5.0/24 network you have been provided

- Configure IP addresses and subnet masks

- Confirm connectivity between systems

Lab Materials and Setup

The materials you'll need for this lab exercise are

- Two Windows 10 systems

- Ethernet switch and two UTP straight-through cables

Getting Down to Business

You will begin this exercise with the assembly of a subnet of the small lab network described earlier, using a switch and two Windows 10 computers. You will then calculate the range of host addresses that you will assign to the computers.

When network administrators plan out their network addressing scheme, they always work to have expansion planned into the design. Typically, a range of addresses will be set aside for router interfaces, servers, and printers. These devices should be statically configured with IP addresses. You don't want their addresses to change, which might happen if they are dynamically configured. Also, even with "reservations" that allow them to get the same IP addresses each time, if the server providing the IP addresses goes down, any devices that depend on that server for addressing, like router interfaces, servers, and printers, would go down as well. You never want to have routers, servers, and printers depend on the availability of another server.

The actual IP addresses assigned to devices (statically or dynamically) can follow one of many different patterns.

For example, the network of 192.168.5.0/24 might be distributed as follows:

Routers:	192.168.5.1–192.168.5.10
Clients:	192.168.5.11–192.168.5.199
Printers:	192.168.5.200–192.168.5.210
Servers:	192.168.5.201–192.168.5.254

However, there is no requirement to assign any device any specific host address. That's completely up to you. After planning the network addressing scheme, you'll configure each system with an appropriate static address and subnet mask and then test the connectivity.

Step 1   Assemble two computers into a small network connected via UTP straight-through cables to an Ethernet switch or the Ethernet switch ports on a wireless router.

Step 2   Now calculate the IP addresses and subnet masks for each of the host computers on this network, using the previous example of how addresses might be distributed.

Pay careful attention to the reserved addresses, and avoid assigning duplicate addresses, as they will create IP address conflicts on the network.

You're just going to practice static configuration now, but of course, client systems should get their addresses dynamically, as you'll do in the next lab exercise.

Computer	IP Address	Subnet Mask
Windows 10 Computer A		
Windows 10 Computer B		

Step 3 Statically configure the PCs:

   a. Open up the first Windows 10 system.

   b. In the Windows search box, type **sharing**.

   c. Click Manage Advanced Sharing Settings, which will appear as the top choice in the dynamically generated menu.

   d. In the address bar at the top, click Network And Sharing Center.

   e. In the pane at the left, click Change Adapter Settings.

   f. Right-click Ethernet and select Properties.

   g. Select Internet Protocol Version 4 (TCP/IPv4) and click the Properties button.

   h. In the General tab, which will open by default, change the radio button selection to Use The Following IP Address. Configure the Windows 10 system with the IP address and subnet mask based on the earlier addressing information. Set the Default Gateway IP Address also based on the earlier discussion. There will be no routers in this topology, so you won't be able to use the IP address configured here.

   i. In the next section on the dialog box, make sure Use The Following DNS Server Addresses is also selected. Assign **9.9.9.9** as the Preferred DNS Server and **8.8.8.8** as the Alternate DNS Server.

➜ **Note**

9.9.9.9 (among other IP addresses) is operated by Quad9, a global public DNS server, with built-in protections for malware and phishing. 8.8.8.8 (among other IP addresses) is operated by Google Public DNS, in existence for "making the web faster and more secure." There are others, including Cloudflare's 1.1.1.1 (among other IP addresses).

   j. Click the OK button, and then click the next OK button.

See Figure 6-6 to see how your configuration should look.

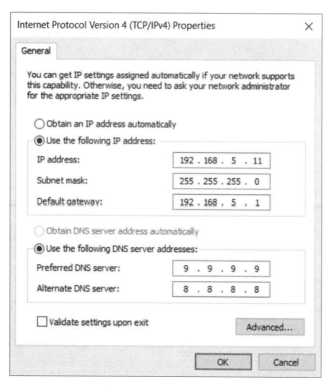

FIGURE 6-6 Configuration of Windows 10 Computer A

Step 4   Repeat the configuration steps with Windows 10 Computer B (and obviously a different IP address).

Step 5   Open up a command prompt on the first Windows 10 system. Type `ping` followed by the IP address of the second Windows 10 system, and press ENTER (for example, `ping 192.168.1.12`). Now, send a ping from the second Windows 10 system to the first Windows 10 system.

You might have to disable firewalls on the systems to let the pings through by typing **Firewall** into the Windows search box, selecting Windows Defender Firewall, clicking Turn Windows Defender Firewall On Or Off, and clicking all radio buttons next to Turn Off Windows Defender Firewall (Not Recommended). These systems are not connected to the Internet, so it's fine.

✖ **Cross Reference**

In Chapter 19, you'll learn how to add rules that let pings through instead of disabling the firewall altogether, which is obviously a much better approach.

The ping utility is a great diagnostic tool that allows a network host to ask another device "Can you hear me?" by sending ICMP (Internet Control Message Protocol) Echo request packets. If the pinged device can hear the pings, it replies with "Yes, I can hear you" by sending ICMP Echo reply packets.

 45 MINUTES

Lab Exercise 6.06: Dynamic IP Address Configuration

One of the reasons that TCP/IP is so widely adopted is that it's extremely flexible. The TCP/IP protocol suite not only works on any number of computer platforms and applications but also interfaces with a variety of advanced network services. One of these important services is Dynamic Host Configuration Protocol (DHCP). DHCP provides valuable functions that make your job as a network tech easier. After seeing what DHCP does and configuring your host to use DHCP, you'll then examine what happens when the DHCP server goes down or becomes unavailable.

Learning Objectives

In this lab exercise, you'll explore and configure the various components of the DHCP client. By the end of this lab exercise, you'll be able to

- Describe the functions of the DHCP service

- Configure PCs to use DHCP

- Explain the four types of DHCP messages exchanged between a DHCP client and DHCP server during the leasing process

- Understand the four DHCP message types

- Recognize some typical DHCP problems and know how to deal with them

Lab Materials and Setup

The materials you'll need for this lab exercise are

- Windows 10 system

- DHCP server service running on a wireless router

Getting Down to Business

In the previous lab exercise, you configured the IP address, subnet mask, and default gateway manually. This is known as *static IP addressing*. Imagine, though, if instead of two computers on a single network (which you had in the previous lab exercise), you were responsible for managing thousands of devices (computers, servers, printers, tablets, phones, etc.) on hundreds of networks. The documentation alone would be staggering! DHCP to the rescue!

Step 1   Describe the function of the DHCP service on a TCP/IP network.

 2h

Step 2   Perform the following substeps on a computer currently connected to a network that uses a wireless router that runs DHCP to enable dynamic addressing.

    a.   In the search box, type **sharing**.

    b.   Click Manage Advanced Sharing Settings, which will appear as the top choice in the dynamically generated menu.

    c.   In the address bar at the top, click Network And Sharing Center.

    d.   In the pane at the left, click Change Adapter Settings.

    e.   Right-click Ethernet and select Properties.

    f.   Select Internet Protocol Version 4 (TCP/IPv4) and click the Properties button.

    g.   In the General tab, which will open by default, change the radio button selection to Obtain An IP Address Automatically. Odds are this radio button selection is already in place, but this is how you'd change a system that was using a static IP configuration to a dynamic IP configuration.

    h.   In the next section on the dialog box, make sure Obtain DNS Server Address Automatically is also selected. Odds are this is set already, too.

    i.   Click the OK button, and then click the next OK button.

Step 3   To view your PC's TCP/IP configuration, including advanced settings such as its DHCP server IP address, type `ipconfig /all` and press ENTER at the command prompt. What is the IP address of your DHCP server?

> **→ Note**
>
> **Don't concern yourself with the IPv6 information at this time. You will be exploring the characteristics and configuration of IPv6 in the lab exercises for Chapter 12.**

Step 4   Network techs sometimes must manually refresh a network host's DHCP lease, such as when a major change has been made to the network's configuration. To release and renew a network host's DHCP lease manually, you must execute two commands. The first is `ipconfig /release`, which, when executed, releases the IP address back into the pool of addresses. There are eight DHCP message types. The `ipconfig /release` command triggers one of them, a DHCP Release message, where the DHCP client tells the DHCP server it is relinquishing the configuration it had received earlier.

The second command is `ipconfig /renew`. When you execute this command, it causes the host to obtain a new DHCP lease. You will now use Wireshark to capture DHCP traffic while you obtain an IP address from a DHCP server.

Run Wireshark on one of the DHCP client systems, but do not start capturing yet. Open a command prompt and execute `ipconfig /release`.

`ipconfig /renew` can be executed to renew an existing lease without running `ipconfig /release` first.

Step 5   Go back to Wireshark and start capturing. As in the previous lab exercise, you are going to use a filter; this time, to isolate DHCP traffic. Use the following display filter: **dhcp**.

Return to your command prompt and execute `ipconfig /renew`. When the renewal is successful, stop capturing in Wireshark.

Step 6   You should see four rows labeled DHCP under the Protocol column, as shown in Figure 6-7 (with the offer highlighted in the DHCP Offer): DHCP Discover, DHCP Offer, DHCP Request, and DHCP ACK. This process, where a client gets a lease, is therefore known as the DORA (Discover, Offer, Request, ACK) process.

→ **Note**

Whenever I teach this in a course, I have a Dora the Explorer doll nearby. At first, students have no idea what its purpose is. But once I start wondering, out load, if there's a good acronym to remember the four DHCP messages sent initially, they figure it out and crack up!

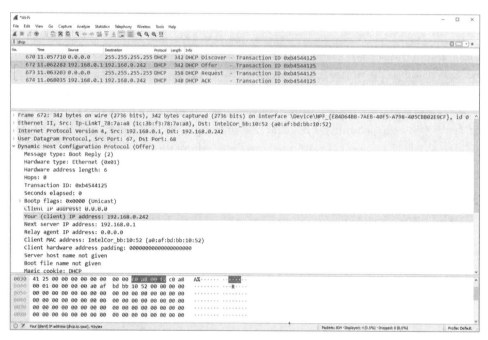

FIGURE 6-7 DHCP's DORA in action

Using RFC 2171 (https://datatracker.ietf.org/doc/html/rfc2131) and your capture, answer the questions in the following step.

7a–7f

Step 7   Examine the DHCP Discover.

    a.   What is the source IP address?

    b.   What is the destination IP address?

    c.   What do you think is the significance of this destination address?

    d.   What port (shown in the UDP header) does a DHCP client use?

    e.   What port (shown in the UDP header) does a DHCP server use?

    f.   Expand the Dynamic Host Configuration Protocol section. Did your system request a particular IP address? If so, why do you think it did so?

▦ **8a–8c**

Step 8 Next, examine the DHCP Offer.

   a. What is the source IP address? Depending on various factors, the destination IP address could be either a flooded broadcast (255.255.255.255) or the actual unicast IP address (this is better than a broadcast) being offered to the DHCP client (the client will be able to open this packet even though it doesn't technically have that IP address yet).

   b. In Wireshark's Packet Details pane, go into the Dynamic Host Configuration Protocol details. What is the IP address the DHCP server is offering?

   c. What other IP information is being offered by the DHCP server?

➜ **Note**

When capturing packets on an enterprise environment, you're likely to see two DHCP Offers, as most enterprise environments deploy two DHCP servers (and other servers in multiples, like DNS) for fault tolerance and load balancing. Windows DHCP clients will request the last IP address used on the interface in the DHCP Discover (it's saved in a registry key). If that address is in the first DHCP Offer that comes back, the DHCP client will snag it. If another address is in the first DHCP Offer that comes back, the DHCP client will wait a bit to see if the requested IP address shows up in another DHCP Offer. If it does, the DHCP client will snag it. If the requested IP address doesn't show up shortly thereafter, the DHCP client will usually take the first offer that came in.

▦ **9a–9d**

Step 9 Now examine the DHCP Request, which is almost identical to DHCP Discover.

   a. What's the source IP address?

   b. What's the destination IP address?

   c. What's the purpose of this step?

   d. What's in the DHCP Request that wasn't in the DHCP Discover?

10a–10c

Step 10   The DORA process concludes with a DHCP ACK, which is almost identical to the DHCP Offer.

    a.   What's the source IP address? Depending on various factors, the destination IP address could be either a flooded broadcast (255.255.255.255) or the actual unicast IP address (this is better than a network broadcast) being offered to the DHCP client (the client will be able to open this packet even though it doesn't technically have that IP address yet).

    b.   What's the purpose of this step?

    c.   What's in the DHCP ACK that wasn't in the DHCP Offer?

Step 11   The three DHCP messages not covered so far are DHCP Decline, DHCP NAK, and DHCP Inform. Jonathan asks you to research these and explain what purpose each of these messages serves.

 12a–12c

Step 12   Open up a command prompt once again and execute `ipconfig /release`. Now disable the DHCP server by simply unplugging your wireless router.

After a moment, execute `ipconfig /renew`.

    a.   What IP address was assigned to the PC?

    b.   Who assigned this address?

    c.   What does this address represent?

🕑 **45 MINUTES**

Lab Exercise 6.07: DHCP Client and DHCP Server

After a great look at how DHCP works from the client side, it's now time to get some valuable hands-on experience with a DHCP server. Technically speaking, servers are software services (that communicate with client services), but most people call the systems, on which these server services run, servers.

Learning Objectives

In this lab exercise, you'll explore and configure both a DHCP client and a DHCP server. By the end of this lab exercise, you'll be able to

- Configure a DHCP client system

- Configure a DHCP server system

- Install the DHCP role on the DHCP server system

- Create a DHCP scope

- Analyze, test, debug, and troubleshoot DHCP traffic

Lab Materials and Setup

The materials you'll need for this lab exercise are

- Windows 10 system

- Windows Server 2019 system

Getting Down to Business

In previous steps, you might have used the DHCP service in a box that we just call router, but now you'll use of a standalone, dedicated DHCP server.

 1a–1j

Step 1   Perform the following substeps to configure the DHCP client system:

a.   Open up the first Windows 10 system.

b.   In the Windows search box, type **sharing**.

c.   Click Manage Advanced Sharing Settings, which will appear as the top choice, in the dynamically generated menu.

d.   In the address bar at the top, click Network And Sharing Center.

e.   In the pane at the left, click Change Adapter Settings.

f.   Right-click Ethernet and select Properties.

g.   Select Internet Protocol Version 4 (TCP/IPv4) and click the Properties button.

h.   In the General tab, which will open by default, change the radio button selection to Obtain An IP Address Automatically.

i.   In the next section on the dialog box, make sure Obtain DNS Server Address Automatically is also selected.

j.   Click the OK button, and then click the next OK button.

 2a–2c

Step 2   Perform the following substeps to configure the system that will run the DHCP server:

a.   Using the same steps as provided earlier to get to Internet Protocol Version 4 (TCP/IPv4) Properties, assign the Windows Server 2019 system the following information:

IP address: **10.0.0.52**

Subnet mask: **255.0.0.0**

Default gateway: (leave blank)

Preferred DNS server: **127.0.0.1** (even though you don't have the DNS role set up on this system)

b.   Give the server a meaningful computer name instead of using the long, awkward one that was generated. Right-click the This PC icon on the desktop and select Properties.

c.   In the Computer Name, Domain, And Workgroup Settings section, click Change Settings. Click the Change… button toward the middle of the dialog box. Enter any name for your computer and then click the OK button. Then click the OK button, Close, and Restart Now. Your server will now reboot.

 3a–3e

Step 3   Perform the following substeps to install the DHCP role on the server system:

a.   The Server Manager window should be opened. If not, click the Start button and then Server Manager.

b.   Click the Add Roles And Features link. Click the Next > button until the Select Server Roles page is displayed.

c.   Select the DHCP Server check box. On the Add Roles And Features Wizard dialog box, click Add Features.

d.   The Select Server Roles page returns with the DHCP Server role check box selected. Click the Next > button.

e.   Complete the installation process.

4a–4o

Step 4   Perform the following substeps to create a DHCP scope on the server:

a.   On the Server Manager console, click Tools, and then click DHCP.

b.   On the DHCP console, expand your server name.

c.   Now create a new DHCP scope to specify the IP address ranges for your DHCP server. To do so, select and right-click IPv4 and then select New Scope.

d.   On the welcome page of the New Scope Wizard, click the Next > button.

e.   On the Scope Name page, specify a DHCP scope name (anything, really), and then click the Next > button.

f.   On the IP Address Range page, specify the start and end IP addresses from which the DHCP server will allocate the IP addresses to the clients. We will use the following information:

Start IP address: **10.0.0.1**

End IP address: **10.0.0.99**

Length: **8**

Subnet mask: **255.0.0.0**

g.   Click the Next > button.

h.   On the Add Exclusions And Delay page, exclude the IP addresses that you want to be not distributed by the DHCP server. This would be for other servers and router interfaces. For example, we will exclude the server's IP address this way:

Start IP address: **10.0.0.52**

End IP address: **10.0.0.52**

i.   Click Add, and then click the Next > button. On the Lease Duration page, review the default lease duration limit, and then click the Next > button.

j.   On the Configure DHCP Options page, make sure that the Yes, I Want To Configure These Options Now radio button is selected and then click the Next > button.

k.   On the Router (Default Gateway) page, in the IP Address text box, type the address of your router. We will use **10.0.0.200** as a default gateway for the DHCP clients. Note that we have no router set up; this is just for display purposes.

l.   Click Add, and then click the Next > button. On the Domain Name And DNS Servers page, enter the IP address of this system, which will later become the DNS server as well: **10.0.0.52** and then click the Next > button.

m. On the WINS Servers page (WINS is old and obsolete), leave it as is and click the Next > button.

n. On the Activate Scope page, make sure that the Yes, I Want To Activate This Scope Now radio button is selected. Click the Next > button and complete the wizard.

o. Refresh the DHCP console. Make sure that the IPv4 node is marked with the green color. Now your DHCP server is configured and ready to allocate TCP/IP settings to the DHCP clients.

 5a–5d

Step 5 Perform the following substeps to initiate the DORA process and watch it in Wireshark:

a. On the Windows 10 system, open up a command prompt and execute the command `ipconfig /release`, which will release the lease your system should have already.

b. Open up Wireshark, and start capturing network traffic.

c. In the filter box type dhcp and press ENTER.

d. In the command prompt of the Windows 10 system, execute `ipconfig /renew`; when the action completes, stop the Wireshark capture and examine the DHCP Discover, DHCP Offer, DHCP Request, and DHCP ACK messages. Execute `ipconfig /all` in the command prompt of the Windows 10 system to see the configuration information given to it by the DHCP server.

Lab Analysis

1. Kelly works for an ISP and has been asked to set up the IP addressing scheme for a new region of the city they are providing with Internet service. She is provided the Class B address of 141.27.0.0/16 as a starting point and needs at least 25 subnets. What is the custom subnet mask for this, how many networks does this allow for, and how many hosts will be available on each subnet?

2. Chris would like you to describe the function of private IP addresses, and list the private IP address ranges for Class A, B, and C IP networks. Can you help out?

3. Ned arrived at work this morning, signed in to his Windows 10 system, and found that he has no Internet access. You respond to the network support call. All of the obvious hardware and configuration settings check out, so you run `ipconfig /all`. The IP address is 169.254.113.97/16. What do you think the problem could be? What might you check next?

4. Francesca is troubleshooting a network connectivity problem. She tries pinging 127.0.0.1, but the command is unsuccessful. What might this indicate?

5. Exzavier is trying to determine if PC A and PC B are on the same network. PC A has an IP address of 172.16.33.1/20 and PC B has an IP address of 172.16.45.254/20. Are they on the same network?

Key Term Quiz

Use the terms in this list to complete the sentences that follow.

arp -a   DHCP Request

default gateway   ipconfig

DHCP ACK   ipconfig /all

DHCP Discover   packet sniffer

DHCP Offer   Wireshark

1. Many utilities are available, both software based and hardware based, that enable you to capture frames and analyze the contents. The generic name for these utilities is a(n) _____, and an excellent free and open-source version is _____.

2. When a PC communicates with another PC over a TCP/IP network, the IP address must be resolved to the MAC address in order for the communication to take place. After the communication is established, the system stores the resolved address in a cache. The command to view this cache is _____.

3. To determine the IP address, subnet mask, and default gateway on a Windows PC, execute _____ at a command prompt. To display even more information, execute _____.

4. The _____ IP address is the IP address of a router that takes traffic off the LAN to other networks and brings traffic from other networks onto your LAN.

5. When a client is negotiating with a DHCP server to obtain an address, the sequence of transmissions is as follows: The client will broadcast a(n) _____ to the LAN. All of the DHCP servers will respond with a(n) _____. The client will broadcast a(n) _____. Finally, the DHCP server will send a(n) _____ confirming the address to the client.

Chapter 7

Routing

Lab Exercises

Taking packets off the LAN and moving them out to other networks, both within an organization's infrastructure and across the Internet, requires a reexamination of a number of concepts, components, and software you have already worked with. For example, you've configured client computers to communicate with other computers on the local area network, as well as computers on remote networks, using the default gateway. Now, you need to look at routing from the perspective of the router itself to understand how packets move from one router to the next, until reaching the destination network.

In addition, you will work with some important technologies that facilitate routing: Network Address Translation (NAT) and port forwarding. These two technologies are critical for communication over the Internet from private networks connected to the Internet.

Setting your small office/home office (SOHO) router up the right way also plays a role in the ensuing routing to and from your network, and this chapter will conclude with that.

 30 MINUTES

Lab Exercise 7.01: tracert

As covered in Chapter 6, when you send a packet to a destination IP address that's not on your LAN (which is considered remote communication), the packet will need to exit your network through your default gateway. What happens after that? Each router consults its routing table to decide on the next router to send the packet to. Within an autonomous system, Open Shortest Path First (OSPF) and Enhanced Interior Gateway Routing Protocol (EIGRP) are the most likely interior gateway protocol (IGP) routing protocols to be used between routers to exchange routes and keep track of destination networks and how best to get to them. Between different autonomous systems, Border Gateway Protocol (BGP) is the only exterior gateway protocol (EGP) that's used, connecting the routers of the largest wide area network (WAN) known as... the Internet. At home, instead of running a dynamic routing protocol, your router has a static route for all packets not on the home LAN to be sent to your Internet service provider (ISP).

A packet is routed through multiple routers until it reaches the destination network. The way the Internet router hierarchy is set up, it doesn't matter if you're sending traffic to a system one state away or thousands of miles away in another country—somehow, someway, the number of routers that your packet passes through will always be somewhere between 10 and 20.

Learning Objectives

In this lab exercise, you'll use a tool that takes ping to the next level, tracert, to see the IP addresses of routers that your packets are passing through to get to destinations on different networks. By the end of this lab exercise, you'll be able to

- Understand paths packets take across the Internet in the routing process

- Use the tracert tool for troubleshooting

Lab Materials and Setup

The materials you'll need for this lab exercise are

- *Mike Meyers' CompTIA Network+ Guide to Managing and Troubleshooting Networks* textbook

- Windows 10 system with Internet connectivity

Getting Down to Business

Jonathan would like you to understand more about what happens to your packets as they leave a LAN and are routed to different destinations around the world. He recommends the tracert utility as both a way to understand routing and to use for future troubleshooting.

 1a–1b

Step 1 Examine tracert (introduced in Chapter 1) from the command prompt and Wireshark.

    a. Open up Wireshark (introduced and covered in Chapter 6) and start sniffing with a display filter of **icmp**.

    b. Open a command prompt.

The ping utility (introduced in Chapter 1 and covered in Chapter 6) is a binary operation. With ping, an ICMP Echo request sent basically says "Can you hear me?" If the destination "hears it," the destination will send an ICMP Echo reply back to the source. If the destination doesn't "hear it," the destination will not send anything back, obviously. If your packets aren't reaching a destination, it might be helpful to understand where the packets are getting lost or filtered. The ping utility can't tell you that, but tracert (pronounced traceroute, which is the name of the utility on non-Windows operating systems) most definitely can!

At the command prompt, execute

```
tracert www.google.com
```

If you're seeing IPv6 addresses in the output, press CTRL-C to cancel the execution and enter the following command, which forces IPv4 to be used:

```
tracert -4 www.google.com
```

The IPv6 packet header is different than the IPv4 packet header, and IPv6 uses ICMPv6 (ICMP for IPv6), while IPv4 uses ICMP. IPv6 is coming up in Chapter 12.

Like other Web sites that get a tremendous amount of traffic, Google's Web pages are located on servers at strategic locations around the world through a content delivery/distribution network (CDN). This way, wherever you are in the world, the time it takes the Web page to load is minimized, because you'll be hitting a server that is geographically closer to you. Sometimes, your traffic could be routed to a less optimally located server, which can be seen with an increase in hops in the output of tracert. If you run the command provided earlier (tracing the route to www.google.com) multiple times, you'll notice varying IP addresses that www .google.com is mapped to through Domain Name System (DNS, which is covered in Chapter 9), as well as a varying number of hops and IP addresses for certain hops, since your packets will be taking different paths, for each new tracert attempt.

➜ **Note**

> **You'll have to wait until your system's DNS cache removes the previous mapping of www.google.com to an IP address or force a new DNS query with ipconfig /flush. Even so, you might get the same IP address again. DNS is coming up in Chapter 9.**

Compare your results to mine, as shown in Figure 7-1.

c.   When the tracert utility completes executing, stop the Wireshark capture.

```
Administrator: Command Prompt                                        —   □   ×
Microsoft Windows [Version 10.0.19042.1110]
(c) Microsoft Corporation. All rights reserved.

C:\WINDOWS\system32>tracert -4 www.google.com

Tracing route to www.google.com [172.217.6.196]
over a maximum of 30 hops:

  1     1 ms     1 ms     1 ms  192.168.0.1
  2     3 ms     5 ms     5 ms  100.65.88.1
  3     4 ms     4 ms     1 ms  172.16.0.3
  4    18 ms     5 ms     5 ms  172.16.0.9
  5    11 ms    15 ms    13 ms  lag-104.ear1.NewYork6.Level3.net [4.30.178.177]
  6     *         *         *    Request timed out.
  7    13 ms    12 ms    14 ms  Google-level3-100G.NewYork6.Level3.net [4.68.75.170]
  8    16 ms    14 ms    16 ms  108.170.225.2
  9    11 ms    13 ms    13 ms  108.170.237.205
 10    12 ms    14 ms    13 ms  lga25s54-in-f4.1e100.net [172.217.6.196]

Trace complete.

C:\WINDOWS\system32>
```

FIGURE 7-1 From the Weissman home in Rochester, New York, to www.google.com

Step 2   Now, let's analyze the output of tracert. Use your output from Step 1 and Figure 7-1 as you go through this step.

You'll notice that there are a certain number of rows with columns. The first column represents the hop number. This is a little misleading, because the last "hop" (10 in Figure 7-1) isn't really a hop. A hop is a router/network that a packet goes through. The last row is the actual destination you're tracing the route to, so technically, it's not a hop.

With tracert, for each hop between the source (the system running tracert) and the destination (the fully qualified domain name [FQDN] or IP address after the tracert command), three ICMP Echo requests are sent. Each of those three ICMP Echo requests receives an ICMP Time-to-Live exceeded error message in return. Examine the first three ICMP Echo requests and ICMP Time-to-Live exceeded messages in Wireshark now.

The time from when each ICMP Echo request was sent to the time when the ICMP error message was received is measured in milliseconds, as shown in the second, third, and fourth columns.

The fifth column represents the IP address of the device that sent the ICMP error message. Compare the IP address in the fifth column in the first row of the command prompt output with the source IP address for the first three ICMP Time-to-Live exceeded messages in Wireshark, and you'll see a match. You should recognize this IP address as your default gateway. In my case, as shown in Figure 7-2, it's 192.168.0.1. That should make a lot of sense, because the first router packets pass through to a remote network will be the one your default gateway interface is a part of!

In fact, all of the IP addresses in the following rows (except the last) represent the interfaces of the other routers that your packet passed through to go the actual destination. You'll notice some rows show an FQDN with the IP address in square brackets. This is the case for router IP addresses enabled for a reverse lookup in DNS.

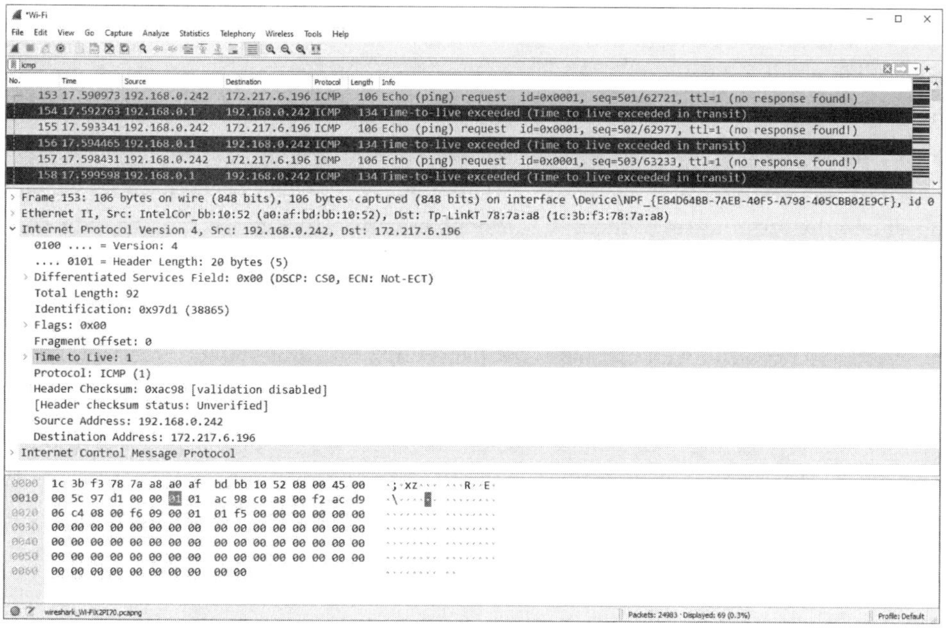

FIGURE 7-2   Understanding how tracert works through Wireshark

Now, the obvious question is: How are you getting all routers to send you ICMP error messages back, which identifies them as hops between you and the actual destination?

In Wireshark, in the Packet Details pane, expand the IP header (click the > next to Internet Protocol Version 4). Notice the "Time to Live" field has a value of 1, also shown in Figure 7-2. Although the name of the field indicates that this value has something to do with actual time, it doesn't. Every time a router sends a packet out of an interface, en route to another router, the router sending the packet decrements the value in this field by 1. If a router decrements a TTL to 0, it does two things:

- It blows up the packet. Well, not really, but it's similar to that. The router simply drops/discards the packet.

- It sends an ICMP Time-to-Live exceeded message (which is a specific type of an ICMP error message) directly to the source of the IP packet, regardless of how many hops away it is.

The purpose of the TTL field is to keep packets from circling endlessly over the Internet in the event of a routing loop. Incidentally, in the IPv6 header, the field was renamed to the more intuitive Hop Limit.

Are the pieces of the puzzle starting to come together now?

The first three ICMP Echo requests sent with your system's source IP address and a destination IP address of the system you're tracing the route to have a TTL of 1 in the IP header. This causes your default gateway to "blow up" the packet and send an ICMP Time-to-Live exceeded message to you with its source IP address in the IP header.

Now, look at the next three ICMP Echo requests, containing the same source IP address and destination IP address as the first three. The IP header is showing a TTL of 2 for each of these. Your router will once again decrement the TTL, but since 2 – 1 is not 0, your router will consult its routing table and forward the packet out of an interface to the next router in the path to the destination. That next router, represented in the second row of output in the command prompt, will "blow up" the packet, because the TTL it sees is 1 (since your default gateway decremented the TTL from 2 to 1) and 1 – 1 is 0. That second router will also send an ICMP Time-to-Live exceeded message to you with its source IP address in the IP header. Check the second row's IP address against the source IP address for the next three ICMP Time-to-Live exceeded messages. This process continues, where the source system will generate the same ICMP Echo request with the same source and destination IP address, but each new set of three ICMP Echo requests will have a TTL in the IP header that is one higher than the TTL in the previous set of three ICMP Echo requests. That allows the packet to make it one router further.

When the actual destination gets the packet, the TTL will always be 1, but since the destination is the other endpoint of communication and not a router, it just sends the packet up OSI and doesn't decrement the TTL or "blow up" the packet.

For some output from tracert, you might have noticed asterisks (*) for part of or all of a hop's output. If one or two attempts have asterisks, either packets got lost or the ICMP Time-to-Live exceeded messages took too long to arrive back on your system. If the latter is the case, you'll still be able to see them in a Wireshark capture, even though the tracert utility had already given up on them. If all three attempts for a hop have asterisks (as shown for the sixth hop in Figure 7-1), that more likely means that the router in question is filtering ICMP (all or just certain types of ICMP messages, like ICMP Echo requests) and is not sending ICMP Time-to-Live exceeded messages. Alternatively, the router could be overworked and might not be capable of responding at that time. However, those routers will still forward the traffic (including ICMP Time-to-Live exceeded messages) from routers closer to the destination, which is why after some asterisks, you'll see things return back to normal with the output. If you just see asterisks from a certain hop all the way down in the output, there is a major filtering issue going on from that point.

> → **Note**
>
> When you go to sleep tonight, you'll have your own time to live. When you go to sleep tomorrow night, your TTL will be one less than it will be tonight. When your TTL is decremented to 0…

 3a–3d

 3e–3f

Step 3

    a. Use the following command to trace the route to a Web site in China:

```
tracert sina.com.cn
```

    b. Use the following command to trace the route to a Web site in Russia:

```
tracert -4 yandex.ru
```

    c. Use the following command to trace the route to a Web site in South Africa:

```
tracert fnb.co.za
```

    d. Use the following command to trace the route to a Web site in Honduras:

```
tracert netsys.hn
```

    e. Go to https://whois.arin.net/ui/. ARIN (American Registry for Internet Numbers) is the regional Internet registry (RIR) responsible for IP addresses in Canada, the United States, and multiple Caribbean and North Atlantic islands. WHOIS is a protocol that queries databases for information about registration related to domain names, IP address blocks, and more. Using ARIN's WHOIS tool, enter the IP addresses of the servers you traced the route to in steps 1a–1d. You'll notice that each of those servers is under the jurisdiction of one of the other four RIRs.

        What are the four IP addresses you saw in steps 1a–1d, and which RIR does each one fall under (based on the output from WHOIS)?

    f. What can you conclude about the number of hops needed to reach servers in each of the different locations in the world covered by each of the five RIRs? Why do you think this is the case?

▦ **4a–4c**

Step 4   Now for some more background on tracert:

a.   The tracert utility isn't perfect. Routing over the Internet is dynamic. The path one packet might take to get to a destination could involve different routers than another packet. Sometimes, when sniffing the tracert traffic in Wireshark, you might see that for a single hop, not one, but two or three router IP addresses will be listed in each of the three ICMP Time-to-Live exceeded messages. The Windows command prompt will only show one IP address for a hop, and it always seems to be the source IP address from the last ICMP Time-to-Live exceeded message.

   Draw a diagram of what this might look like, including the source, destination, and five routers in between.

b.   Actually, it can get even more inconsistent than that. Imagine if two or three packets from the same set have a different number of routers to traverse to get to the destination. It's going to be rare, but imagine if in the middle of the set of three ICMP Echo requests for a specific hop routing tables of the Internet backbone routers slightly change, and now there will be fewer or more hops for an ICMP Echo request compared to the previous ICMP Echo request of the same hop. That could make for really jagged output for tracert.

   Draw a diagram of what this might look like, including the source, destination, and initially five routers in between, changing to four routers in between.

   Draw a diagram of what this might look like, including the source, destination, and initially five routers in between, changing to six routers in between.

c.   If one ms value appears strikingly high (compare the 18 ms in the first attempt to the 5 ms in the second and third attempts at the fourth hop in Figure 7-1), that does not mean there was a problem at that particular hop. The time value only shows how long it took from the ICMP Echo request until your system got the ICMP Time-to-Live exceeded message. The additional latency could have been at that hop or an earlier hop. Maybe it was at your default gateway. Maybe it was actually latency on your own system. There's no way of ever knowing.

   Did any of your hops have an anomalous value?

d.   The Windows implementation of tracert not only differs in name from other operating systems' traceroute but also in how it works under the hood as well. Windows sends ICMP Echo requests, but for operating systems with traceroute, UDP datagrams with high destination port numbers are sent. The TTL field in the IP header will be incremented for each new hop the same way, but when the UDP datagram actually makes it to the destination, the destination will send an ICMP port unreachable message (another type of an ICMP error message) back, and that's how the source knows the trace is complete.

Sometimes ICMP (all ICMP messages or specific ICMP messages, like Echos) will be filtered by routers, and you'll see lots of asterisks from a Windows **tracert**. In that case, a non-Windows **traceroute** might yield better results. On the other hand, some routers will filter UDP datagrams with the port numbers used by the non-Windows traceroute (starting with 33434 and incrementing with each new UDP datagram), and you'll see lots of asterisks from a non-Windows **traceroute**. In that case, a Windows **tracert** might yield better results.

✖ Cross Reference

Port scanning is covered in Chapter 21.

e. The Verizon Fios network handles ICMP packets *differently*, and because of this, if you use Windows's tracert on Fios, you'll very strangely see everything as two hops, where the first hop is your default gateway and the second hop isn't really a hop, but the actual destination. Some customers on the Verizon Fios Community forums suspect that it has something to do with Verizon's IPv6 deployment. By the time you're reading this, it could be fixed.

Step 5 Now for some tracert fun!

a. Execute the following tracert:

```
tracert -h 50 bad.horse
```

b. Execute the following to see options to tracert, including -h:

```
tracert /?
```

By default, tracert uses a maximum number of 30 hops (as shown at the top of all tracert output). The -h option is followed by a number to specify a new maximum number of hops, 50 in this case to allow the trace to bad.horse to complete.

c. Read about the bad.horse story here: https://www.a2wd.com/traceroute-bad-horse/. There used to be a similar one for Star Wars, but it is no longer active. Read about it at the following links:

https://news.ycombinator.com/item?id=5192656

https://beaglenetworks.net/post/42707829171/star-wars-traceroute

d. Whenever I teach tracert in a course, I conclude the lesson with "Actually, guys, I'm sorry. Everything I just taught you is wrong. Sorry about that! Let's just watch this video that explains tracert better than anyone can." Now it's your turn to watch this legendary video by NextGenHacker101 in 2008 that has close to 2 million views and still gets comments today: https://youtu.be/SXmv8quf_xM.

→ **Note**

> Since NextGenHacker101 typed http://, it was misinterpreted as part of the domain name, and
> he was actually routed to an ad server by his ISP, Time Warner. He didn't get anywhere near the
> Google Web server. That was back in the days of Windows XP. On Windows 10, if you put the
> protocol (http or https) and :// after tracert, you'll get an error message.

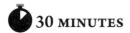 **30 MINUTES**

Lab Exercise 7.02: NAT and Port Forwarding

Network Address Translation (NAT) is a technology that enables many network clients on a TCP/IP network
to share a single public IP address and, in essence, a connection to the Internet. The inside hosts use their own
unique private IP addresses internally, but out on the Internet, all hosts from within that network use and share
the same single public IP address. Industry-level routers and SOHO routers have built-in NAT functionality.
While there are many different flavors of NAT, the one most often referred to simply as NAT is Port Address
Translation (PAT), which maps an inside socket (local IP address, local source port, and protocol) to a
translated/pseudo socket (shared public outside IP address with a source port that's unique in the NAT
mapping table).

NAT was designed for one reason and one reason only: to slow down the depletion of IPv4 addresses.
NAT was not designed for any form of security. Thinking NAT is security is an example of "security through
obscurity," relying on something being kept secret for security and thinking that hiding vulnerabilities is the
same as securing them.

If NAT was, in fact, essential network security, why are so many devices in homes and organizations
around the world infected with malware? The following Web sites explain this in greater detail:

- https://blog.webernetz.net/why-nat-has-nothing-to-do-with-security/

- https://blog.ipspace.net/2011/12/is-nat-security-feature.html

- https://www.internetsociety.org/blog/2015/01/ipv6-security-myth-3-no-ipv6-nat-means-less-security/

Even though NAT blocks unsolicited direct access from computers on the Internet to computers on
a private network behind NAT, phishing attacks involving malicious links and files, as well as users simply
visiting malicious sites, will allow a way in for the cybercriminals.

What if you want to host a Web site or an online game? Nobody would be able to directly access your
computer with NAT enabled, since state is established with packets leaving your private inside network. When
servers on the private inside network must be accessed from the outside world directly—for example, Web
servers, File Transfer Protocol (FTP) servers, and more—port forwarding is the way it's done.

Learning Objectives

In this lab exercise, you will learn about NAT and port forwarding. By the end of this lab exercise, you'll be able to

- Implement NAT on a SOHO router

- Analyze various addresses used by your packets behind one or more NATs

- Configure port forwarding to allow applications to pass through the router from the outside world into your private LAN

Lab Materials and Setup

The materials you'll need for this lab exercise are

- *Mike Meyers' CompTIA Network+ Guide to Managing and Troubleshooting Networks* textbook

- Windows 10 system with Internet connectivity

- SOHO router

Getting Down to Business

It's time to get some hands-on experience with both NAT and port forwarding. Jonathan is expecting a report from you on both of these technologies, so it's time to get cracking.

 1a–1b

Step 1   Examine the public IP address your packets are using in the source IP address field when they reach their destinations.

    a.   Go to https://whatismyipaddress.com/. You'll see an IPv6 address if your ISP is giving you native IPv6 (covered in Chapter 12) connectivity. For now, focus on the IPv4 address shown.

    b.   Search the WHOIS database at https://whois.arin.net/ui/ for that IP address. You should see information relating to your ISP.

 2a

 2b

Step 2   Examine the private IP address your packets are using in the source IP address field when they are still local on your LAN.

    a.   From the command prompt, execute

```
ipconfig /all
```

       Notice that your Ethernet or Wi-Fi (depending on which connection you're using) IPv4 address is an RFC 1918 private address (discussed in Chapter 6).

→ **Note**

> If you do have native IPv6 connectivity from your ISP, one of your IPv6 addresses will match what you saw in Step 1a.

    b.   Where does the address from Step 2a turn into the address from Step 1a?

 3a–3b

 3c

Step 3   Nowadays, there likely is a third address involved besides the two you've already examined.

Many ISPs are rolling out native IPv6 connectivity, but some still aren't there yet. For the ISPs that aren't yet giving customers IPv6 addresses, they simply do not have enough public IPv4 addresses (referred to from this point simply as public IP addresses) to give to all of their customers. For the ISPs that are giving customers IPv6 addresses, they have to figure out a way to allow their customers to access IPv4-only Web sites and resources if the customers are given IPv6 addresses. Carrier-grade NAT (CGNAT), also known as Double NAT, is the solution in both cases.

In the past, with NAT, your ISP gave a public IP address to your outside router interface. The NAT service inside of your router changed all private inside source IP addresses in one of the ranges specified in RFC 1918 (https://datatracker.ietf.org/doc/html/rfc1918) into that public IP address (and, in certain cases, also changed source port numbers in TCP segments and UDP datagrams) for packets on the way out. That's the IP address you would have seen in Step 1a. The public IP address was changed back into the private inside IPv4 address on the way back in (port numbers that had been changed were changed back as well at this point). Now, with CGNAT, it's even more involved!

    a.   Log in to your router. In most cases, this is done by entering the IP address of your default gateway in URL address bar and pressing ENTER.

    b.   In one of the available screens, locate the IPv4 address assigned to your outside router interface. In my case, it's 100.65.93.13.

        With CGNAT, your outside router interface that connects to the ISP does not get a public IP address anymore! Your ISP gives it an address in a special reserved range of addresses, 100.64.0.0/10 (like mine, 100.65.93.13), which is only to be used by ISP GCNAT deployments per RFC 6598 (https://datatracker.ietf.org/doc/html/rfc6598).

        Now, your outgoing packets have their RFC 1918 private address changed to an address within the 100.64.0.0/10 range and make their way to your ISP. There, your ISP's NAT service changes that 100.64.0.0/10 address into a public IP address, shared by other customers of the ISP! That's Double

NAT! Then the whole process for return packets plays out the other way. The public IP address is turned back into the 100.64.0.0/10 address at the ISP, and then the 100.64.0.0/10 address is turned back into the RFC 1918 private address used in your LAN.

    c. Why do you think a new reserved range of addresses was needed for ISP CGNAT deployments instead of just using the vast address ranges in RFC 1918?

 4a–4b

 4c–4d

Step 4

    a. Open Wireshark and start sniffing with a display filter of **icmp**.

    b. From the command prompt, execute

        `ping 1.1.1.1.`

    c. Which IP address is used as the source for the ICMP Echo requests and the destination for the ICMP Echo replies?

    d. Fully explain what's happening to the source IP address if you're using CGNAT. What three addresses are used for the source IP address and why?

 5a–5c

Step 5   NAT and its variant, CGNAT, break the end-to-end principle of networking, as your IP address changes twice before packets reach their destination. Furthermore, the overhead involved can cause great latency, with addresses being crossed out and replaced. Since NAT and CGNAT are stateful, that could introduce problems in terms of scalability, reliability, and especially security. However, NAT and CGNAT still allow your outbound traffic to reach their destinations and the replies to come back, if your infrastructure requires NAT or CGNAT.

    What if you wanted to host a Web server, an FTP server, or another resource inside your LAN? How would anyone be able to access them if you're behind a NAT or CGNAT? Let's start with NAT first and then discuss how this would work with CGNAT.

    a. In your router's configuration utility, find the screen that allows you to configure port forwarding, as shown in Figure 7-3.

    In Figure 7-3, any traffic hitting the public IP address on the outside interface of the router that has a destination port of 21 (for FTP) will be sent to port 21 of the private inside IP address of 192.168.1.246, as the public IP address in the destination IP address field will be replaced with 192.168.1.246, and sent to that private inside host. Likewise, any traffic hitting the public IP address

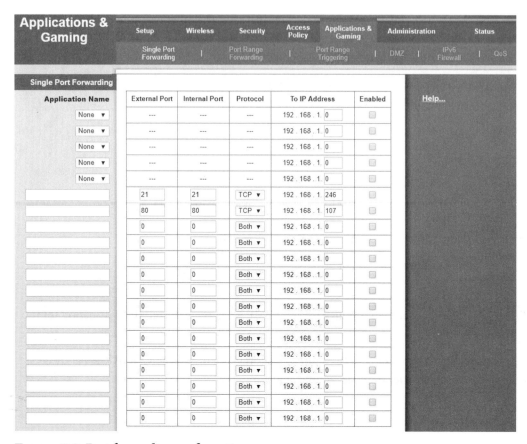

FIGURE 7-3 Port forwarding configuration

on the outside interface of the router that has a destination port of 80 (for HTTP) will be sent to port 80 of the private inside IP address of 192.168.1.107. It's not necessary for the two port numbers to match, but it doesn't make sense not to (security through obscurity is not security). This is like NAT in reverse for unsolicited traffic coming from outside your LAN.

b.   But wait a minute, now! How can this even be possible with CGNAT if the outside router interface has an IP address in the special 100.64.0.0/10 range? The answer is…it isn't. If you are behind a CGNAT and want to host services, you'd have to pay extra to your ISP (some charge $10 a month) for an actual static public IP address to be assigned to your outside router interface, turning your CGNAT back into NAT.

c.   If you are behind a NAT or CGNAT with a static public IP address, create an entry mapping all inbound traffic with a destination port of 80 to be sent to port 80 on an inside system. Then, have a friend from their home network open a browser and type the IP address of the public IP address assigned to your outside router interface. By default, HTTP uses port 80. You don't need to actually be running a Web server for this step. In Wireshark on the inside system, you should see an HTTP GET request, which will fail, but the request proves that the system behind NAT received unsolicited traffic.

→ **Note**

To make this work, you'll have to disable Windows Defender Firewall (which is stateful) or write a rule to allow certain traffic in (skip to that lab exercise in Chapter 19). Depending on your router as well, you might have to allow unsolicited inbound traffic.

 **30 MINUTES**

Lab Exercise 7.03: Router Configuration

In order for your router to route both efficiently and securely, certain settings and configurations need to be in place. Some are fine to be left at their defaults; others should be changed based on your and your LAN's needs.

Learning Objectives

In this lab exercise, you will explore the settings, configurations, and options of your SOHO router. By the end of this lab exercise, you'll be able to

- Configure your router for efficiency

- Configure your router for security

Lab Materials and Setup

The materials you'll need for this lab exercise are

- *Mike Meyers' CompTIA Network+ Guide to Managing and Troubleshooting Networks* textbook

- Windows 10 system with Internet connectivity

- SOHO router

Getting Down to Business

Jonathan would like you to examine your SOHO router to make sure your infrastructure at home is up to speed with the efficiency and security of JSW, since you'll be working remotely from home at various points in time.

Step 1   What is the SSID? Why did you choose that SSID?

Step 2   Is the guest network enabled? Why or why not?

⌨

Step 3   Do you have different settings for the 2.4-GHz network vs. the 5.0-GHz network?

⌨

Step 4   Which encryption is enabled?

⌨

Step 5   Which 802.11 version is used?

⌨

Step 6   What QoS policies are implemented? If none, can you suggest and implement a couple?

⌨

Step 7   What security and firewall settings are in place?

⌨

Step 8   What tasks do the system tools allow you to do from an administrative perspective?

Lab Analysis

1. Dorothy wants to know how tracert is different than ping. What do you tell her?
2. Rose asks you to explain the purpose of the TTL field in the IP header. What's your response?
3. Blanche wants to know why the number of routers packets pass through is very similar, despite destinations being very geographically separated. What's the reason?
4. Sophia wants to understand how NAT and CGNAT are different. Can you help her out?
5. Andrew asks for some tips on setting up his SOHO router. What tips can you offer?

Key Term Quiz

Use the terms in this list to complete the sentences that follow.

CGNAT	tracert
hop	WPA2
NAT	

1. The use of _____ allows one public IP address to be shared by a LAN using private addressing for Internet-bound traffic.

2. The source IP address in a packet will go through three different addresses with the usage of _____.

3. A _____ is a router/network that a packet passes through.

4. The utility that allows you to follow the path that a packet takes as it travels through routers and networks is _____.

5. Encryption for Wi-Fi networks is provided by _____.

Chapter 8

TCP/IP Applications

Lab Exercises

Obviously, one of the reasons you are spending all of this time and effort studying the minute details of network infrastructure, besides the fact that it's fun, is to better provide networking services to users. The most popular applications—World Wide Web, e-mail, Web conferencing, audio and video streaming, file transfers, Voice over IP, and more—all require the configuration of specific components of the TCP/IP suite of protocols.

At the Application layer (Layer 7), protocols like DNS, DHCP, FTP, SSH, HTTP, TLS, SMTP, and more, can be found. At the Transport layer (Layer 4), either TCP or UDP will be chosen to encapsulate the Layer 7 protocols. Network layer (Layer 3) protocols include IP, ICMP, and IGMP. Layer 4 protocols, as well as Layer 3 protocols like ICMP and IGMP, are encapsulated by IP at Layer 3.

To effectively perform the management of even the smallest network, administrators must develop a strong command of the network applications and the mechanisms they use to communicate over TCP/IP.

 **30 MINUTES**

Lab Exercise 8.01: Transport Layer and Network Layer Protocols

All of the Application layer data-related communications that take place with the TCP/IP protocol suite will be encapsulated at the Transport layer inside of either TCP segments or UDP datagrams. At the Network layer, IP packets encapsulate TCP segments and UDP datagrams. In addition, the Network layer features two specialized protocols, ICMP, which provides for error and informational messages, and IGMP, which provides for communication related to multicast group membership.

Learning Objectives

In this lab exercise, you'll explore the TCP, UDP, ICMP, and IGMP protocols. Chapter 6 covered IP in great depth. By the end of this lab exercise, you'll be able to

- Define TCP (Transmission Control Protocol)

- Define UDP (User Datagram Protocol)

- Define ICMP (Internet Control Message Protocol)

- Define IGMP (Internet Group Management Protocol)

Lab Materials and Setup

The materials you'll need for this lab exercise are

- *Mike Meyers' CompTIA Network+ Guide to Managing and Troubleshooting Networks* textbook

- Internet access

Getting Down to Business

Jonathan notices that you have been aggressively studying IP addressing and routing. After some discussion, he agrees that you are really getting a handle on the IP component of the TCP/IP protocol suite. He thinks it would be an excellent time to delve into the other protocols that enable the TCP/IP protocol suite for network communication.

You agree, fire up a browser, and dive into some research on the protocols that work hand in hand with IP to communicate information from one system to another over the network.

✖ Cross-Reference

For further information on TCP, UDP, ICMP, and IGMP, review the "TCP," "UDP," "ICMP," and "IGMP" sections in Chapter 8 of the *Mike Meyers' CompTIA Network+ Guide to Managing and Troubleshooting Networks* textbook.

Step 1 Research TCP and provide a short summary of its features. Make sure to include how it fits in the OSI model. Define the communication methods used (such as connection-oriented or connectionless, acknowledged or unacknowledged, guaranteed or non-guaranteed) and some of the Application layer protocols that require it for their functionality.

Step 2   Research UDP and provide a short summary of its features. Make sure to include how it fits in the OSI model. Define the communication methods used (such as connection-oriented or connectionless, acknowledged or unacknowledged, guaranteed or non-guaranteed) and some of the Application layer protocols that require it for their functionality.

Step 3   Research ICMP and provide a short summary of its features. Make sure to include how it fits in the OSI model. Describe the two general types of categories that ICMP message fall under, with examples of each.

✔ **Hint**

   Lab exercises dealt with ICMP in Chapters 1, 6, and 7.

Step 4   Research IGMP and provide a short summary of its features. Make sure to include how it fits in the OSI model. Describe its purpose and give examples of how it's used.

 **30 MINUTES**

Lab Exercise 8.02: Ports

By this point, you should appreciate the complexity of the TCP/IP suite's many network functions. To the novice technician, it might seem as if these many capabilities could spill over into one another, but TCP/IP does a great job of keeping its different programs and services separate. It does this by using logical ports.

Learning Objectives

In this lab exercise, you'll define the function of TCP/IP logical ports and review the common port number assignments. You'll also use several utilities that will allow you to explore and analyze protocols, ports, and services. By the end of this lab exercise, you'll be able to

- Define the function of TCP/IP logical ports

- List some of the well-known port number assignments

- Explore the various protocols, ports, and services employed in typical network communication

- Use netstat to collect information about protocols, ports, programs, and services

Lab Materials and Setup

The materials you'll need for this lab exercise are

- *Mike Meyers' CompTIA Network+ Guide to Managing and Troubleshooting Networks* textbook

- Windows 10 system with Internet access

Getting Down to Business

The way network communication goes in and out of a machine physically (at Layer 1, the Physical layer of the OSI model) is through the network interface card (NIC). Those 1s and 0s are entering and exiting your machine through the NIC (which exists at both Layer 1 and Layer 2, the Data Link layer, of the OSI model), which is the connection from your machine to the rest of the world. The way network communication goes in and out of a machine logically, though, is through a program or service. A service is a program that runs in the background, independent of a sign-in, in Windows. In Linux, the term daemon is used instead of service. Furthermore, in Linux, the term service refers to a command that calls scripts that control daemon processes. A process is an instantiation of a program or service and can be further broken down into execution units known as threads. Windows client machines, for instance, will have a workstation service running in the background that allows them to create and maintain network connections with the Server Message Block (SMB) protocol to server services that allow for access to remote files and printers.

When you start a Web server, you're starting a specific server service that isn't associated with or connected to the signed-in user. The service runs in the background, so it is able to run when the system is rebooted and no user is signed in.

→ **Note**

> **Technically speaking, a server is a service (software) that responds to client requests. Just like a server is a service that could have an application front-end, so, too, some clients are implemented as services. A client service makes a request to a server service. For example, a DHCP client service makes a request to a DHCP server service. Clients can be implemented as applications as well. The term server, though, is often used for the machines (hardware) on which server services run.**

Well, how does network communication go in and out of a program or service?

Let's say a single machine is running both a File Transfer Protocol (FTP) server and a Web server. If they are both accessible by the same IP address, how does the traffic for the FTP server get to the FTP server and the traffic for the Web server get to the Web server?

Think about an apartment building with a grid of mailboxes in the lobby. The man in apartment 21, Frank Thomas Peterson, checks his mail with a key to mailbox 21, and the woman in apartment 80, Helen Theresa Thomasina Parker, checks her mail with a key to mailbox 80. The mailman brought their mail to the same building. They both live in the same building with the same street address. This is like two different servers that are accessible through the same IP address. However, when traffic is destined for the man in apartment 21, it is noted on the front of the envelope. The same goes for mail addressed to the woman in apartment 80. Similarly, the way into and out of a program or service is through a port. A port is a logical endpoint of communication that identifies a program or service, and is represented by a number.

> **→ Note**
>
> The term port is used instead of port number. For example, you'd read, write, say, or hear *port 21* instead of *port number 21.*

So, in addition to source and destination MAC addresses and source and destination IP addresses, there are source and destination ports. MAC addresses are found in frame headers at Layer 2 (Data Link layer) of the OSI model. IP addresses are found in IP packet headers at Layer 3 (Network layer) of the OSI model. Port numbers are found in either TCP segment headers or UDP datagram headers at Layer 4 (Transport layer) of the OSI model.

Based on the destination port, the operating system on the destination machine knows which program or service to send the data to, in the same way that the mailman knows to put the mail for apartment 21 in the mailbox for apartment 21 and the mail for apartment 80 in the mailbox for apartment 80.

Well-known ports use port numbers from 0 to 1023, and are reserved for major protocols and services. FTP servers send and receive control traffic on port 21 (which explains why I chose to name the man in apartment 21 Frank Thomas Peterson). Web servers running HTTP send and receive unencrypted traffic on port 80 (which is why I chose to name the woman in apartment 80 Helen Theresa Thomasina Parker). Web servers send and receive encrypted traffic on port 443 with Transport Layer Security (TLS).

Registered ports use port numbers from 1024 to 49,151 and are assigned by the Internet Assigned Numbers Authority (IANA) for specific organizations that want a common port to be used for their programs or protocols. However, these port numbers can be used by any system if not in use. In fact, operating systems will use certain port numbers in this range and treat them like dynamic ports (coming up next). Registered port numbers are locally significant to a system. It's not like using a registered IP address, which has global scope.

Dynamic ports use port numbers from 49,152 to 65,535 and are used by client applications on an as-needed basis. For example, a browser might open port 60,000 to send a request to a Web server that will be listening for requests on port 80. The Web server's response is sourced from port 80 and is destined for the port the browser opened. After the communication between the browser and the Web server is complete, the browser will close the port it opened, but the Web server's port will remain open for new incoming connections. The browser, or any other program/service running on the machine, will subsequently open a different port in the dynamic range for its next request. As mentioned earlier, operating systems will sometimes use unused ports in the registered port number range for the same purpose.

A port can be classified as being in one of three states: open, closed, or filtered. There's really just one difference between an open port and a closed port. Open ports have programs or services listening on them, whereas closed ports don't. For example, if you start a FileZilla FTP server, port 21 is open. Stop the FileZilla FTP server, and port 21 is closed. If you start an Apache HTTP Server Web server, port 80 is now open. Stop the Apache HTTP Server Web server, and port 80 is now closed.

A filtered port is a port that's either open or closed, but it can't be determined because packet filtering keeps the scans from getting to the port. The filtering could come from a dedicated firewall device, router rules, or a host-based firewall. Sometimes an ICMP error message will be sent in response to a filtered port. However, often, filtering devices will just drop traffic and won't send responses.

Firewalls don't open ports. Firewalls don't close ports. Firewalls filter ports.

If a network-based firewall is set to deny some or all traffic to a Secure Shell (SSH) server that sends and receives traffic on port 22, you still have an SSH server running on a machine. The firewall didn't close port 22 on the machine. If you run the netstat utility on the machine running the SSH server service, you'll see that port 22 is indeed open. Any host inside the network, therefore, will be able to access the SSH server, since the network-based firewall that's filtering port 22 doesn't affect it. When a host-based firewall on the SSH server is filtering either some or all incoming traffic on port 22, if the service is started, port 22 is still open.

Let's say I'm teaching a class in the Finger Lakes Community College (FLCC) Victor Campus Center. Think of the class in the Networking and Cybersecurity Lab as a program or service that's running. Think of the room number (VC206) as the port number that lets students know where to enter. While class is in session, the port is open. After class, we all leave, the lights go off, and the door is locked. The port is closed.

Picture yourself trying to enter FLCC's Victor Campus Center, but the security guard at the front door doesn't let you in. That guard is the firewall. You can't get to my classroom door to even determine whether class is in session (open port) or not (closed port) because you're being filtered by the firewall (filtered port).

Step 1   In your own words, explain the purpose of a logical port.

Step 2   Fill in the protocols/services associated with these commonly used ports. If you need some help, check out https://www.iana.org/assignments/service-names-port-numbers/service-names-port-numbers.xhtml.

Port	Protocol/Service
21	
22	
25	
53	
67/68	
80	
88	
143	
389	
443	
3389	

3a–3d

Step 3 You can view a listing of the active ports using the `netstat` command prompt utility. You took a brief look at this utility in Chapter 1, but now you're going to go deeper into its capabilities.

With `netstat`, you have a number of options to customize the output of the list. Run the `netstat /?` command, and provide a description of the following options:

a. `netstat -a`

b. `netstat -b`

c. `netstat -n`

d. `netstat -o`

When you want to run multiple options at a time, you don't need to specify a new - for each one. For example, `netstat -b -a -n -o` can simply be written as `netstat -bano`. The `-b` option requires the command prompt to be run as an administrator (type **cmd** in the search box, right-click Command Prompt, and select Run As Administrator, and click the Yes button).

➜ Note

Make use of the help function of utilities in order to learn about more advanced features. When in doubt, type the utility name, a space, and /? to the end of the command. For example, type `ping /?` **to explore the ping options.**

Step 4 Jonathan calls you over to see a system that he suspects may contain active malware. Before running your company's standard anti-malware program, he wants you to run `netstat`. Why would he want you to do this? Which netstat option would be a good choice to use in this case?

Step 5 Now, run `netstat` without any options.

You'll recall that each Session layer connection is represented by a local and foreign socket (the column headers use the term "address"). A socket is an endpoint of an active network communication link (on each of the two communicating sides), represented by an IP address and port number, as well as a Layer 4 protocol (TCP or UDP). The local socket is on the machine you're using, while the remote socket is on the machine your machine is communicating with. The last column in the `netstat`

output deals with TCP connection states and is explained here: http://www.tcpipguide.com/free/t_
TCPOperationalOverviewandtheTCPFiniteStateMachineF-2.htm.

Step 6   Now launch a Web browser, navigate to www.flcc.edu, and immediately after (if you're not quick enough, the connection could be closed and the output would not show it) run `netstat -bano`. Recall that the `-b` option requires you to run the Windows command prompt as Administrator. Find the row that corresponds to that connection.

You can ping www.flcc.edu to get its IP address.

Step 7   After waiting a few moments, if you run `netstat -bano` once again, you'll find that the status of some of the connections will change or disappear. To have `netstat` run itself repeatedly, put a number after `netstat` that represents an interval of seconds for `netstat` to rerun itself. For example, `netstat 15 -bano` will automatically run the command every 15 seconds. To stop it, press CTRL-C.

60 MINUTES

Lab Exercise 8.03: HTTP

In essence, most people mistakenly equate the World Wide Web with the Internet. In reality, the Internet is the infrastructure of connected networks, devices, and resources, while the World Wide Web is the multimedia content accessed through a browser using hyperlinks. This mistake is likely due to the fact that the World Wide Web, using HTTP (Hypertext Transfer Protocol) and TLS (Transport Layer Security), is arguably the most widely used TCP/IP application. That said, one of the best ways to develop and practice the skills needed to both understand and support TCP/IP applications, as well as ports, is to install, configure, and test a Web server.

There are two important components associated with hosting a Web site. The first, and the one that you'll be concerned with the most as a network support technician, is the installation, configuration, and management of the Web server itself. A close second would be the development and layout of the actual content (the Web pages) as a Web designer.

Learning Objectives

In this lab exercise, you'll use Apache HTTP Server to set up a simple one-page Web site. By the end of this lab exercise, you'll be able to

- Install and configure a Web server

- Create a simple Web site

- Access the created Web site through a Web browser on a separate system

- Analyze the communication between the client and server through Wireshark and netstat

Lab Materials and Setup

The materials you'll need for this lab exercise are

- A Windows 10 system with Internet connectivity

- Another system on the same network (phone, tablet, or PC)

Getting Down to Business

WampServer is an environment for developing Web applications for Windows. The *W* in "Wamp" stands for Windows, the operating system that this platform is run on. (Alternatively, there is LAMP for Linux and MAMP for macOS.) The *a* stands for Apache HTTP Server, the world's most used Web server. The *m* stands for the MariaDB (which is the default in WampServer) relational database management system (RDBMS), a fork of the world's most used open-source RDBMS, MySQL, which is also included in WampServer (Oracle Database has the number-one spot in terms of market share when including proprietary RDBMSs). The *p* stands for PHP, the world's most used server-side scripting language. Bundling these applications together in one environment is of great benefit for Web developers.

Step 1   Download and install WampServer.

   a.   On your Windows 10 system, download the latest version of WampServer from https://sourceforge .net/projects/wampserver/files/latest/download.

   b.   Double-click the .exe installer file in your Downloads folder to start the installation. Click the Yes button in the User Account Control dialog box. With English showing as the language, click the OK button. Click the radio button next to I Accept The Agreement and click the Next > button. After that, you'll see an important setup screen that starts with an Information heading and "Please read the following important information before continuing," shown in Figure 8-1. Pay close attention to the information in red text, five rows from the top: "Make sure you are 'up to date' in the redistributable packages VC9, VC10, VC11, VC13, VC14 and VC15."

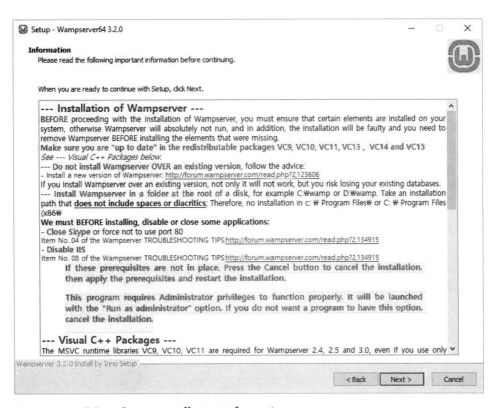

FIGURE 8-1 WampServer installation information

c. To ensure that you have all of the Microsoft Visual C++ redistributable packages needed, click the Start button or in the search box, type **programs**, and select Add Or Remove Programs. Next, in the Search This List box, type **C++**. If you are missing one or more of the redistributable packages in the setup screen, follow the instructions provided in the setup screen to download them. Unfortunately, the first two links are bad links, so if you need VC9 Packages (Visual C++ 2008 SP1), you should use Google to search for the new official Microsoft links. Alternatively, follow the instructions at the very end of the setup screen (from "If you have a 64-bit Windows…"), as shown in Figure 8-2.

d. Back in the WampServer installer, after ensuring all the required elements are in place, click the Next > button. Keep the default destination location and click the Next > button. Click the Install button on the Ready To Install screen. Then you'll be presented with a question: "Do you want to choose another Browser installed on your system?"

If you don't have the Google Chrome browser or the Mozilla Firefox browser, download and install one or both now:

- Google Chrome: https://www.google.com/chrome/

- Mozilla Firefox: https://www.mozilla.org/en-US/firefox/new/

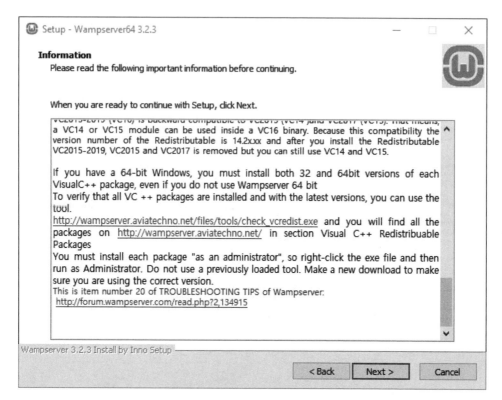

FIGURE 8-2 WampServer installation information continued

e. Back in the WampServer installer, in response to the browser question, click the Yes button and browse to C:\Program Files (x86)\Google\Chrome\Application or C:\Program Files\Google\Chrome\Application (your Chrome executable will be stored in one of these two locations) and then click chrome.exe to select Chrome. Alternatively, browse to C:\Program Files\Mozilla Firefox and then click firefox.exe to select Firefox.

f. When prompted, "Do you want to choose another text editor installed on your system?" click the No button. Read the information on the next screen and click the Next > button. Then click the Finish button on the final screen of the installer.

g. Launch Wampserver64 via a shortcut on the desktop or by clicking the Start button, or in the search box, typing **Wampserver64** and selecting Wampserver64.

h. You'll see the WampServer icon in the notification area on the taskbar (if you don't see the WampServer icon, click the arrow to expand the icons list). It should turn green, which means you're good to go! Click it to open the program menu, as shown in Figure 8-3.

If the WampServer icon turned red or orange, you'll need to troubleshoot. Odds are it has to do with something in the Information screen shown in Figure 8-1. Skype and its use of port 80 is a likely culprit.

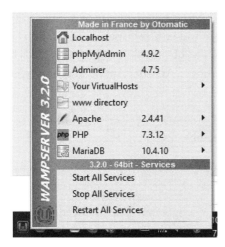

FIGURE 8-3 The WampServer menu

Step 2 Open a Windows command prompt, type `netstat -an`, and then press ENTER. You should now see an entry, possibly at the very top, that looks like this:

```
Proto   Local Address           Foreign Address         State
TCP     0.0.0.0:80              0.0.0.0:0               LISTENING
```

What does all of this mean?

Step 3 What is the difference between the following IP addresses found in the Local Address column: 0.0.0.0, 127.0.0.1, and the actual IP address bound to your NIC?

Step 4 Why does the output of `netstat -an` show asterisks instead of an IP address and port in the Foreign Address column and nothing in the State column for UDP?

 a–c

Step 5 Create a default Web page for your Web site.

    a. Click the green WampServer icon.

    b. Click www directory to bring you to the root folder for the Web server. In the menu bar, click the View tab, and make sure there is a check in the box marked File Name Extensions.

    c. To create a default Web site, right-click a blank area inside the root folder, mouse over New, and then select Text Document. Change the filename and extension to **index.html** (make sure you don't call it index.html.txt, and click Yes in the rename pop-up), which will be the default page that loads for your Web site. Right-click the file and select Open With | Choose Another App | Notepad. Type **Hello, World!** in the file, save it, and then exit Notepad.

    If there is an index.php file in the www directory, rename it to something else—for example, noindex.php. This will allow your index.html file to be loaded by default.

 6a–6b

Step 6 There are two configuration changes on the system running WampServer that you need to make to allow other systems to access your Web server.

    a. From the WampServer menu, mouse over Apache, and select httpd-vhosts.conf, which will open that file in Notepad. Change the line "Require local" to "Require all granted." Save and close the file. From the WampServer menu, select Restart All Services.

    b. In the search box type **firewall**, and select Windows Defender Firewall. In the pane on the left, select Advanced Settings. In the pane on the left select Inbound Rules. From the men bar at the top, select Action and then New Rule…. Select the radio button next to Port and click the Next > button. Keep the default TCP radio button selection, and in the Specific Local Ports: textbox enter **80**. Click the Next > button. With the default selection of Allow The Connection set, click the Next > button. With default checks in the checkboxes next to Domain, Private, and Public, click the Next > button. In the Name: textbox enter **My Web site**, enter a description of your choice in the Description (optional) box, and click the Finish button.

 a–d

 e

Step 7 Access the Web page you created in the previous step from a local system, and capture the related traffic in Wireshark.

    a. Start sniffing with Wireshark on the Windows 10 system you're running WampServer on.

    b. Open a browser on a second system on the same network as the Windows 10 system you're running WampServer on. This second system could be a phone, tablet, or PC. In the address bar, clear everything, and type just the IP address of the system that's running the Web server (for example, 192.168.1.52) and press ENTER. You should see the simple Web site you just made. If you see a Server Configuration page, there is an index.php file (referenced in Step 5c) in the www directory. Rename that file and try again, or simply enter **/index.html** after the Web server's IP address in the address bar (to explicitly specify what to load) and press ENTER.

c. Quickly execute `netstat -n` from a command prompt on the Windows 10 system running WampServer to see the connection's sockets listed in the output from the command. If need be, from the client, reload Web site again to generate new output for netstat.

d. What do you see in Wireshark, related the connection?

e. In this step, what specifically is the Web client and what specifically is the Web server?

→ **Note**

To access the Web site from the same system that the server service is running, open up a browser on that system, enter the loopback address (127.0.0.1) in the address bar (or 127.0.0.1/index.html), and press ENTER.

Step 8 On the Windows 10 system running WampServer, click the green WampServer icon, mouse over Apache, mouse over Service Administration 'wampapache64', and select Stop Service. The WampServer icon should now turn orange, which means, in this case, that the Web server component of WampServer has been stopped, although the MariaDB service (which was started earlier too) is still running. Can you spot the MariaDB service's port (a simple Google search will help you out with the number) in the output of `netstat -an`?

Step 9 On the Windows 10 system running WampServer, open a command prompt, execute `netstat -an`. The entry seen earlier in Step 2 should no longer be present. Why do you think this is the case?

45 MINUTES

Lab Exercise 8.04: FTP

Transferring files between computers is a very important process that all networks require. In relation to Lab Exercise 8.03 that you just performed, files from the Web designer's computer are sent to the system running the Web server using FTP, which was designed for the uploading and downloading of files between clients and servers.

Learning Objectives

In this lab exercise, you'll set up both an FTP client and an FTP server using FileZilla. Then, you'll transfer data between the two. By the end of this lab exercise, you'll be able to

- Install, configure, and manage an FTP server

- Install an FTP client and transfer files

- Analyze the communication between the client and server through Wireshark and netstat

Lab Materials and Setup

The materials you'll need for this lab exercise are

- Two Windows 10 systems with Internet connectivity (one for the server service and one for the client service)

Getting Down to Business

You can use FTP through a command-line interface (CLI) or a graphical user interface (GUI). This lab exercise uses a popular GUI FTP application for Windows called FileZilla.

 1a–1d

 1d

Step 1   Download, install, and run the FTP server and FTP client on separate systems.

   a.   Go to https://filezilla-project.org/download.php?show_all=1 and then download, install (keeping all default selections), and run the FileZilla FTP client on one system. Be sure to decline all additional requested packages. To run the FTP client, click the Start button or in the search box, type FileZilla, and select FileZilla.

   b.   Go to https://filezilla-project.org/download.php?type=server and then download, install (keeping all default selections, including port 14148, which is the default admin port for the server, not for FTP clients to connect to), and run the FileZilla FTP server on the other system.

   c.   When the FTP server interface opens automatically on the system running the FTP server (to manually open it, click the Start button or in the search box, type FileZilla, and select Administer FileZilla Server), click the Connect to FileZilla FTP Server button. On the Connection window, click the OK button. On the Do you trust this server? window, click the Yes button.

> → **Note**
>
> **You'll see three icons on the desktop: Administer FileZilla Server (as mentioned above, this opens up the GUI that allows you to create users and perform other administrative tasks), Start FileZilla Server (this just starts the server service and opens port 21), and Stop FileZilla Server (this just stops the server service and closes port 21).**

d.   After you start the server, from a command prompt, execute `netstat -an`. The output will include the following rows:

```
TCP    0.0.0.0:21             0.0.0.0:0              LISTENING
TCP    127.0.0.1:14148        0.0.0.0:0              LISTENING
```

Why does the first row, shown above, have 0.0.0.0 as part of its socket, while the second row, shown above, has 127.0.0.1 as part of its socket?

 2a–2f

Step 2   Create an FTP user.

a.   On the system on which you installed the FileZilla FTP server, in the Administration interface, click Server from the menu bar item, then click Configure…

b.   In the left pane, select Users, and then click the Add button.

c.   Type **bob** for the username and press ENTER.

d.   There will be a check in the checkbox next to User is enabled, by default. From the Credentials: dropdown, select Require a password to log in. Type **bob** into the textbox below the dropdown (see Figure 8-4, which includes Step 2e, as well).

→ **Note**

A password like this is, of course, not recommended, but is being used here for demonstrative purposes.

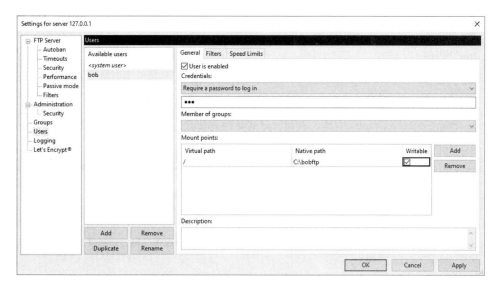

FIGURE 8-4   FileZilla FTP server

 e. In the Mount points: section, click the Add button. Put / for the Virtual path and C:\bobftp for the Native path. Then, put a check in the Writable checkbox (see Figure 8-4).

 f. Click the OK button to save the configuration and close the window.

Step 3 On the system running the FTP server, using Windows Explorer, create a folder called **bobftp** off of the root of the C:\ drive.

Step 4 Start sniffing with Wireshark on the system on which you installed the FTP server. Use a display filter of **ip.addr** == followed by the IP address of the system running the FTP client (for example, **ip.addr == 192.168.1.52**), to restrict the output to related packets.

 5i–5l

Step 5 Allow FTP through the firewall.

 a. On the system running the FTP server, in the search box, type **firewall** and select Windows Defender Firewall.

 b. In the pane at the left, select Allow An App Or Feature Through Windows Defender Firewall.

 c. Click the Change settings button at the top.

 d. Click the Allow another app... button.

 e. In the Add an app window that opens, click the Browse button.

 f. Browse to the C:\Program Files\FileZilla Server folder.

 g. Double-click FileZilla Server.exe.

 h. Click the Add button.

 i. Verify that filezilla-server.exe (it may display without the .exe extension) has been added to the Allowed Apps And Features list.

 j. Make sure there are checks in the checkboxes for Private and Public (you'll have to add the check for the Public checkbox) for filezilla-server.exe.

 k. Click the OK button to close the window.

 l. Close the Windows Defender Firewall by clicking the X in the top right.

 m. Open a command prompt as an admin and execute the following command, which disables stateful inspection (and possible blocking) of FTP traffic, allowing the custom rule created to function as expected for passive mode FTP traffic:

```
netsh advfirewall set global StatefulFTP disable
```

In a rare deviation from "No news is good news," regarding output in the command prompt, you'll see "Ok."

6c–6d

Step 6

a. On the system on which you installed the FileZilla FTP client, at the top of the client application, type in the IP address of the FTP server (execute `ipconfig` from a command prompt on that system to get it) in the Host: box.

b. Provide the username of **bob** and password of **bob** in the Username: and Password: boxes. Leave the Port box blank, as FTP will use its default port for establishing the connection (see Figure 8-5).

c. Click the Quickconnect button.

d. In the Unknown certificate window, click the OK button.

 7a–7d

7c–7d

Step 7 Analyze the results.

a. What do you see in Wireshark, on the system running the FTP server, related to the FTP control traffic?

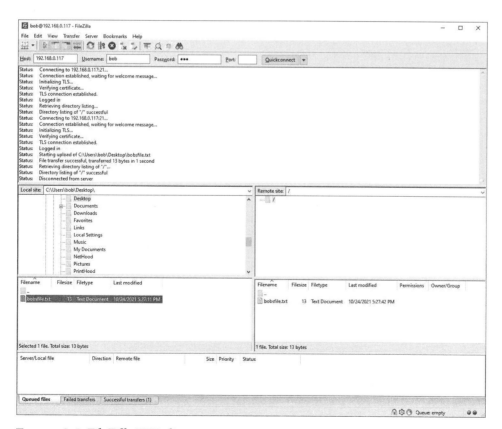

FIGURE 8-5 FileZilla FTP client

    b.   Execute `netstat -an` in a command prompt.

    c.   Based on what you saw in Wireshark and in the command prompt output, what port is being used by the FTP server for control information?

    d.   Based on what you saw in Wireshark and in the command prompt output, what port is being used by the FTP client for control information?

 8a–8b

Step 8   Create and transfer a file.

    a.   With Wireshark still running on the system with the FTP server, on the system with the FTP client, create a text file called **bobsfile** on the desktop, and type a sentence into that file.

    b.   In the FileZilla FTP client on the same system, in the Local Site: pane, browse to the desktop. From the pane below, where you can see the files on the desktop, drag and drop bobsfile.txt to the pane to its right (showing the message "Empty directory listing), which represents the FTP server's directory for the user bob (See Figure 8-5).

Step 9   On the system running the FTP server, use Windows Explorer to browse and open the file that was just uploaded to the server.

 10a–10d

 10c–10d

Step 10   Analyze the results.

    a.   What do you see in Wireshark on the server related to the FTP data traffic?

    b.   On the system running the FTP server, open a command prompt and run `netstat -an`.

    c.   Based on what you saw in Wireshark and in the command prompt, what is being received over TLS, and what ports are being used by the FTP server?

    d.   Based on what you saw in Wireshark and in the command prompt, what is being sent over TLS and what ports are being used by the FTP client?

Step 11   In the past, port 20 was used by FTP servers for the data transfer. Why isn't it used anymore? Use this link as a reference: http://slacksite.com/other/ftp.html.

30 MINUTES

Lab Exercise 8.05: The TCP Three-Way Handshake and Beyond

You've heard much about the TCP three-way handshake up to this point, but now it's time to actually see it in action. In order to form a bidirectional line of communication at Layer 4 with the sequencing, acknowledging, connection-oriented features, and guaranteed delivery of TCP, each host needs to acknowledge a TCP segment sent from the other side.

Learning Objectives

In this lab exercise, you'll analyze the TCP three-way handshake with Wireshark. Seeing the sequence and acknowledgment numbers will solidify your knowledge of the steps involved. By the end of this lab exercise, you'll be able to

- Analyze a connection between two systems in Wireshark

- Understand how the TCP three-way handshake works

- Understand what happens after the TCP three-way handshake

- Observe and record specific TCP flags related to the connection

- Understand how the other TCP flags work

- Observe and record sequence and acknowledgment numbers related to the connection

Lab Materials and Setup

The materials you'll need for this lab exercise are

- *Mike Meyers' CompTIA Network+ Guide to Managing and Troubleshooting Networks* textbook

- Windows 10 system with Internet access

Getting Down to Business

Before starting this lab exercise, it would be a great idea to review the "TCP" section in Chapter 8 of the *Mike Meyers' CompTIA Network+ Guide to Managing and Troubleshooting Networks* textbook; it contains a great look at the TCP three-way handshake.

Step 1   Pick a Web site, any Web site! From a command prompt, ping that FQDN (fully qualified domain name). You don't even need an ICMP Echo reply (covered in Chapter 6), just DNS (coming up in Chapter 9) to turn that FQDN into its corresponding IP address. For example, even though www.flcc.edu is blocking ICMP Echo requests in this case, you're able to see its IP address of 192.156.234.2:

```
c:\Users\jswics>ping www.flcc.edu

Pinging www.flcc.edu [192.156.234.2] with 32 bytes of data:
Request timed out.
Request timed out.
Request timed out.
Request timed out.

Ping statistics for 192.156.234.2:
    Packets: Sent = 4, Received = 0, Lost = 4 (100% loss),
```

Open Wireshark, and start capturing packets. Add a display filter of **ip.addr** == followed by the IP address seen in the ping attempt (in the www.flcc.edu example, it would be **ip.addr == 192.156.234.2**), which will limit the display to packets to and from the Web server, and press ENTER. Open a browser, and head to the FQDN you pinged. After the page loads, stop the Wireshark capture.

Step 2   Look at the first three rows in the Wireshark capture, as shown in Figure 8-6 with SYN (synchronize) flags and ACK (acknowledgment) flags shown. Although not shown in Figure 8-6, your display might include other packets in between the TCP three-way handshake rows. If so, no worries, just focus on the relevant rows. What TCP flags are set for each step of those TCP segments of the TCP three-way handshake?

Step 3   Select the row with the first step of the TCP three-way handshake in the Packet List pane. In the Packet Details pane, click the > next to Transmission Control Protocol to see its fields, and select the Sequence Number field. Look in the Packet Bytes pane to see the actual sequence number in hex (see Figure 8-7). What is the actual sequence number in your capture?

```
File  Edit  View  Go  Capture  Analyze  Statistics  Telephony  Tools  Internals  Help
●  ◎  ⦿  ◢  ▣  ⬚  ⊞  ✕  ⧉  | Q  ⟵  ⟶  ⊚  ⬚  ⬚  | ▤▣ | Q  Q  Q  ⊡ | ⬚  ⬚  ⬚  ✕ | ⬚
Filter:  ip.addr==75.126.29.106                     ▼ Expression...  Clear  Apply  Save
No.   Time     Source              Destination        Protocol  Length  Info
    14 7.670580 192.168.1.145       75.126.29.106      TCP       66 59056→80 [SYN] Seq=0 Win=8192 Len=0 MSS=1460 WS=4 SACK_PERM=1
    15 7.713672 75.126.29.106       192.168.1.145      TCP       66 80→59056 [SYN, ACK] Seq=0 Ack=1 Win=14600 Len=0 MSS=1460 SACK_PERM=1 WS=128
    16 7.713764 192.168.1.145       75.126.29.106      TCP       54 59056→80 [ACK] Seq=1 Ack=1 Win=65700 Len=0
```

FIGURE 8-6 The TCP three-way handshake

```
⊟ Transmission Control Protocol, Src Port: 59056 (59056), Dst Port: 80 (80), Seq: 0, Len: 0
    Source Port: 59056 (59056)
    Destination Port: 80 (80)
    [Stream index: 3]
    [TCP Segment Len: 0]
    Sequence number: 0        (relative sequence number)
    Acknowledgment number: 0
    Header Length: 32 bytes
  ⊞ .... 0000 0000 0010 = Flags: 0x002 (SYN)
    Window size value: 8192
    [Calculated window size: 8192]
  ⊞ Checksum: 0x825f [validation disabled]
    Urgent pointer: 0
  ⊞ Options: (12 bytes), Maximum segment size, No-Operation (NOP), Window scale, No-Operation (NOP), No-Operation (NOP), SACK permitted


0020  1d 6a e6 b0 00 50 ef 8a  0b 0a 00 00 00 00 80 02   .j...P..........
0030  20 00 82 5f 00 00 02 04  05 b4 01 03 03 02 01 01    .._.... ........
0040  04 02                                               ..
```

FIGURE 8-7 The first sequence number

  a–b

Step 4   Select the row with the second step of the TCP three-way handshake in the Packet List pane.

   a.   In the Packet Details pane, expand the TCP segment fields, and select the Sequence Number field. Look in the Packet Bytes pane to see the actual sequence number in hex. What is the actual sequence number in your capture?

   b.   Click the field called Acknowledgment Number. Look in the Packet Bytes pane to see the actual acknowledgment number in hex. What is the actual acknowledgment number in your capture? It should be one more than the sequence number you got in Step 3. This value will be *x+1* to the *x* sequence number you recorded in the previous step.

Step 5   Select the row with the third step of the TCP three-way handshake in the Packet List pane. In the Packet Details pane, expand the TCP segment fields, and select the Acknowledgment Number field. Look in the Packet Bytes pane to see the actual acknowledgment number in hex. What is the actual acknowledgment number in your capture? It should be one more than the sequence number you got in Step 4. This value will be *y+1* to the *y* sequence number you recorded in the previous step.

Step 6   List the four numbers in hex that follow the *x, x+1, y, y+1* pattern, and explain how they prove that a TCP three-way handshake occurred.

Step 7   After the TCP three-way handshake, the client will send a request and the server will acknowledge that request. Then, the server will send what was requested in multiple TCP segments. The client will acknowledge them by acknowledging every other or every third one (for efficiency, instead of acknowledging each one, as TCP ACKs are cumulative).

The sequence numbers in the client's request and the server's response start exactly where they left off for each side in the TCP three-way handshake and increment by the size of data. The subsequent acknowledgment numbers for each side will increment the sequence numbers by one. For example, let's say the TCP three-way handshake values (using simple base 10 values in this example) were

- Client: SYN 75 (Step 1)

- Server: SYN 300 ACK 76 (Step 2)

- Client: ACK 301 (Step 3)

If the client's HTTP GET Request was 500 bytes, those bytes would be numbered 76–575, since the last acknowledgment number (the only acknowledgment number at this point) it heard from the server was 76, which means "start your next sequence number with 76." The server, upon receipt of the HTTP GET request, sends an acknowledgment number of 576, which means "I got through byte 575. Start your next sequence number with 576." If the client has no more requests then or later in the connection, it simply doesn't send anything.

Then, the server will send multiple TCP segments of data in response, starting with a sequence number of 301, which is the last (the only) acknowledgment number from the client. If the server sent three segments of 1000 bytes each: the bytes would be numbered 301–1300 for the first, 1301–2300 for the second, and 2301–3300 for the third. If the client got all three, it would send an acknowledgment number of 3301, which means "I got through 3300. Start your next sequence number at 3301."

If the client only got the first, it would raise the ACK flag and send an acknowledgment number of 1301. If the client only got the first two, it would send an acknowledgment number of 2301. If the client got the first and third, it would send an acknowledgment number of 1301, since TCP acknowledgments are cumulative and only acknowledge a consecutive set of bytes. The loss of the second segment breaks up the continuity between the first and the third segments. Therefore, an acknowledgment number of 3301 would imply that segments 1, 2, and 3 were all received.

In this case, a special TCP option known as SACK (selective acknowledgment) in the TCP header containing the acknowledgment number of 1301 will contain information that bytes 2301–3300 were received as well, letting the server know it only needs to resend the second segment containing bytes 1301–2300. When the client gets the missing second segment, it can now send an acknowledgment number of 3301, since it already has the third segment.

That is exactly how we can say TCP is guaranteed. When a segment's bytes aren't acknowledged, that lets the sender know that it needs to retransmit them.

See if you can follow, further down in your capture, to see this in action, where the sequence numbers go up by the size of the actual data.

Step 8   A TCP connection can be terminated gracefully with the FIN (*finis*—spelled as such in RFC 793, referencing the Latin word meaning "the end") flag from each side (with an ACK sent in response from the other side) or abruptly with the RST (reset) flag. Reasons for sending an RST to abort a connection include receiving an invalid header, not having enough resources present to support the connection, not receiving any response from the other side, and even optimizing—getting rid of the other side as quickly as possible instead of a graceful close with FINs that takes more time and resources. Furthermore, some servers will not send anything at the end and simply let the connection time out as a TCP timer will kick in and close the connection. Sometimes the client will send the first FIN, while other times the server will send the first FIN. It varies by protocol and service. For example, an SSH client will send the first FIN to an SSH server, when the user terminates the connection, while a Web server will send the first FIN to a Web browser, when it gets an ACK for the last segment in the exchange.

The normal way a TCP connection goes through a graceful teardown process is as follows, where Side A represents the side (either client or server) initiating the teardown process and Side B represents the other side (either client or server):

- Side A: FIN (Step 1)
- Side B: ACK (Step 2)
- Side B: FIN (Step 3)
- Side A: ACK (Step 4)

The sequence number in each FIN will be what it was from where the last data segment (which will also be the same number as the last acknowledgment number received from the other side). The ACK will increment this number by one.

Termination consists of four steps (a couple of two-way handshakes) because when the first FIN is received by a system, it has to let its application process know about it and then wait for a response. If the application is ready to terminate the connection itself, a FIN will be sent. If the application has more data to send, it can continue to send more data in this now "half-closed" connection and eventually send the FIN (which will elicit an ACK from the side that sent the first FIN) when all data has been sent and acknowledged.

It's like when someone says "Bye. I have to go!" in a phone conversation and the other person says "No, wait. I have something else to tell you!"

RFC 793 explains that after a connection is established, the ACK flag is always set in subsequent segments. That's why when the FINs are set, the ACK flags will be set as well. However, the FIN-ACK combination is not analogous to the SYN-ACK combination. In the TCP header for each of the ACKs that are sent in response to the FINs, the Acknowledgment Number field values increment the Sequence Number field values by one, the same way it was done in the TCP three-way handshake.

Visit a few Web sites and see how the connection is closed: FINs and ACKs? RSTs? Nothing? It will vary greatly by server.

→ **Note**

For completeness purposes, here are the other two standard flags in the TCP flags section of the TCP header:

The URG (urgent) flag is a relic of the past and is not really used by modern protocols. It used to be a way to tell a destination system to prioritize data in a segment at a location specified by the Urgent Pointer field in the TCP header.

The PSH (push) flag is used to tell the sending system to push the data down and out immediately without waiting for a buffer to accumulate (which would normally happen for efficient data transfer when many TCP segments are sent), as well as to tell the receiving system to push the received data up to the receiving application without waiting for a buffer to accumulate (which would normally happen for efficient data transfer when many TCP segments are received). The PSH flag is used at the end of an HTTP or TLS session, when there's no more data to be sent or received, as well as during an SSH session, where the keystrokes need to be sent immediately to a remote system, in addition to other instances. Without the PSH flag, there could be significant latency, making the communication unbearable.

→ **Note**

Unskilled Attackers Pester Real Security Folks is the mnemonic to remember the six standard TCP flags (there are three nonstandard ones as well): URG, ACK, PSH, RST, SYN, FIN.

Lab Analysis

1. Scott asks you to explain the main operational difference between TCP and UDP. How does this difference affect which services use TCP or UDP?

2. Ann wants to know how ports open and close. She also wants to know what effect firewalls have on the actual opening and closing of ports. Can you help her?

3. Harrison wants you to give him a quick rundown of the TCP three-way handshake. Can you quickly summarize it for him?

4. Meir, while capturing packets with Wireshark, pings one of the other computers on his network. He examines the output of the capture and finds the section relating to the ping activity. What is the underlying protocol you would expect Meir to observe?

Key Term Quiz

Use the terms in this list to complete the sentences that follow.

21   netstat -b

Apache HTTP server   SMTP (Simple Mail Transfer Protocol)

ICMP (Internet Control Message Protocol)   TCP (Transmission Control Protocol)

IGMP (Internet Group Management Protocol)   UDP (User Datagram Protocol)

IMAP (Internet Message Access Protocol)

1. A command that will allow you to explore all of the current connections and the associated program or service involved with the connection is _____.

2. _____ and _____ are defined at the Transport layer of the OSI model, whereas _____ and _____ are defined at the Network layer of the OSI model.

3. When working with e-mail, _____ is associated with sending e-mail and _____ is associated with receiving e-mail.

4. _____ listens on port 80.

5. FTP servers listen for requests from clients and send responses to clients on port _____.

Chapter 9
Network Naming

Lab Exercises

As demonstrated in the last few chapters, you can cable some systems together and configure (statically or dynamically) their IP addresses, subnet masks, and default gateways to create a very basic TCP/IP network. Over this network, users can send information to and receive information from each other. You can even add a Web server to this small network and host some resources for clients to access. However, without the addition of some sort of naming convention and resolution process, you'll soon find that the use and management of this network becomes fairly tedious. Then, consider what happens when your internal devices need to access resources from other networks from other parts of the world. What happens then?

Without a naming convention and resolution process, you'll be stuck using IP addresses for everything. Instead of typing something like www.flcc.edu into your Web browser, you'll need to enter the IP address of the FLCC (Finger Lakes Community College) Web server. No one can keep track of all the IP addresses of all the resources out there. Furthermore, some sort of centralized directory listing would be impossible to maintain. Even further, IP addresses of resources change from time to time, so a directory listing could have lots of outdated information at any given point in time.

Initially, in the 1970s, a text file called HOSTS.TXT was manually maintained and shared by Stanford Research Institute (SRI) for the Advanced Research Projects Agency Network (ARPANET). The file mapped networks, gateways, and hostnames to IP addresses for member organizations. Changes were e-mailed to SRI, and a new HOSTS.TXT was compiled once or twice weekly. Over time, the size of this file grew to an unmanageable level, and the network traffic and processing requirements in terms of distributing the file became untenable. Furthermore, duplicate names were not allowed, but there was no mechanism to stop anyone from inserting a conflicting name into HOSTS.TXT and breaking the system. For example, a legitimate host could be prevented from receiving traffic. As the ARPANET grew with each year, sometimes by the time an update to HOSTS.TXT was received and processed, a host had already changed addresses or a new host was added, and the file was outdated upon receipt.

An amazing repository of actual HOSTS.TXT files has been collected through the years, and it can be accessed here: https://emaillab.jp/dns/hosts/.

Operating systems today have a text file called hosts (lowercase with no extension) that maps hostnames, or fully qualified domain names (FQDNs), to IP addresses. This file can be used by both malware and anti-malware programs. Malware can write to this file, redirecting network traffic from intended Web sites to Web sites controlled by attackers that contain malware. However, this has become less common in recent years with other protection mechanisms now in place that make malicious entries into the hosts file worthless. Anti-malware programs use the hosts file too, redirecting known FQDNs for ads, malware, and more, to the loopback address (127.0.0.1) or to an invalid address (0.0.0.0), which means your machine will never reach out to those undesirable Web sites in the event that a link for one of them was clicked or a site you were on redirected you to one of them. If you're running a Web server on a machine, redirecting traffic to 0.0.0.0 is more desirable, since it won't be eating up CPU cycles and RAM, and traffic will be rejected instantly.

For many years, Dan Pollock has been maintaining and frequently updating a hosts file you can copy and paste into your actual hosts file (C:\Windows\System32\drivers\etc\hosts on Windows and /etc/hosts on Linux and macOS) that redirects your machine away from undesirable Web sites as anti-malware programs do. The base HTML file, which redirects to 127.0.0.1, is located at https://someonewhocares.org/hosts/, but there are variations in the menu at the right that include a text version, an RSS feed, an IPv6 version (which also includes IPv4) in both HTML and text formats, a version that redirects to 0.0.0.0 in both HTML and text formats, and an IPv6 version of that 0.0.0.0 version in both HTML and text formats, as well as versions of 127.0.0.1 and 0.0.0.0 for old Macs.

The problems with HOSTS.TXT were solved with 1983's RFC 882 (https://datatracker.ietf.org/doc/html/rfc882) and RFC 883 (https://datatracker.ietf.org/doc/html/rfc883), which were superseded by 1987's RFC 1034 (https://datatracker.ietf.org/doc/html/rfc1034) and RFC 1035 (https://datatracker.ietf.org/doc/html/rfc1035).

The solution was a powerful new protocol, Domain Name System (DNS).

> ➜ **Note**
>
> There is an erroneous belief by some that the hosts file is consulted before the DNS resolver cache. That's just not true. The contents of the hosts file are merged into the DNS resolver cache, along with any DNS query responses. When you clear the DNS resolver cache, any entries in the hosts file will repopulate in the DNS resolver cache.

 **30 MINUTES**

Lab Exercise 9.01: DNS Queries, DNS Responses, and DNS Resolver Cache

Jonathan suggests you first review the DNS hierarchical process and then see DNS in action in both the command prompt and Wireshark.

Learning Objectives

In this lab exercise, you'll start your exploration of DNS. By the end of this lab exercise, you'll be able to

- Describe the DNS hierarchal process
- Understand the DNS query and response process
- Understand how the DNS resolver cache works

Lab Materials and Setup

The materials you'll need for this lab exercise are

- *Mike Meyers' CompTIA Network+ Guide to Managing and Troubleshooting Networks* textbook

- Windows 10 system with Internet access

Getting Down to Business

Having recently finished Chapter 9 on network naming in the *Mike Meyers' CompTIA Network+ Guide to Managing and Troubleshooting Networks* textbook, you know that you are going to have to implement DNS for the JSW systems. Time to jump in!

→ **Note**

For all the commands in this chapter, press ENTER after every command to execute them.

Step 1   Place the following steps in numerical order, from first to last (10), in the DNS hierarchical process.

____ Authoritative TLD DNS server gives a referral to the destination domain's authoritative DNS servers.

____ DNS client adds the response to its DNS resolver cache.

____ Local DNS server queries one of the authoritative TLD DNS servers.

____ Destination domain's authoritative DNS server gives the DNS response to the local DNS server.

____ Root server gives a referral to authoritative TLD DNS servers.

____ DNS client queries one of its local DNS servers.

____ Local DNS server queries one of the destination domain's authoritative DNS servers.

____ DNS client checks its DNS resolver cache.

____ Local DNS server caches the response and gives the DNS response to the DNS client.

____ Local DNS server queries one of the 13 root servers.

Step 2   Open a command prompt. To view your PC's TCP/IP configuration, including IP addresses of the DNS servers, execute `ipconfig /all`. What are the IP addresses of your DNS servers?

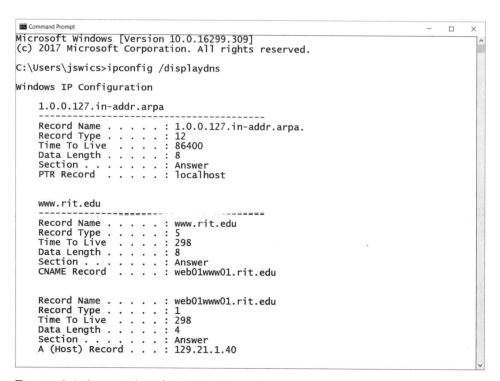

```
Command Prompt                                                    —   □   ×
Microsoft Windows [Version 10.0.16299.309]
(c) 2017 Microsoft Corporation. All rights reserved.

C:\Users\jswics>ipconfig /displaydns

Windows IP Configuration

    1.0.0.127.in-addr.arpa
    ----------------------------------------
    Record Name . . . . . : 1.0.0.127.in-addr.arpa.
    Record Type . . . . . : 12
    Time To Live  . . . . : 86400
    Data Length . . . . . : 8
    Section . . . . . . . : Answer
    PTR Record  . . . . . : localhost


    www.rit.edu
    ----------------------------------------
    Record Name . . . . . : www.rit.edu
    Record Type . . . . . : 5
    Time To Live  . . . . : 298
    Data Length . . . . . : 8
    Section . . . . . . . : Answer
    CNAME Record  . . . . : web01www01.rit.edu


    Record Name . . . . . : web01www01.rit.edu
    Record Type . . . . . : 1
    Time To Live  . . . . : 298
    Data Length . . . . . : 4
    Section . . . . . . . : Answer
    A (Host) Record . . . : 129.21.1.40
```

FIGURE 9-1 `ipconfig /displaydns` **output**

Step 3 A PC's DNS resolver cache in RAM stores recently resolved entries received from its DNS servers. To view a display of resolved addresses cached on your PC, execute `ipconfig /displaydns`. You should see a list of results similar to what's shown in Figure 9-1. (More explanation of this output is provided in Lab 9.02, Step 5.)

 4a–4c

 4a, 4d

Step 4 Generate a DNS query and response for www.flcc.edu. In the past, I had students go to www.flcc.edu from a browser for this next step. However, with DNS over HTTPS (DoH) now being implemented by browsers, including Google Chrome and Mozilla Firefox, these DNS queries and DNS responses are now encrypted and not readable through Wireshark anymore. Therefore, effective for this edition and in-class demos, I recommend using ping from the command prompt instead.

✖ **Cross Reference**

DoH and DoT are covered in the next chapter.

a. Manually clear the DNS resolver cache by executing `ipconfig /flushdns` and then immediately execute `ipconfig /displaydns`. How do the results compare to the time you displayed your DNS resolver cache in the previous step?

b. Start sniffing with Wireshark, using a display filter of **dns**, or for even more specific results, filter by **dns.qry.name == www.flcc.edu**. Now, execute `ping www.flcc.edu`.

c. In the Packet List pane, find and select the DNS query response for the A (IPv4 host address) resource record of www.flcc.edu (see Figure 9-2). In the Packet Details pane, expand the Domain Name System (response) section in the UDP datagram, and then expand the Answers section to reveal the IP address given to your system for www.flcc.edu (also shown in Figure 9-2). You'll also notice in Figure 9-2 a DNS query and DNS response for the AAAA (IPv6 host address) record for www.flcc.edu. In this case, the FLCC Web server isn't enabled for IPv6, so there is no answer in the DNS response for the AAAA resource record, but rather the SOA (start of authority) resource record, which contains domain/zone information.

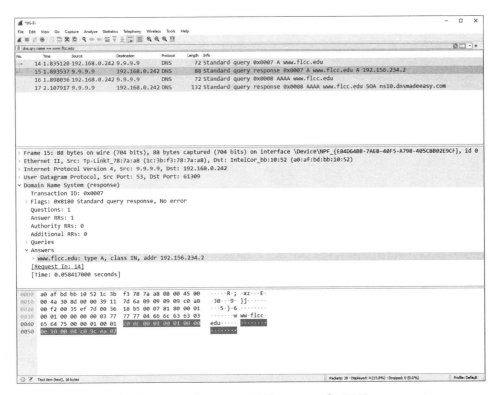

FIGURE 9-2 Wireshark capture showing a DNS query and a DNS response

> **→ Note**
>
> To search by string in Wireshark (with or without a display filter in place), click Edit in the menu bar and then Find Packet.... A new bar will appear at the top. In that bar, change the dropdown Display filter to String, type www.flcc.edu in the search box, and click the Find button.

d. Referring to the OSI model, DNS, at Layer 7, is in the UDP datagram at Layer 4. The data is then encapsulated by a Layer 3 IP packet. Finally, the IP packet is encapsulated by a Layer 2 frame.

Why do you think DNS uses UDP for DNS queries and replies (aside from responses greater than 512 bytes, which are rare, and a zone transfer, which is when a primary DNS server sends a copy of its zone containing DNS records to a secondary DNS server for that domain, which both use TCP)?

> **→ Note**
>
> A zone is part of the DNS namespace under the management and administration of a single organization. A zone can consist of more than one subdomain, and different zones can exist on the same DNS server.

Step 5   Go through both the DNS query and DNS response in the Packet Details pane and answer the following questions. What port do DNS servers use? What ports do DNS clients use? What is the answer to the query, "What's the IP address of www.flcc.edu?"

 6a–6f

 6g

Step 6   See how the DNS resolver cache works.

a. Start sniffing with Wireshark, using a display filter of **dns or icmp**, which will show packets containing either DNS or ICMP.

b. In the command prompt, clear the DNS resolver cache once again by executing `ipconfig /flushdns`, and then execute `ping www.syracuse.edu`. You should see the DNS query and DNS response in Wireshark, followed by the ICMP Echo requests and ICMP Echo replies.

c.   You'll notice from the command prompt output that the FQDN is resolved into its corresponding IP address.

d.   Execute `ipconfig /displaydns` to see the records from www.syracuse.edu in the DNS resolver cache. You should notice a TTL (Time to Live) of around 50 seconds, which means your PC will keep the related information cached for this amount of time. It was originally 60 (which you can see if you drill down in the corresponding packet in Wireshark), so what you see for a value will be how quickly after the ping you displayed the cache. In fact, with the capture stopped, from the menu bar, click File, click Save, type a name and select a location, and click the Save button (the extension will default to pcapng: Packet Capture Next Generation). You can create a great repository of saved captures from your hands-on activities for future reference in this fashion. I'd like you to save this one in particular for Step 5 of Lab Exercise 9.02.

e.   Execute `ipconfig /displaydns` again, and you'll notice the TTL is decrementing with each second.

f.   Try it yet again, and it will be even lower, as it ticks down to 0, when the related information will be removed from the DNS resolver cache.

g.   In fact, if you execute `ping www.syracuse.edu` again while still sniffing in Wireshark, you'll notice the ICMPs again, but you will not see the DNS query and response for the A resource records (IPv4 host addresses), since they are in the cache. As of this writing, Syracuse University doesn't have IPv6 enabled for their Web server, so you will once again see the DNS query and response for the AAAA resource records (IPv6 host addresses). When will you see the DNS query and response for the A records related to this ping again?

✖ Cross Reference

More on A and AAAA resource records, as well as others, is coming up in the next lab exercise.

 30 MINUTES

Lab Exercise 9.02: nslookup

Jonathan thinks it's time for you to look at a great utility, nslookup (name server lookup), that does not use the operating system's DNS resolver library for its queries, but rather operates on its own. There will be times when you'll need this tool to troubleshoot and diagnose issues. When name resolution fails, this tool will give you a great behind-the-scenes look at DNS in terms of domain names, IP addresses, DNS servers, mail servers, and more.

Learning Objectives

In this lab exercise, you'll learn how to use the nslookup utility. By the end of this lab exercise, you'll be able to

- Troubleshoot DNS issues
- Diagnose DNS problems

Lab Materials and Setup

The materials you'll need for this lab exercise are

- *Mike Meyers' CompTIA Network+ Guide to Managing and Troubleshooting Networks* textbook
- Windows 10 system with Internet connectivity

Getting Down to Business

Users complain about not being able to access a Web site. You have an idea what the problem is, and you decide to run a few troubleshooting and diagnostic tests to see if they will provide answers to this conundrum and get the network running at optimum performance!

 1a–1d

 1d

Step 1

    a.   Start sniffing with Wireshark, using a display filter of **dns**. As you go through each step, notice the DNS queries and DNS responses in Wireshark.

    b.   Open a command prompt, type nslookup, and press ENTER, which will run the utility in interactive mode. To break out of this mode, press CTRL-C.

> **→ Note**
>
> **You can also run nslookup in non-interactive mode by typing in the rest of a command after nslookup.**

    c.   You'll notice the FQDN and IP address of your default server and a > prompt. At the > prompt, type set q=ns and press ENTER, which will set the query type to NS, the name server DNS resource record type that identifies authoritative DNS servers (DNS servers that have zone files to consult for responses instead of using a cache like a local DNS server does, querying for its clients).

    d.   Now, just type . (a period) and press ENTER (see Figure 9-3). What do you see as output?

```
Command Prompt - nslookup                                    —   □   ×
Microsoft Windows [Version 10.0.16299.309]
(c) 2017 Microsoft Corporation. All rights reserved.

C:\Users\jswics>nslookup
Default Server:  dns.quad9.net
Address:  9.9.9.9

> set q=ns
> .
Server:  dns.quad9.net
Address:  9.9.9.9

Non-authoritative answer:
(root)   nameserver = j.root-servers.net
(root)   nameserver = k.root-servers.net
(root)   nameserver = l.root-servers.net
(root)   nameserver = m.root-servers.net
(root)   nameserver = a.root-servers.net
(root)   nameserver = b.root-servers.net
(root)   nameserver = c.root-servers.net
(root)   nameserver = d.root-servers.net
(root)   nameserver = e.root-servers.net
(root)   nameserver = f.root-servers.net
(root)   nameserver = g.root-servers.net
(root)   nameserver = h.root-servers.net
(root)   nameserver = i.root-servers.net
>
```

FIGURE 9-3 nslookup showing the root servers

Step 2 At the > prompt, type com. and press ENTER Notice, as shown in Figure 9-4, that it's com followed by . and not .com (with the dot before com). The . at the end prevents your system from appending anything after this (which it could do based on your configuration), and it's the proper way to end an FQDN. Furthermore, queries never begin with a . (as in .com).

```
Command Prompt - nslookup                                    —   □   ×
Microsoft Windows [Version 10.0.16299.309]
(c) 2017 Microsoft Corporation. All rights reserved.

C:\Users\jswics>nslookup
Default Server:  dns.quad9.net
Address:  9.9.9.9

> set q=ns
> com.
Server:  dns.quad9.net
Address:  9.9.9.9

Non-authoritative answer:
com      nameserver = d.gtld-servers.net
com      nameserver = c.gtld-servers.net
com      nameserver = i.gtld-servers.net
com      nameserver = e.gtld-servers.net
com      nameserver = h.gtld-servers.net
com      nameserver = f.gtld-servers.net
com      nameserver = m.gtld-servers.net
com      nameserver = a.gtld-servers.net
com      nameserver = g.gtld-servers.net
com      nameserver = b.gtld-servers.net
com      nameserver = j.gtld-servers.net
com      nameserver = l.gtld-servers.net
com      nameserver = k.gtld-servers.net
>
```

FIGURE 9-4 nslookup showing the authoritative DNS servers for the .com top-level domain (TLD)

In a similar fashion, one at a time, execute queries for (without the commas, but with dots) net., edu., gov., and other top-level domains (TLDs) you can think of. What do you see as output?

Step 3   At the > prompt, one at a time, execute queries for (without the commas) rit.edu., flcc.edu., syr.edu., and naz.edu. (without the commas, but with dots). See Figure 9-5. What do you see as output?

→ **Note**

> You will not get the expected results if you type www (or any hostname) in front of any of the listed domains in this step. nslookup will display the start of authority (SOA) resource record for the domain (which contains domain/zone information) instead of the DNS servers. The reason is because NS records are for an entire domain, not a specific machine, like a Web server named www (which typing www before the domain implies).

```
Command Prompt - nslookup                                          —   □   ×
Microsoft Windows [Version 10.0.16299.309]
(c) 2017 Microsoft Corporation. All rights reserved.

C:\Users\jswics>nslookup
Default Server:  dns.quad9.net
Address:  9.9.9.9

> set q=ns
> rit.edu.
Server:  dns.quad9.net
Address:  9.9.9.9

Non-authoritative answer:
rit.edu nameserver = accuvax.northwestern.edu
rit.edu nameserver = ns1a.rit.edu
rit.edu nameserver = ns2a.rit.edu
> flcc.edu.
Server:  dns.quad9.net
Address:  9.9.9.9

Non-authoritative answer:
flcc.edu        nameserver = ns.flcc.edu
flcc.edu        nameserver = ns4.flcc.edu
flcc.edu        nameserver = ns7.suny.edu
flcc.edu        nameserver = ns8.suny.edu
flcc.edu        nameserver = ns9.suny.edu
flcc.edu        nameserver = dns3.flcc.edu
>
```

FIGURE 9-5 nslookup showing the authoritative DNS servers for the rit.edu and flcc.edu domains

Step 4 At the > prompt, type set q=mx and press ENTER. Now, instead of the NS (name server) records for the domain, nslookup will display the MX (mail exchange) resource records, which identify a domain's mail servers. Once again, one at a time, execute queries for (without the commas) rit.edu., flcc.edu., syr.edu., and naz.edu. (without the commas, but with the dots at the end). What do you see as output?

Step 5 At the > prompt, type set q=a and press ENTER. Now nslookup will show the A (IPv4 address) resource record(s) for each query. Type www.rit.edu. (with or without the dot at the end this time) and press ENTER to get the IPv4 address of the RIT Web server.

What is the IPv4 address of the RIT Web server?

You'll notice the output contains web01www01.rit.edu for the name, and the Wireshark capture shows a CNAME (canonical name) record in response with the same FQDN (web01www01.rit.edu).

In this case, the CNAME record allows RIT to maintain an internal naming standard for the Web server of web01www01.rit.edu, but not require Web site visitors to type in that long name. Instead, www will be mapped to web01www01. Instead of requiring another query along the lines of "OK, what's the IPv4 address of web01www01.rit.edu," the DNS server, in addition to the CNAME record, gives out the corresponding A record for web01www01.rit.edu. (Refer also back to Figure 9-1.)

CNAMEs are also used for geographical load balancing in DNS, where, for instance, if you go to www.cnn.com in New York, you'll be given a CNAME for a content delivery network (CDN) server close to you, which will be different than the CNAME given to someone from another country, which will refer to a server closer to them.

Finally, refer back to your saved capture from Lab Exercise 9.01, Step 6d. When you expand the DNS response that contains the IPv4 address of the Syracuse University Web server, you'll notice a CNAME as well as four A resource records in the Answers section of the Domain Name System (response) section (at the time of writing, which may be different by the time you're doing this). The systems administrator at Syracuse University created A records that map the domain itself to the IPv4 address of the Syracuse University Web server. The CNAME record changes any query for www.syracuse.edu into a query for syracuse.edu, which has four corresponding A records, representing four different potential ways to reach a Web server (returned in a round-robin order in each DNS response for load balancing and fault tolerance). Doing it the other way, mapping an FQDN to a domain, will cause failure in a zone since, in most cases, the root of the zone can't be a CNAME. Another option is to make an A record for both the domain itself and the FQDN. Now you know the real reason why you can leave off the www when going to Web sites!

Step 6   At the > prompt, type `set q=aaaa` and press ENTER. Now, nslookup will show the AAAA (IPv6 address) resource record(s) for each query. Type `www.rit.edu.` (with or without the dot at the end this time) and press ENTER to get the IPv6 address of the RIT Web server. What is the IPv6 address of the RIT Web server? IPv6 addresses are four times the length of IPv4 records ($32 \times 4 = 128$), which is why this DNS resource record was named AAAA.

Step 7   With nslookup, you can change the DNS server from your default DNS server that the queries go to by default by simply typing `server` followed either by the IP address or FQDN of another DNS server.

Type `server 8.8.8.8` or `server 8.8.4.4` to have any subsequent queries through nslookup go to one of these Google Public DNS Servers. Then execute a few of the earlier queries (see Figure 9-6). Where can you see proof that the queries went to the new servers in both the command prompt and Wireshark?

```
Command Prompt - nslookup                                        —  □  ×
Microsoft Windows [Version 10.0.16299.309]
(c) 2017 Microsoft Corporation. All rights reserved.

C:\Users\jswics>nslookup
Default Server:  dns.quad9.net
Address:  9.9.9.9

> server 8.8.8.8
Default Server:  google-public-dns-a.google.com
Address:  8.8.8.8

> set q=a
> www.rit.edu.
Server:  google-public-dns-a.google.com
Address:  8.8.8.8

Non-authoritative answer:
Name:    web01www01.rit.edu
Address:  129.21.1.40
Aliases:  www.rit.edu

> set q=mx
> rit.edu.
Server:  google-public-dns-a.google.com
Address:  8.8.8.8

Non-authoritative answer:
rit.edu  MX preference = 10, mail exchanger = mx03a-in01r.rit.edu
rit.edu  MX preference = 10, mail exchanger = mx03b-in01r.rit.edu
rit.edu  MX preference = 5, mail exchanger = mx03c-in01r.rit.edu
rit.edu  MX preference = 5, mail exchanger = mx03d-in01r.rit.edu
>
```

FIGURE 9-6 nslookup using a non-default DNS server

8a–8b

Step 8 As shown in earlier steps, the queries for NS and MX records return FQDNs, not IP addresses. What if you wanted the actual IP addresses for DNS servers and mail servers? Simple! Execute a query to find out the FQDN of the server first, and then take the answer that comes back in a DNS response and use that as the question in a DNS query for either an A or AAAA record!

   a. Find the FQDN of a DNS server from a domain, and then find its IP address.

   b. Find the FQDN of a mail server from a domain, and then find its IP address.

Step 9 At the > prompt, type `set q=ptr` and press ENTER. Now, nslookup will display the PTR (pointer) resource records. In essence, PTR resource records are the inverse of A and AAAA records, as they map a given IP address (either IPv4 or IPv6) to an FQDN. Type `129.21.1.40` and press ENTER. Notice in the output that the answer is the FQDN web01www01.rit.edu (the CNAME for www.rit.edu), which you saw earlier mapped to 129.21.1.40. Also notice that the octets of the IP address in the query are in reverse order with a TLD of in-addr.arpa, which is the TLD for DNS reverse zones. In order to use IP addresses in DNS this way, the IP address must be inverted. The reason why is very interesting. DNS goes from the more specific to the more general, for example, www (the hostname) to flcc (the second-level domain, SLD) to edu (the TLD). As you learned in Chapter 6, IP addresses go from the more general (the network ID) to the more specific (host ID). As a result, IP addresses have to be reformatted to be used in a reverse lookup zone hierarchy.

Step 10 Answer either what's being asked for (DNS query) or what's being returned (DNS response) in DNS. Choose from the following choices for each RR (resource record) type, which can be used more than once:

   • FQDN

   • IPv4 address

   • IPv6 address

   • domain

   • Either an IPv4 or an IPv6 address

RR type	The DNS query gives this to the DNS server	The DNS response gives this to the DNS client
A		
AAAA		
NS		
MX		
PTR		

 **45 MINUTES**

Lab Exercise 9.03: DNS Client and DNS Server

DNS allows a distributed database of name-to-IP-address and other mappings, called *zones*, to be stored on dedicated DNS servers and be accessed by clients to resolve mappings.

From the Internet DNS root servers to simple intranet DNS servers, the goal is to make access to resources as transparent to the end user as possible, while keeping administrative overhead to a minimum. Even entry-level network techs are expected to have some understanding of DNS server configuration and maintenance.

Learning Objectives

In this lab exercise, you'll install a DNS server. At the end of this lab exercise, you'll be able to

- Install and configure a DNS server on a Microsoft Windows Server 2019 system
- Configure DNS server entries to resolve hostnames to IP addresses

Lab Materials and Setup

The materials you'll need for this lab exercise are

- *Mike Meyers' CompTIA Network+ Guide to Managing and Troubleshooting Networks* textbook
- Windows 10 system
- Windows Server 2019 system

Getting Down to Business

It's time to dive in and configure a Windows Server 2019 system to provide DNS services. This will really solidify your knowledge of DNS! You hope to have this up and running before Jonathan returns to check on your progress.

1h

Step 1 Perform the following substeps to configure the DNS client:

    a. Open up the Windows 10 system.

    b. In the search box, type **sharing**.

    c. Click Manage Advanced Sharing Settings, which will appear as the top choice in the dynamically generated menu.

    d. In the address bar at the top, click Network And Sharing Center.

    e. In the pane at the left, click Change Adapter Settings.

    f. Right-click Ethernet and select Properties.

    g. Select Internet Protocol Version 4 (TCP/IPv4) and click the Properties button.

    h. In the General tab, which will open by default, change the radio button selection to Use The Following IP Address. Use the following information:

        • IP address: 192.168.1.18

        • Subnet mask: 255.255.255.0

        • Default gateway: (leave blank)

    In the next section, make sure Use The Following DNS Server Addresses is also selected. Assign 192.168.1.81 as the Preferred DNS Server, and leave the Alternate DNS Server field blank.

    i. Click the OK button, followed by the Close button, on the remaining dialog box. Click OK twice and close the Network Connections window.

 2a, 2c

Step 2 Perform the following substeps to configure the DNS server:

    a. Using the same steps provided earlier, assign the Windows Server 2019 system the following information:

        • IP address: 192.168.1.81

        • Subnet mask: 255.255.255.0

        • Default gateway: (leave blank)

        • Preferred DNS server: 127.0.0.1

        • Alternate DNS server: (leave blank)

b. Let's also give the server a hostname instead of using the long awkward one that was generated. Right-click the This PC icon on the desktop and select Properties.

c. In the Computer Name, Domain, And Workgroup Settings section, click Change Settings. Click the Change button toward the middle of the dialog box. Enter a better name for your computer and click OK. Then click OK, Close, and Restart Now. Your server will now reboot.

 3g

Step 3 Perform the following substeps to install the DNS role on the server:

a. On the Windows Server 2019 system, open Server Manager by clicking Start and then clicking Server Manager.

b. Click the Add Roles And Features link. Click Next until the Select Server Roles page is displayed.

c. Select the DNS Server check box. On the Add Roles And Features Wizard dialog box, click Add Features.

d. In the Add Roles Wizard, if the Before You Begin page appears, click Next.

e. In the Roles list, click DNS Server, and then click Next.

f. Read the information on the DNS Server page, and then click Next.

g. On the Confirm Installation Options page, verify that the DNS Server role will be installed, and then click Install.

 4e–4f

Step 4 Perform the following substeps to configure the DNS zone on the server:

a. On the Server Manager console, click Tools and open the DNS Manager console.

b. Expand Domain Server, select and right-click Forward Lookup Zones, and then select New Zone.

c. Navigate to the Zone Type page, and make sure that the Primary Zone radio button is selected.

d. Clear the Store The Zone In Active Directory check box, and then click Next.

e. On the Zone Name page, type **jonathan.weissman** and then click Next.

f. Navigate to the Dynamic Update page, make sure that the Do Not Allow Dynamic Updates radio button is selected, and then click Next and finish the wizard.

5b

Step 5 Perform the following substeps to add resource records (RRs) to the DNS Forward Lookup Zone:

    a. On the DNS Manager console, expand Forward Lookup Zones. Select and right-click the created zone, and then select New Host (A or AAAA).

    b. On the New Host dialog box, specify the name and IP address of your host and then click Add Host. Make the following two A records:

        • **professor** for the host name and **192.168.1.81** for the IP address (the server's IP address)

        • **rochester** for the host name and **192.168.1.99** for the IP address (an IP address that doesn't exist)

    c. Click **Done** once you have added the desired hosts.

 6d–6e

Step 6 Perform the following substeps to test out the DNS resource records from the client:

    a. Open up the Windows 10 system.

    b. Start Wireshark on the client, and filter by **dns**.

    c. You might have to disable firewalls on the systems to let the pings through by typing **Firewall** into the Windows search box, selecting Windows Defender Firewall, clicking Turn Windows Defender Firewall On Or Off, and clicking all radio buttons next to Turn Off Windows Defender Firewall (Not Recommended). These systems are not connected to the Internet, so it's fine. Furthermore, in Chapter 19, you'll see how to add rules that let pings through instead of disabling the firewall altogether, which is obviously a much better approach.

    d. Type `ping professor.jonathan.weissman.` (with the dot at the end). You should see the ping successfully get replies from your server in the command prompt. You should also see the DNS query and DNS reply in Wireshark.

    e. Type `ping rochester.jonathan.weissman.` (with the dot at the end). Even though the ping fails, since there is no host at 192.168.1.99, you'll see that the DNS query gets a DNS response in both the command prompt and Wireshark, mapping the name rochester.jonathan.weissman to its corresponding IP address of 192.168.1.99.

Lab Analysis

1. Janaye wants you to explain why DNS is said to be hierarchical. Can you help her out?

2. Owen would like to know the purpose of the DNS resolver cache. What would you tell him?

3. Robyn is interested in understanding the purpose of the nslookup utility. How do you respond?

4. Charles wants to know why an NS query doesn't return an IP address. Can you explain it to him?

5. Alexandria wants to know what a zone is in relation to configuring a DNS server. What's your response?

Key Term Quiz

Use the terms in this list to complete the sentences that follow.

A   `ipconfig /flushdns`

FQDN (fully qualified domain name)   nslookup

`ipconfig /displaydns`   ping

1. When troubleshooting DNS, you could use the _____ utility to query a DNS server.

2. The _____ record maps a name to an IPv4 address.

3. You can run the _____ utility with the _____ to test if DNS is configured correctly. If this task returns an error, you can run the command with the IP address to further clarify if there is a problem with DNS.

4. The _____ command removes entries from RAM.

5. The _____ command shows the names and IP addresses that have been resolved for you by your DNS server.

Chapter 10

Securing TCP/IP

Lab Exercises

There are a number of mechanisms, protocols, and utilities that make using the Internet safer for sharing private data and conducting business transactions. In broad terms, this is accomplished by securing the TCP/IP suite of protocols following the guidelines of the CIA triad, which looks to secure the confidentiality, integrity, and availability of data.

Using a digital certificate from a reputable certificate authority (CA) is a must. Using Secure Shell (SSH) for remote management to encrypt traffic to and from an SSH server is a must. Using Transport Layer Security (TLS) to encrypt traffic to and from a Web server is a must.

 45 MINUTES

Lab Exercise 10.01: Certificate Authorities

Creating and implementing a public key infrastructure (PKI) to secure the transfer of data can be achieved using various inexpensive encryption applications. This is all well and good, but are you going to trust sending private information, such as credit card numbers or Social Security numbers, to an organization that hasn't verified its integrity? Even if a Web site has implemented security using PKI, you still want verification that the organization is a valid, respectable outfit and that this is really their Web site.

A number of organizations have established themselves as reputable providers of digitally signed certificates and are known as CAs. A company that wants to do business over the Internet will apply with one of these organizations for a digital certificate for their Web server. This certificate not only provides secure communications through encryption, but it also validates the company's integrity by providing a digital signature from a reputable certificate authority.

→ **Note**

> A root certificate authority is the "root" of the chain of trust and signs certificates of intermediate CAs. The intermediate CAs, in turn, sign the certificates of clients of the root CA. This reduces the effects of a compromised CA and allows for flexibility in terms of the certificate parameters, for example, different lifetimes for certificates depending on the intermediate CA.

Digital certificates and certificate authorities are not just for Web sites with logins and sensitive information. Cybercriminals will try to exploit all resources transmitted between Web browser and Web server, especially ads. Instead of an ISP or hotel ad, you'll get the attacker's ad, which, of course, could include malware. Other resources that can be exploited include HTML, scripts, images, and cookies. Furthermore, a collective browsing profile of users, including behaviors, intentions, and even identities, can be collected from capturing unencrypted Web traffic. Knowing a user went to a certain medical Web site or read a certain medical article, for example, could reveal a certain health condition that the user was keeping secret. Finally, there are new cutting-edge additions to the Web experience as well as certain technologies that actually require the use of TLS. For more, check out this great question and answer Web site: https://doesmysiteneedhttps.com/.

Learning Objectives

In this lab exercise, you'll examine the solutions provided by various certificate authorities. By the end of this lab exercise, you'll be able to

- Analyze various product offerings from certificate authorities
- Recommend a specific product based on needs

Lab Materials and Setup

The materials you'll need for this lab exercise are

- *Mike Meyers' CompTIA Network+ Guide to Managing and Troubleshooting Networks* textbook
- Windows 10 system with Internet access

Getting Down to Business

JSW's client, the Department of Transportation (DOT), has decided to add a customer response page to its Web site, where commuters can report traffic concerns, such as road hazards and damage, or make suggestions for improvements. To keep inappropriate comments to a minimum, the DOT has asked JSW to implement a members-only site and require commuters to provide some personal data and create a username and password. To ensure the security of the commuters' personal data, Jonathan is going to secure the site and assign a PKI certificate to it.

Jonathan asks you to research CAs and put together a report on the costs and benefits of the various products. Due to the public nature of the client, Jonathan recommends that you narrow your research to mid-level and top-of-the-line products.

1b

 1b

Step 1

a.   On your Windows 10 system, open up the Mozilla Firefox browser. If you don't have Firefox, get it at https://www.mozilla.org/en-US/firefox/new/.

b.   Click the "hamburger menu" (the button with three equal horizontal lines at the top right that looks like a hamburger), click Settings toward the bottom, click Privacy & Security in the left pane, scroll all the way down to the Certificates section, and click the View Certificates ... button. Scroll through the list and note any names that you recognize. These are all the CAs (at different hierarchical levels) recognized by Mozilla Firefox. Close the Certificate Manager window when you're done. Figure 10-1 shows Firefox's Certificate Manager.

 2b

 2b

Step 2

a.   On your Windows 10 system, open up the Google Chrome browser. If you don't have Chrome, get it at https://www.google.com/chrome/.

FIGURE 10-1 Firefox's Certificate Manager

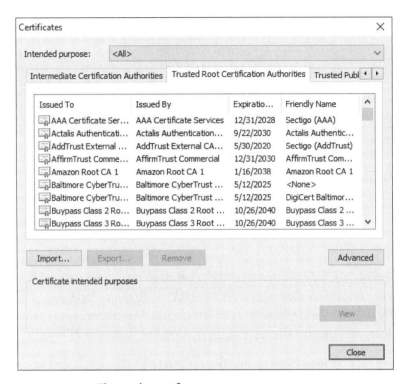

FIGURE 10-2 Chrome's certificates

b. Click the three vertical dots button (some call this the "kebab menu" because it looks like a kebab) at the top right, click Settings toward the bottom, click Privacy & Security in the left pane which brings the Privacy And Security box to the top of the main pane, click Security in the Privacy And Security box in the main pane, and scroll down to the bottom and click Manage Certificates. Browse through the Intermediate Certification Authorities and Trust Root Certification Authorities tabs and list any names that you recognize. These are all the CAs (at different hierarchical levels) recognized by Google Chrome. Click the Close button when you're done. Figure 10-2 shows Firefox's certificates.

→ **Note**

You can see the OS view of certificates, which is used by browsers as well. Click the Start button or in the search bar, type certlm.msc for the local machine, click certlm.msc, and click the Yes button. In a similar fashion, open certmgr.msc for the current user (there won't be a Yes button to click for this one).

Step 3 Jonathan suggests you do some research on what digital certificates are before looking into CAs. He wants you to read the information at the following links and write a one-page summary of what digital certificates are and why they are absolutely needed. In that summary, he also asks you to address the

Troy Hunt blogs that discuss three different types of certificates, with the declarations that EV certificates are "dead" and "really, really dead."

- https://www.cloudflare.com/learning/ssl/what-is-an-ssl-certificate/

- https://www.entrust.com/resources/hsm/faq/what-digital-signing-certificates-time-stamping

- https://opensrs.com/blog/2015/05/dv-ov-or-ev-how-to-offer-the-right-ssl-certificate/

- https://www.troyhunt.com/extended-validation-certificates-are-dead/

- https://www.troyhunt.com/extended-validation-certificates-are-really-really-dead/

- https://www.keyfactor.com/blog/what-are-extended-validation-certificates-and-are-they-dead/

Step 4   With the background on digital certificates you acquired in the previous step, Jonathan now wants you to look into actual CAs. A digital certificate will allow visitors of the DOT Web site to feel safe and secure. Without a digital certificate in place for the Web server, browsers display icons and words indicating the site is not secure, possibly scaring away visitors and potential clients.

As shown in Steps 1 and 2, browser support for a CA is mandatory for that CA to be able to do business.

Jonathan hands you the following list of six CAs, the top-ranked CAs in terms of usage and market share in 2021, asking you to evaluate their various offerings and make a recommendation for JSW to contract with. As part of this task, you are asked compare the CAs in at least five different categories of your choice, with a chart and explanation.

- IdenTrust

- DigiCert

- Sectigo

- GoDaddy

- GlobalSign

- Let's Encrypt

 30 MINUTES

Lab Exercise 10.02: Secure Ports, OpenSSH, and TLS

In Chapter 8, you examined the TCP and UDP ports of various programs and services. Now that you have been working with secure TCP/IP applications, you will spend some time analyzing the connection between secure applications, their port numbers, and the associated functions the secure applications provide, thinking about recommendations you can make for JSW to implement. Then, you will use Wireshark to see the difference between ports used for unencrypted communications and ports used for encrypted communications.

Learning Objectives

In this lab exercise, you'll work with various TCP/IP security components. By the end of this lab exercise, you'll be able to

- List some of the well-known ports for security protocols

- Explore the results of utilizing some of the secure protocols used in typical network communications

- Install, configure, and use OpenSSH

- Understand the differences between SSH and Telnet

- Understand the differences between HTTPS (HTTP over TLS) and HTTP

Lab Materials and Setup

The materials you'll need for this lab exercise are

- *Mike Meyers' CompTIA Network+ Guide to Managing and Troubleshooting Networks* textbook

- Two Windows 10 systems with Internet access

Getting Down to Business

You want to explore some protocols involved in creating secure connections. While you're at it, go ahead and examine some of the other components that help keep TCP/IP secure, their function, port numbers, and associations.

Step 1   Fill in the secure protocols/services associated with the given ports. Once again, use https://www.iana.org/assignments/service-names-port-numbers/service-names-port-numbers.xhtml as a reference.

Port	Protocol/Service
22	
49	
88	
443	
587	
636	
993	
1812, 1813	

Step 2   In Chapter 8, you used FileZilla's FTP server and FTP client applications. Jonathan wants you to research and document the differences between these similarly sounding technologies:

- **a.**   FTPS (FTP-TLS/FTP Secure)
- **b.**   SFTP (SSH File Transfer Protocol)
- **c.**   FTP over SSH

Step 3   The OpenSSH connectivity tool allows an OpenSSH client to remotely sign in to a system running an OpenSSH server. During this session, SSH encrypts all traffic between the OpenSSH client and the OpenSSH server, thwarting man-in-the-middle (MITM) attacks, including eavesdropping, connecting hijacking, and more. SSH is used by systems administrators (and others) for remote management of systems and programs, software patch deployment, execution of commands, file management, and more.

Perform the following steps on both Windows 10 systems to install the OpenSSH Client and OpenSSH Server, so that either could be the client or server using OpenSSH.

- **a.**   In the search bar, type **settings**, and select Settings.
- **b.**   Click Apps, under Apps & Features and select Optional Features.
- **c.**   Check to see if the OpenSSH Client or OpenSSH Server is already installed. The OpenSSH Client should be.
- **d.**   To install the OpenSSH Server, click Add A Feature at the top of the window, put a check in the checkbox next to OpenSSH Server, and click the Install (1) button. If the OpenSSH Client was not installed, you can select both the Open SSH Server and OpenSSH Client checkboxes and click the Install (2) button.

Installing the OpenSSH Server automatically will create and enable the firewall rule named OpenSSH-Server-In-TCP, which allows unsolicited SSH traffic (port 22) inbound to your system. This is needed since Windows Defender Firewall is stateful and will not allow anything unsolicited inbound otherwise.

Step 4   Start and configure the OpenSSH Server.

- **a.**   On the system that will be acting as the server, type **PowerShell** in the search box, right-click Windows PowerShell, select Run As Administrator, and click the Yes button.
- **b.**   Type the following to start the sshd service and press ENTER:

```
Start-Service sshd
```

- **c.**   If you want the service to start automatically each time your system boots up, execute the following command:

```
Set-Service -Name sshd -StartupType 'Automatic'
```

d. See the firewall rule:

```
Get-NetFirewallRule -Name *ssh*
```

e. The following code shows the manual way to create the firewall rule. This is all one command, so don't press ENTER until the very end of the second line.

```
New-NetFirewallRule -Name sshd -DisplayName 'OpenSSH Server (sshd)' -Enabled True
-Direction Inbound -Protocol TCP -Action Allow -LocalPort 22
```

 5c–5f

 5f

Step 5 Connect to the OpenSSH Server.

a. On the system that will be acting as the server, start sniffing in Wireshark with a display filter of **tcp.port == 22**.

b. On the system that will be acting as the client, type **PowerShell** in the search box, right-click Windows PowerShell, select Run As Administrator, and click the Yes button.

c. Execute the following command:

```
ssh username@servername
```

where username is the username that you're signed in with currently on the system running the SSH server and servername is the IP address of the system running the SSH server (use **ipconfig** to get it). The computer/hostname could be used as well if DNS has a record, but that's not likely at this point, so using the IP address is what you'll do here.

For example,

```
ssh cscprof@192.168.0.242
```

You'll see the following message (with different values):

```
The authenticity of host '192.168.0.242 (192.168.0.242)' can't be established.
ECDSA key fingerprint is SHA256:AUe22kLn+c/3clOXqBpfR3YS7CC0NoKITSvhbktyMDQ.
Are you sure you want to continue connecting (yes/no/[fingerprint])?
```

d. Type **yes** and press ENTER. You'll then see something that looks like this (customized to your IP address and username):

```
Warning: Permanently added '192.168.0.242' (ECDSA) to the list of known hosts.
cscprof@192.168.0.242's password:
```

e. Provide the password and press ENTER.

→ **Note**

To remove the system from the list of known hosts, browse to C:\Users\%USERNAME%\.ssh (%USERNAME% is a variable that will resolve into your actual username, so you can type it as is) and either delete the known_hosts file or remove the entry (using Notepad or any text editor) from the file.

Now, you'll see a prompt that looks like this:

```
cscprof@JWEISSMAN C:\Users\cscprof>
```

Guess what? It's like you're now sitting in front of the other system!

f.   Type

```
ipconfig
```

and press ENTER. You'll see output of the remote system, not the system you're signed in locally to, now. You can send pings and traceroutes from the remote system as if they were sent directly from that system. The replies will come back to that system, not the system you're on (although the command prompt output will).

In Wireshark on the client, you should notice the capture starts with the TCP three-way handshake and continues with the key exchange. After that, you'll see a bunch of encrypted packets, and that's why SSH should be used.

In Wireshark, click one of the packets showing Client: Encrypted Packet Or Server: Encrypted Packet in the Packet List pane. In the Packet Details pane, expand the SSH Protocol section, then expand the SSH Version 2 section, and you'll see the Encrypted Packet: field with gibberish that you can't read or understand. You won't be able to see the commands you're typing or the output you're receiving. That's a good thing!

Look inside the TCP header. What port is the server using for sending and receiving? What port is the client using for sending and receiving?

 6a–6d

 6d–6e

Step 6   SSH debuted in 1995. Before then, and unfortunately in some cases since then, the notorious Telnet has served the same purpose, but with one big difference: Telnet doesn't do any encryption. That means client-to-server and server-to-client communications are in plaintext. Just think of all the juicy things an MITM attacker can do with those packets!

Using the sample Telnet packet captures at https://packetlife.net/captures/protocol/telnet/, work through the following steps:

- **a.** Look inside the TCP header. What port is the server using for sending and receiving? What port is the client using for sending and receiving?

- **b.** How do the contents and ports differ from the previous step?

- **c.** Right-click one of the rows in the Packet Details pane, mouse over Follow, and select TCP Stream. You'll see a window that opens, with the conversation put together from the separate TCP segments.

- **d.** What is the password that was captured?

- **e.** Why do you think some characters appear a second time after the first?

→ **Note**

There are tons of other great packet captures to see and download (to add to your collection) at https://packetlife.net/captures/.

 7c, 7e

 7e–7f

Step 7   Generate your own Telnet traffic. Not only will you not put yourself at risk, you're in for some great entertainment!

- **a.** Download the PuTTY terminal emulator from https://www.chiark.greenend.org.uk/~sgtatham/putty/latest.html (I recommend the standalone 64-bit x86: putty.exe). Then, launch PuTTY.

- **b.** On the Basic Options For Your PuTTY Session screen (with Session, the top choice, selected in the Category: pane), select the Telnet radio button (which will populate the Port textbox with 23).

- **c.** In the Host Name (or IP address) textbox, enter **towel.blinkenlights.nl** and click the Open button.

- **d.** Optionally, start the "Star Wars Main Theme (Full)" video here: https://youtu.be/_D0ZQPqeJkk.

- **e.** In Wireshark, click a row showing Telnet Data . . . in the Info column of the Packet List pane, and expand the Telnet section in the Packet Details pane. What do you see? Click the next row with Telnet Data . . . in the Info column. And the next! And the next! How is this different than SSH?

- **f.** Look inside the TCP header. What port is the server using for sending and receiving? What port is the client using for sending and receiving?

7a–7d

 7d

Step 8   TLS encrypts all traffic between a Web browser and a Web server (it is also used for e-mail, instant messaging, and Voice over IP [VoIP]), thwarting MITM attacks like SSH does for remote management, as described earlier.

    a.   Start sniffing in Wireshark with a display filter of

```
ipv6.addr == 2620:8d:8000:0:aba:ca:daba:217 || ip.addr == 129.21.1.40
```

    This filter covers both the IPv6 and IPv4 addresses of the RIT Web server and will match the one you're sending traffic to, based on your infrastructure.

    b.   Open a browser and go to https://www.rit.edu/. After it loads completely, stop the capture.

    c.   In Wireshark, click one of the packets showing TLSv1.3 in the Packet List pane. In the Packet Details pane, expand the Transport Layer Security section, then expand the TLSv1.3 Record Layer: section, and you'll see the Encrypted Application Data: field with gibberish that you can't read or understand. You won't be able to see any requests from the browser or any replies from the server. That's a good thing!

    d.   Look inside the TCP header. What port is the server using for sending and receiving? What port is the client using for sending and receiving?

 8a–8c

 8c, 8d

Step 9   Sites that don't use digital certificates send and receive data in plaintext, which could lead to MITM attacks and compromise sensitive personally identifiable information (PII).

    a.   Start sniffing in Wireshark with a display filter that matches the two possible IP addresses of www.insecam.org at the time of publication and an http of

```
ip.addr == 104.21.44.66 || ip.addr == 104.21.44.66 && http
```

    If there were changes to the Web site's IP addresses and you're not seeing results, use either ping or nslookup to discover the new IP address(es) of www.insecam.org and use that/those in your display filter.

    b.   Open a browser and go to http://insecam.org/. After it loads completely, stop the capture.

    c.   Select the row with HTTP/1.1 200 OK (text/html) in the Info column of the Packet List pane. Expand the Line-Base Text Data: Text/html section in the Packet Details pane.

    Look inside the TCP header. What port is the server using for sending and receiving? What port is the client using for sending and receiving?

    d.   How do the contents and ports differ from the previous step?

45 MINUTES

Lab Exercise 10.03: Kerberos

When you sign in to a Windows domain, an incredible set of events happens under the hood to verify your password. Of course, passwords are not stored in plaintext, but in hashed format.

On Windows systems, password hashes are stored in the SAM (expanded as both Security Account Manager and Security Accounts Manager) database file, located in C:\Windows\ System32\config. On Windows domain controllers running Active Directory, password hashes are stored in the C:\Windows\ NTDS\NTDS.dit file.

On a Windows system, your password will be hashed and compared to the stored hash in the SAM file. On a domain, a protocol named after a three-headed guard dog of Hades, from the world of Greek mythology, kicks in to authenticate users. Jonathan would like you understand how Kerberos works.

Learning Objectives

In this lab exercise, you'll examine the intricacies of Kerberos. By the end of this lab exercise, you'll be able to

- Explain the many steps of the Kerberos process

Lab Materials and Setup

The materials you'll need for this lab exercise are

- *Mike Meyers' CompTIA Network+ Guide to Managing and Troubleshooting Networks* textbook
- Windows 10 system with Internet access

Getting Down to Business

Jonathan directs you to two great resources on Kerberos, including a superbly illustrated video made by Don Jones and a Web page by Lynn Root that claims to treat you like you're a 5-year-old. It's time to dig in!

Step 1

    a. Watch "MicroNugget: How Kerberos Works in Windows Active Directory | CBT Nuggets" at https://youtu.be/kp5d8Yv3-0c. The illustrations, the animations, and the color coding make it really easy to understand.

    b. Go to https://www.roguelynn.com/words/explain-like-im-5-kerberos/ and spend as much time as you need to fully understand the Kerberos protocol. There's a quiz Jonathan wants you to take in the next step.

Step 2   Based on the knowledge of Kerberos you gained in the previous step, fill in the blanks in the following chart, which mirrors the process you saw in the Web page in the previous step. Two cells have been filled in for clarity.

Use the following items to fill in the blank cells in the Sent From, Sent To, and Meant For columns:

- Client
- HTTP Server
- KDC (AS)
- KDC (TGS)

Use the following items to fill in the blank cells in the Encrypted With column:

- Client Secret Key
- HTTP Service Secret Key
- Not Encrypted
- TGS Secret Key
- TGS Session Key

	Sent From	Sent To	Meant For	Encrypted With
TGT	KDC (AS)			
TGS Session Key				
TGT	Client			
Authenticator				
Plaintext Request				
HTTP Service Session Key				
Ticket for HTTP Service				
Ticket for HTTP Service				
Authenticator	Client			
Authenticator	HTTP Server			

 45 MINUTES

Lab Exercise 10.04: DoH and DoT

After the previous chapter's coverage of DNS, you should appreciate two new technologies that are finally seeing the light of day. They sound very similar, DoH (DNS over HTTPS) and DoT (DNS over TLS). HTTPS is implemented through TLS, so what is the actual difference? You're about to find out!

Learning Objectives

In this lab exercise, you'll explore cutting-edge browser security for DNS. By the end of this lab exercise, you'll be able to

- Understand the similarities and differences between DoH and DoT

- Configure DoH in multiple browsers

Lab Materials and Setup

The materials you'll need for this lab exercise are

- *Mike Meyers' CompTIA Network+ Guide to Managing and Troubleshooting Networks* textbook

- Windows 10 system with Internet access

- Google Chrome and Mozilla Firefox browsers

Getting Down to Business

Wouldn't it be great if ISPs, companies, and cybercriminals couldn't sniff your DNS queries and responses? Two new protocols look to grant you privacy in that area. However, these protocols do not come with controversy of their own!

Step 1 Read the following articles and then write a one-page summary of what you learned about DoH and DoT:

- https://www.cloudflare.com/learning/dns/dns-over-tls/

- https://www.dnsfilter.com/blog/dns-over-tls

- https://spectrum.ieee.org/the-fight-over-encrypted-dns-boils-over

- https://securityboulevard.com/2020/06/dns-over-tls-and-dns-over-https/

- https://www.securitymagazine.com/articles/91674-disappearing-dns-dot-and-doh-where-one-letter-makes-a-great-difference

- https://www.zdnet.com/article/uk-isp-group-names-mozilla-internet-villain-for-supporting-dns-over-https/

- https://support.mozilla.org/en-US/kb/firefox-dns-over-https

- https://www.zdnet.com/article/dns-over-https-will-eventually-roll-out-in-all-major-browsers-despite-isp-opposition/

 2c

Step 2   Enable and configure DoH in Mozilla Firefox. (Mozilla and Cloudflare pioneered DoH in 2018.)

   a.   Open the Firefox browser.

   b.   Click the "hamburger menu" (the button with three equal horizontal lines at the top right), click Settings toward the bottom, scroll down to the Network Settings section, and click the Settings… button. In the Connection Settings window, put a check in the checkbox at the bottom next to Enable DNS Over HTTPS.

   c.   In the Use Provider dropdown box you can keep the default selection of Cloudflare (Default), select NextDNS, or select Custom. If you select Custom, a textbox will appear for you to type in the IP address of the DoH server you'd like to use.

   d.   Click the OK button.

 3c

Step 3   Enable and configure DoH in Google Chrome.

   a.   Open the Chrome browser.

   b.   Click the three vertical dots button (some call this the "kebab menu") at the top right, click Settings toward the bottom, click Privacy & Security in the left pane which brings the Privacy And Security box to the top of the main pane, click Security in the Privacy And Security box in the main pane, and scroll down to the bottom and find the Use Secure DNS section. If the slider on the right is in the off position, click on the right to put it in the on position.

   c.   With the With Your Current Service Provider radio button selected, the message "Secure DNS may not be available all the time" is very telling. What this really means is that Chrome will check if your DNS server is on a whitelist of approved servers for DoH. If it is, Chrome will send an encrypted query (using DoH) to that DNS server's DoH component. If it's not, Chrome will treat it like regular DNS and send an unencrypted query to that DNS server. If your ISP doesn't want you to use DoH (referenced in links from Step 1, you're not going to get DoH through Chrome unless you change the radio button selection to the second radio button labeled With, followed by a dropdown list containing Custom (with a textbox to enter the custom provider's IP address), as well as actual choices, including Cloudflare (1.1.1.1), Google (Public DNS), NextDNS, CleanBrowsing (Family Filter), and OpenDNS.

Lab Analysis

1. Mary wants to know why EV certificates are "really, really dead." How do you respond?

2. Tresia wants to know what type of encryption Kerberos uses. What do you tell her?

3. Matt asks you to explain to him what Telnet and SSH have in common and how they differ. What's your explanation?

4. Nathan is curious about what DoH and DoT have in common and how they differ. How do you reply?

5. Ian wants you to tell him about controversies with DoH and DoT. Can you help him out?

Key Term Quiz

Use the terms in this list to complete the sentences that follow.

authentication server (AS)	HTTPS
certificate authority (CA)	KDC
DoH	SSH
DoT	ticket granting server (TGS)
TLS	

1. When an organization provides secure services over the Internet, they will obtain a certificate from a(n) _____ such as Comodo or DigiCert that verifies the public key is legitimate.

2. Port 443 is used by _____ and _____.

3. Port 853 is used by _____.

4. Due to the fact that it transmits in plaintext, you should never use Telnet, but instead use _____, which encrypts traffic in both directions.

5. Components of the Kerberos key distribution center (KDC) include the _____ and the _____.

Chapter 11

Switch Features

Lab Exercises

Switches can do much more than receive frames on one port and send them out to one or more other ports. On managed switches, virtual local area networks (VLANs) can create broadcast domains at Layer 2, trunking can bring all traffic from all VLANs across to other switches, Layer 3 functionality can be implemented if the switch is a multilayer switch, and Switched Port Analyzer (SPAN) can make copies of frames going in and out of certain ports and send them to monitor systems that are connected to other ports.

The lab exercises in this chapter are written for a lab with actual hardware (switches, routers, and computers), but alternatively, they can be done in Cisco's network simulation tool, Packet Tracer. You can set up a full topology in software and adapt the instructions in this chapter to your simulation. Head to https://www.netacad.com/courses/packet-tracer to get started, if necessary.

 **60 MINUTES**

Lab Exercise 11.01: VLANs and SVIs

All devices in a local area network (LAN) are in the same broadcast domain. That means when one of them sends a broadcast frame, all other devices receive and process it. By default, all switch ports are in the same broadcast domain. If you wanted to create two broadcast domains, you could set up two different switches and put them on different networks.

VLANs offer the capabilities of creating broadcast domains within a single switch. When a system in a VLAN sends a broadcast, that broadcast message does not go beyond the VLAN. Having fewer hosts receive and process broadcasts not meant for them improves efficiency, since there are less CPU processing requirements. It also improves security, since fewer hosts will see traffic that the switches flood from any single other host whether the traffic is a multicast, broadcast, or unknown unicast (a destination unicast MAC address that's not in the SAT). Furthermore, security policies can be configured for specific VLANs. Finally, using one or more switches with multiple VLANs allows for a more flexible network topology. Users and their devices can be logically grouped in switches, through VLANs, by department or by users that need to work together for a certain amount of time, instead of physically by actual locations.

Learning Objectives

In this lab exercise, you'll create two VLANs on a Cisco multilayer switch. You'll then verify that two systems connected to the same switch but different VLANs cannot communicate with one another until you enable inter-VLAN routing with switched virtual interfaces (SVIs). By the end of this lab exercise, you'll be able to

- Configure VLANs
- Configure access ports
- Configure an SVI
- Configure inter-VLAN routing
- Send traffic from one VLAN to another VLAN

Lab Materials and Setup

The materials you'll need for this lab exercise are

- *Mike Meyers' CompTIA Network+ Guide to Managing and Troubleshooting Networks* textbook
- Cisco Catalyst multilayer switch (any of these series or something similar: 3560, 3650, 3750, 3850)
- Rollover/console cable
- USB-to-serial adapter/converter (if your rollover/console cable is 8P8C-to-serial)
- Two Windows 10 systems

✔ Tech Tip

You will also be working with the Cisco command-line interface (CLI) in the Cisco IOS (Internetworking Operating System). Only the commands needed to complete this chapter's lab exercises will be introduced.

Many of the commands you will use will be run from privileged EXEC mode (the prompt will look like this: `Switch#`**) or higher modes that require you to go through privileged EXEC mode first. This mode is normally password protected, but if the password is lost or forgotten, it is easy to reset the password if you have physical access to the device. You can use the process described at this link: https://www.cisco.com/c/en/us/support/docs/switches/catalyst-2950-series-switches/12040-pswdrec-2900xl.html.**

Getting Down to Business

Jonathan is working with a customer who is implementing VLANs, and would like to know if you would like to learn how to configure VLANs. As usual, you jump at the chance to work with a mentor.

Before you can start this lab exercise, you'll need to set up the hardware and software involved. After connecting a switch to your PC, you're going to download and install software that will allow you to send keystrokes from your keyboard to the switch and receive output from the switch on your monitor.

1. Connect the 8P8C side of the rollover/console cable to the console port on the switch and the USB side (with or without an adapter) to a USB port on your PC.

→ **Note**

The 8P8C connector is almost always incorrectly referred to as RJ45. See https://www.arrow.com/en/research-and-events/articles/rj45-connectors for more.

2. Download the PuTTY terminal emulator from https://www.chiark.greenend.org.uk/~sgtatham/putty/latest.html (I recommend the standalone 64-bit x86: putty.exe). Then, launch PuTTY.

3. On the Basic Options For Your PuTTY Session screen, make sure that the Serial button is selected.

4. Assuming you've connected the rollover/console cable (or adapter) to a USB port on your machine, click the Windows button (or click in the Windows 10 search box on the taskbar), type **Device Manager**, and select Device Manager.

5. Expand the Ports (COM & LPT) section, and note the port used by your USB-to-Serial Comm port. Figure 11-1 shows that it's COM5 for me. If you're using an 8P8C to USB cable without an adapter,

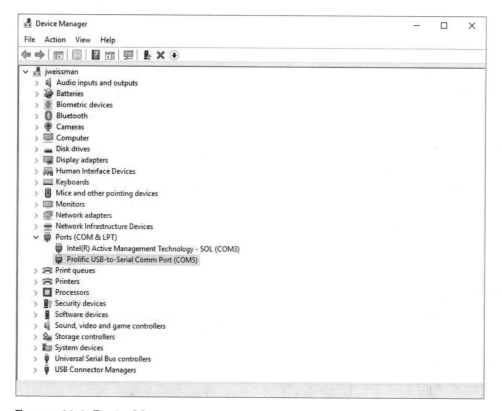

FIGURE 11-1 Device Manager

click Action, then click Add Legacy Hardware. Click the three Next > buttons that follow, find and select Ports (COM & LPT), click the three Next > buttons that follow, and finally click the Finish button.

6. Back in PuTTY, change the serial line port to the port identified in Device Manager.

7. In the Category: pane on the left, click Serial.

8. Under Options Controlling Local Serial Lines, verify the following settings (the last one should be the only non-default value):

   • Serial Line To Connect To: **COM***x* (where x represents the port you identified earlier)

   • Speed (Baud): **9600**

   • Data Bits: **8**

   • Stop Bits: **1**

   • Parity: **None**

   • Flow Control: **None**

9. Click Open. You may have to press ENTER in the PuTTY command-line window before you see a prompt, where you can type commands.

→ **Note**

Press ENTER after every command in this chapter to execute them.

Step 1   To set up the small network, power on the switch (Switch 1) and then plug the first computer (Host A) into port number 1. Connect the second computer (Host B) to port number 2. See Figure 11-2.

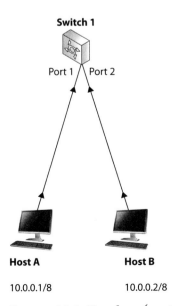

FIGURE 11-2 Topology (version 1)

Depending on the actual switch you're using, the interfaces could be called GigabitEthernet 0/1 and GigabitEthernet 0/2, FastEthernet 0/1 and FastEthernet 0/2, or something else like GigabitEthernet 1/0/1 and GigabitEthernet 1/0/2. Adapt the instructions in this chapter (port number 1, etc.) to your actual interfaces.

> ➔ **Note**
>
> **Although the terms port and interface are frequently used interchangeably, you plug a connector into a port and you configure an interface in the Cisco IOS. Think of the interface as a representation of the physical port in software. Also, don't confuse port, here, with the logical TCP/UDP ports discussed in Chapter 8.**

Step 2 On both systems, you might have to disable firewalls on the machines to let the pings through, by typing **Firewall** into the Windows search box, selecting Windows Defender Firewall, clicking Turn Windows Defender Firewall On Or Off, and clicking all radio buttons next to Turn Off Windows Defender Firewall (Not Recommended). These machines are not connected to the Internet, so it's fine. Furthermore, in Chapter 19, "Protecting Your Network," we'll see how to add rules that let pings through, instead of disabling the firewall altogether, which is obviously a much better approach.

Configure Host A with an IP address and subnet mask of 10.0.0.1/8 and Host B with an IP address and subnet mask of 10.0.0.2/8.

Step 3 Open a command prompt and verify that you can ping from each computer to the other.

Step 4 Back in PuTTY, if you see

```
Would You Like To Terminate Autoinstall? [Yes/No]
```

type **Yes** and press ENTER.

If you see

```
Would you like to enter the initial configuration dialog? [yes/no]:
```

type **no** and press ENTER.

You'll see:

```
Press RETURN to get started!
```

Press ENTER again.

You'll be brought to the user EXEC mode prompt (which allows basic monitoring commands). By default, the prompt will look like this:

```
Switch>
```

5a–5e

Step 5 The switch you're using may already be in some state of configuration, as opposed to the default out-of-box state. If you had any trouble pinging between the computers or there seems to be some VLANs or something else already configured, use the following steps to reset the switch:

a. Type **enable** and press ENTER. You will now be in privileged EXEC mode (which allows for some configuration and management). The > will be replaced by #, and the prompt will look like this:

```
Switch#
```

b. Type **delete vlan.dat** and press ENTER to get rid of any possible VLANs that may be configured on the switch. Press ENTER at the two prompts that follow (the second might vary based on your model and IOS), shown here:

```
Delete filename [vlan.dat]?
Delete flash:/vlan.dat? [confirm]
```

c. Type **erase startup-config** and press ENTER to erase the startup-config file stored in NVRAM, which is subsequently copied to the running-config file in RAM and used during the booting process. Press ENTER at the following prompt that looks like this:

```
Erasing the nvram filesystem will remove all configuration files! Continue? [confirm]
```

d. Type **reload** and press ENTER to reload without the existing elements that you just cleared and press ENTER again.

If you see the following prompt:

```
System configuration has been modified. Save? [yes/no]:
```

type **no** and press ENTER.

➡ **Note**

This is often a confusing question. If you executed the command to erase the startup-config file, and you answer yes to the above question, that would copy the running-config file from RAM back to NVRAM as the startup-config file, and you'll have a startup-config file, once again.

Press ENTER at the following prompt:

```
Proceed with reload? [confirm]
```

At this point, the switch will reload. When you see

```
Press RETURN to get started!
```

press ENTER, and you'll be in user EXEC mode.

e. To check what interfaces your switch has, from user EXEC mode, type **show ip interface brief** and press ENTER. Anytime output consists of multiple pages and the output scrolling pauses, press ENTER to advance line by line or SPACEBAR to advance page by page. To break out of the output and go back to the prompt, press CTRL-C.

Step 6   From user EXEC mode, to display a list of VLANs that currently exist, type **show vlan** and press ENTER. You should see that there are a few default VLANs for different network technologies. Notice that VLAN 1 is the default VLAN. This shows you that VLANs are always in effect on a switch. All ports by default are in VLAN 1, and that's a single broadcast domain. The far-right column shows you which ports are members of the VLAN.

    7a–7g

Step 7   To create a VLAN named Finance and another one called Marketing, type the following commands, pressing ENTER after each command.

a.   You'll start at the Switch> prompt. Enter **enable**.

You will now be in privileged EXEC mode. The prompt will look like this: Switch#.

b.   Enter **configure terminal**.

You will now be in global configuration mode (which allows for major configuration and management of the switch). Now the prompt looks like this: Switch(config)#.

c.   Enter **vlan 101**.

You will now be in VLAN configuration mode (where VLANs are created and configured). You've also just created VLAN 101. Now the prompt looks like this: Switch(config-vlan)#.

d.   Enter **name Finance**.

You've just assigned the name Finance to VLAN 101. You will return to the Switch(config-vlan)# prompt. If you did this correctly, you won't get any feedback. As I like to say in regard to output in a CLI, "No news is good news!"

e.   Enter **vlan 102**.

You've just created VLAN 102. The prompt remains Switch(config-vlan)#.

f.   Enter **name Marketing**.

You've just assigned the name Marketing to VLAN 102. The prompt remains Switch(config-vlan)#.

g.   Enter **end**.

This moves you back down to privileged EXEC mode. CTRL-Z does the same thing. To move down one level at a time, use the exit command instead.

You might see a syslog message from the switch. If so, press ENTER to get back to the prompt.

Step 8 At this point, you should be at the privileged EXEC mode prompt of

```
Switch#
```

To view the newly created VLANs, execute the following command:

```
Switch#show vlan
```

From this point forward, both the prompts and commands (which will be in bold as they have been earlier) will be shown. For example, in this step, just type **show vlan**. Also, remember to press ENTER after each command to execute them.

Step 9 To configure port 1 as an access port and to place it in VLAN 101 (frames coming into this port will be logically associated with VLAN 101), the Finance VLAN, execute the following commands. Note that the prompt will change as you move through the commands.

```
Switch#configure terminal
Switch(config)#interface GigabitEthernet 0/1
Switch(config-if)#switchport mode access
Switch(config-if)#switchport access vlan 101
Switch(config-if)#exit
```

➜ **Note**

Here are some tips for working in the Cisco IOS. Commands in the Cisco IOS can be shortened, but are always shown in this chapter in their full versions. In each mode, you just need to type in enough of a command to distinguish it from other commands in the same mode. For example, in user EXEC mode, all of the following get you to privileged EXEC mode: en, ena, enab, enabl, enable. Just an e by itself wouldn't work, since the exit command also exists at that mode, and it would be ambiguous which command was entered.

You can also press TAB at any point to have tab completion fill in the rest of the command.

When entered at the beginning of the prompt or after whitespace, the ? symbol shows you the next possible commands. When entered right after a character without whitespace, the ? symbol shows you possible completions of the part of the command you're currently entering. Each time you press the ? symbol, results are displayed and the prompt is conveniently returned to the way it was before you pressed the ? symbol.

The UP ARROW key cycles through previous commands, while the DOWN ARROW key takes you back in the other direction.

After the first command, you'll see output like this:

```
Enter configuration commands, one per line. End with CNTL/Z.
```

An access port is a port on a switch that connects to an end device (the actual source or destination of network traffic), like a PC.

Step 10   In a similar fashion, to configure port 2 as an access port and place it in VLAN 102 (frames coming into this port will be logically associated with VLAN 102), the Marketing VLAN, type the following commands:

```
Switch(config)#interface GigabitEthernet 0/2
Switch(config-if)#switchport mode access
Switch(config-if)#switchport access vlan 102
Switch(config-if)#end
```

Step 11   To verify that the ports are placed in the appropriate VLANs, execute the following command to display VLANs:

```
Switch#show vlan
```

Keep in mind that frames belong to a VLAN, but not PCs, protocols, or applications.

Step 12   Now that you have the ports that each system is connected to in different VLANs, the two systems should not be able to ping each another anymore. Try pinging each from the other.

VLANs are security boundaries and broadcast domains. Unless a Layer 3 device is used, only systems within a single VLAN and IP subnet will be able to communicate with one another and not with systems in other VLANs or subnets. Furthermore, if two systems in the same IP subnet are configured for different VLANs (not following the best practice of putting each subnet in its own single VLAN), they will never be able to communicate under any circumstance, since Layer 3 devices only take traffic out of and bring traffic into a network/subnet/broadcast domain and have nothing to do with communication within a network/subnet/broadcast domain.

> **→ Note**
>
> There technically is a "hack" to allow two devices in the same subnet but different VLANs to communicate. It's done with a crossover cable connected to two ports of different VLANs, but you'll need physical access to the switch for that. If an attacker has physical access to a switch, there will probably be better things they'd like to do to it, though.

Step 13 Now you will implement inter-VLAN routing to allow the two separate VLANs to communicate with each other. To enable inter-VLAN routing, you will first assign an IP address to each VLAN virtual interface in interface configuration mode (notice the prompt change from global configuration mode's prompt of Switch(config)# to interface configuration mode's prompt of Switch(config-if)# when you specify an interface). A VLAN interface is known as a switched virtual interface (SVI) and acts just like a router interface. As such, it needs to be configured with an IP address and a subnet mask.

Then, you will need to enable routing on the switch with the ip routing command.

Note that the prompt will change as you move through the commands. Start in privileged EXEC mode. You'll recall, to get there from user EXEC mode, the command is enable, which is why privileged EXEC mode is also referred to as enable mode.

```
Switch#configure terminal
Switch(config)#interface vlan 101
Switch(config-if)#ip address 10.101.0.1 255.255.0.0
Switch(config-if)#no shutdown
Switch(config)#interface vlan 102
Switch(config-if)#ip address 10.102.0.1 255.255.0.0
Switch(config-if)#no shutdown
Switch(config-if)#exit
Switch(config)#ip routing
Switch(config)#end
```

After the second command you'll see output like this:

```
%LINK-5-CHANGED: Interface Vlan101, changed state to up
%LINEPROTO-5-UPDOWN: Line protocol on Interface Vlan101, changed state to up
```

After the fifth command you'll see output like this:

```
%LINK-5-CHANGED: Interface Vlan102, changed state to up
%LINEPROTO-5-UPDOWN: Line protocol on Interface Vlan102, changed state to up
```

→ Note

I've decided to match the VLAN numbers to the second octets of the IP addresses, which is a nice design touch, but not an actual requirement.

Step 14 To verify that the IP addresses have been assigned to the appropriate VLANs, execute the following enable mode command:

```
Switch#show ip interface brief
```

Step 15   Now, you must place the computer systems in the correct networks. Configure Host A with an IP address of 10.101.0.10/16 and a default gateway of 10.101.0.1. Configure Host B with an IP address of 10.102.0.10/16 and a default gateway of 10.102.0.1. See Figure 11-3.

Step 16   Now, ping each machine from the other. With inter-VLAN routing in place, the pings should be successful.

The next lab exercise picks right up from this point. If you're not continuing at this point, you'll have to reestablish the topology and configuration. On the switches, from enable mode, you can execute the command

```
Switch#copy running-config startup-config
```

to copy the running-config file from RAM to the startup-config file in NVRAM, which will be used by the switch the next time it boots up.

FIGURE 11-3 Topology (version 2)

 **60 MINUTES**

Lab Exercise 11.02: Trunking

When using just one switch, as you did in Lab Exercise 11.01, the VLAN configuration is as simplified as can be. However, when using multiple switches, it gets a little more involved. When using VLANs between multiple switches, VLAN trunking allows traffic from more than one VLAN (all by default, but VLANs can be pruned from trunk links automatically or manually) to traverse a link from one switch to another from a trunk port on one switch to a trunk port on another switch. Broadcast, multicast, and unknown unicast (a destination unicast MAC address that's not in the SAT) traffic are only sent out of access ports that are associated with the same VLAN as the frame. Unicast traffic is sent out an access port associated with the same VLAN as the frame, where there is a matching entry in the SAT.

VLAN trunking is done through VLAN tagging, which involves the insertion of a 4-byte IEEE 802.1Q VLAN tag/header, which will be encapsulated inside of the frame's Ethernet header. This tag contains multiple fields, with the one most relevant here being the VLAN ID field, which identifies frames to be in a specific VLAN. The tag is inserted by a switch before sending the frame out of a trunk port, along a trunk link, to a trunk port of another switch. The other switch will now use this tag to decide which ports the frame should be sent out of. Tags are removed before frames are sent out of access ports, so devices connected to access ports never see tagged frames (with a couple of rare exceptions by certain VLAN-aware end devices). Tags are meant for adjacent switches, so they'll know how to forward the frames properly to the respective VLANs.

Learning Objectives

In this lab exercise, you'll trunk traffic from multiple VLANs between two switches. By the end of this lab exercise, you'll be able to

- Configure trunk ports

- Establish a trunk link

- Send traffic from multiple VLANs on a switch to VLANs on another switch over a trunk link

Lab Materials and Setup

The materials you'll need for this lab exercise are

- *Mike Meyers' CompTIA Network+ Guide to Managing and Troubleshooting Networks* textbook

- The topology and configuration from Lab Exercise 11.01 completed

- A second switch to add to the topology—this one should be a traditional Layer 2 switch, like the Cisco Catalyst 2950 or 2960 (if not possible, you can use another multilayer switch)

- Two more computers to add to the topology, which will be connected to the new switch

Getting Down to Business

As mentioned, this lab exercise continues right where the previous one left off. If you are doing this after a break, you'll need to reestablish the topology and configuration from where the previous lab exercise left off.

Step 1   Connect a Layer 2 switch (Switch 2) to the multilayer switch (Switch 1) from the previous lab exercise with a crossover cable using port 3 on each switch.

Step 2   Connect the two PCs to the Layer 2 switch (Switch 2) with a straight-through cable.

Connect the first PC (Host C) to port 1.

Connect the second PC (Host D) to port 2.

See Figure 11-4.

Step 3   Configure the first computer (Host C) with an IP address of 10.101.0.20/16 and a default gateway of 10.101.0.1.

Configure the second computer (Host D) with an IP address of 10.102.0.20/16 and a default gateway of 10.102.0.1.

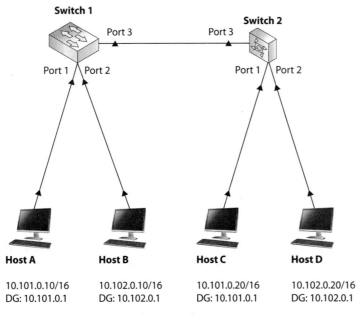

Host A	Host B	Host C	Host D
10.101.0.10/16	10.102.0.10/16	10.101.0.20/16	10.102.0.20/16
DG: 10.101.0.1	DG: 10.102.0.1	DG: 10.101.0.1	DG: 10.102.0.1

FIGURE 11-4 Topology (version 3)

Step 4 Configure the port that Host C is connected to as an access port whose frames will be associated with VLAN 101.

Configure the port that Host D is connected to as an access port whose frames will be associated with VLAN 102.

Step 5 Now, for the trunking.

On the Layer 2 switch, execute the following commands:

```
Switch#configure terminal
Switch(config)#interface FastEthernet 0/3
Switch(config-if)#switchport mode trunk
```

After the first command, you'll see output like this:

```
Enter configuration commands, one per line. End with CNTL/Z.
```

This explicitly makes the interface connected to the multilayer switch a trunk link.

On the multilayer switch, execute the following commands (this device requires an extra command, as you'll see) in the following modes (your interface will vary):

```
Switch(config)#interface GigabitEthernet 1/0/3
Switch(config-if)#switchport trunk encapsulation dot1q
Switch(config-if)#switchport mode trunk
```

After the third command, you'll see output similar to this:

```
%LINEPROTO-5-UPDOWN: Line protocol on Interface GigabitEthernet1/0/3, changed state
to down
%LINEPROTO-5-UPDOWN: Line protocol on Interface GigabitEthernet1/0/3, changed state
to up
```

Press ENTER to return to the prompt.

> **Note**
>
> **Without the command specifying the encapsulation type on devices that require the command,
> you'll see the following message:**
> ```
> Command rejected: An interface whose trunk encapsulation is "Auto" can
> not be configured to "trunk" mode.
> ```

Step 6   There are four PCs in your topology now:

- Each PC is connected to a switch with a second PC on a different VLAN/subnet.

- Each PC is connected to another switch with a PC in the same VLAN/subnet and another PC in a different VLAN/subnet.

From each PC, ping the other three.

Inter-VLAN communication and trunking are in effect!

Once again, the next lab exercise picks right up from this point. If you're not continuing at this point, you'll have to reestablish the topology and configuration. On the switches, from enable mode, you can execute this command:

```
Switch#copy running-config startup-config
```

to copy the running-config file from RAM to the startup-config file in NVRAM, which will be used by the switch the next time it boots up.

 60 MINUTES

Lab Exercise 11.03: Routed Ports

You've configured SVIs on the multilayer switch thus far, and those switched virtual interfaces are, in fact, Layer 3 interfaces. However, the actual physical ports on the multilayer switch are still at Layer 2. Turning an interface on a multilayer switch from a Layer 2 switch interface into a Layer 3 router interface allows the switch to connect to another router at Layer 3 and, in turn, other networks.

Learning Objectives

In this lab exercise, you'll establish Layer 3 functionality on a multilayer switch. By the end of this lab exercise, you'll be able to

- Configure an interface on a multilayer switch as a routed port

- Send traffic through the routed port

Lab Materials and Setup

The materials you'll need for this lab exercise are

- *Mike Meyers' CompTIA Network+ Guide to Managing and Troubleshooting Networks* textbook

- The topology and configuration from Lab Exercise 11.01 and Lab Exercise 11.02 completed

- A router (the first) to add to the topology—this one could be a Cisco 2651 or Cisco 2621 device

- Another switch (the third), a Layer 2 or multilayer one (your choice) to add to the topology

- Another PC (the fifth) to add to the topology

Getting Down to Business

As mentioned, this lab exercise continues right where the previous one left off. If you are doing this after a break, you'll need to reestablish the topology and configuration from where the previous lab exercise left off.

Step 1 Connect a router (Router 1) into the multilayer switch (Switch 1) with a straight-through cable. Connect the cable into port 4 on the switch and port 0 on the router.

Step 2 On the multilayer switch (Switch 1), from privileged EXEC mode, execute these commands (your interface will vary):

```
Switch(config)#interface GigabitEthernet 1/0/4
Switch(config-if)#no switchport
```

The first command moves you from privileged EXEC mode to interface configuration mode.

After the second command you'll output like this:

```
%SYS-5-CONFIG_I: Configured from console by console no switchport
```

By default, all ports on a multilayer switch are Layer 2 ports. To turn a Layer 2 switch port into a Layer 3 router port, all you need to do is execute the command

```
no switchport
```

which undoes the default configuration of

```
switchport
```

Step 3 On the multilayer switch (Switch 1), enter the following commands (your interface will vary). Output after commands from this point forward will be now shown inline:

```
Switch#configure terminal
Enter configuration commands, one per line. End with CNTL/Z.
Switch(config)#interface GigabitEthernet 1/0/4
Switch(config-if)#ip address 10.103.0.1 255.255.0.0
Switch(config-if)#no shutdown
```

This configures the routed port with an IP address and subnet mask on the network of the router interface it's connected to.

Step 4   On the router, enter the following commands (your interfaces will vary):

```
Router>enable
Router#configure terminal
Enter configuration commands, one per line. End with CNTL/Z.
Router(config)#interface GigabitEthernet 0/0/0
Router(config-if)#ip address 10.103.0.2 255.255.0.0
Router(config-if)#no shutdown
%LINK-5-CHANGED: Interface GigabitEthernet 0/0/0, changed state to up
%LINEPROTO-5-UPDOWN: Line protocol on Interface GigabitEthernet 0/0/0, changed state to up
```

That configures one of the router interfaces to be on the same subnet that the multilayer switch (the device it's connected to) is on. Now, to configure the other router interface that connects to a new subnet:

```
Router(config-if)#interface GigabitEthernet 0/0/1
Router(config-if)#ip address 10.104.0.1 255.255.0.0
Router(config-if)#no shutdown
%LINK-5-CHANGED: Interface GigabitEthernet 0/0/1, changed state to up
%LINEPROTO-5-UPDOWN: Line protocol on Interface GigabitEthernet 0/0/1, changed state to up
```

Step 5   Refer to Figure 11-5 for this step and the next one.

Connect a new switch (Switch 3) to the router with a straight-through cable. Connect the cable into port 1 on the switch and port 1 on the router.

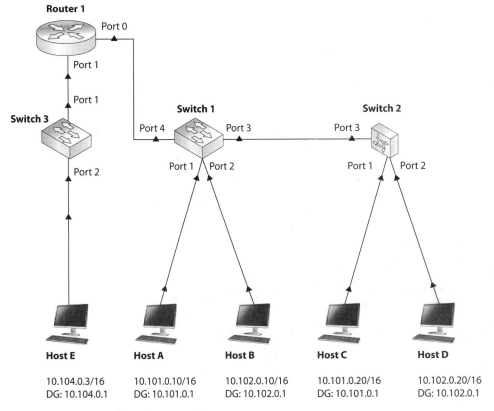

FIGURE 11-5 Topology (version 4)

→ **Note**

Even though a router port connects to another router port with a crossover cable, in this case, since the physical hardware is still a switch port, a straight-through is still used, despite the port being turned into a router port through the IOS.

Step 6   Connect a PC (Host E) into the switch with a straight-through cable. Connect the cable into port 2 on the switch.

Configure the PC with an IP address of 10.104.0.3/16 and a default gateway of 10.104.0.1.

Step 7   Now, routes for networks need to be added to the router:

```
Router#configure terminal
Enter configuration commands, one per line. End with CNTL/Z.
Router(config)#ip route 10.101.0.0 255.255.0.0 10.103.0.1
Router(config)#ip route 10.102.0.0 255.255.0.0 10.103.0.1
Router(config)#end
Router#
%SYS-5-CONFIG_I: Configured from console by console

Router#show ip route
Codes: L - local, C - connected, S - static, R - RIP, M - mobile, B - BGP
D - EIGRP, EX - EIGRP external, O - OSPF, IA - OSPF inter area
N1 - OSPF NSSA external type 1, N2 - OSPF NSSA external type 2
E1 - OSPF external type 1, E2 - OSPF external type 2, E - EGP
i - IS-IS, L1 - IS-IS level-1, L2 - IS-IS level-2, ia - IS-IS inter area
* - candidate default, U - per-user static route, o - ODR
P - periodic downloaded static route

Gateway of last resort is not set

10.0.0.0/8 is variably subnetted, 6 subnets, 2 masks
S 10.101.0.0/16 [1/0] via 10.103.0.1
S 10.102.0.0/16 [1/0] via 10.103.0.1
C 10.103.0.0/16 is directly connected, GigabitEthernet 0/0/0
L 10.103.0.2/32 is directly connected, GigabitEthernet 0/0/0
C 10.104.0.0/16 is directly connected, GigabitEthernet 0/0/1
L 10.104.0.1/32 is directly connected, GigabitEthernet 0/0/1

Router#
```

→ **Note**

Depending on the device you're using, you may not see the local routes marked with an L, which represent actual interfaces on the device.

Step 8 Now, a route for the new network needs to be added to the multilayer switch:

```
Switch#configure terminal
Switch(config)#ip route 10.104.0.0 255.255.0.0 10.103.0.2
Switch(config)#end
Switch#
%SYS-5-CONFIG_I: Configured from console by console
```

Step 9 Have each PC ping the other four.

Step 10 Use tracert on each PC for the other four.

 **60 MINUTES**

Lab Exercise 11.04: SPAN

When a PC sends a frame into a switch, the switch associates the source MAC address in the Ethernet frame with the port on which the frame arrived in a table known as a source address table (SAT), content addressable memory (CAM) table, and MAC address table. If the switch then gets a frame with that MAC address as the destination MAC address in an Ethernet frame, the switch sends the frame just to the port that MAC address is associated with.

→ **Note**

> Don't confuse the table described here with an ARP cache. The SAT maps MAC addresses to ports, while the ARP cache maps IP addresses to MAC addresses.

A switch floods broadcasts, standard multicasts, and unknown unicasts (a destination unicast MAC address that's not in the SAT) out of all ports except the port on which the message originated. That's why, for example, in Chapter 6, you were able to sniff all ARP requests (broadcasts) from all devices on your network, but you were able to just sniff ARP replies (unicasts) to your device.

Let's say a company wants to implement an intrusion detection system (IDS) to inspect traffic flowing through a switch for security, or even for troubleshooting and debugging purposes. An IDS—for example, Snort—could be installed on a system and plugged into a switch. However, the switch will not send frames to the port that the IDS is connected to. The SPAN (switched port analyzer) feature, also known as port mirroring and port monitoring, changes everything. A switch can be instructed to send transmitted frames, received frames, or both in relation to a certain switch port to another port, where an analyzer will be receiving them.

You probably wouldn't want to send all traffic in both directions from a certain VLAN to a specific port, as that could overload the SPAN destination port. The general rule is to capture what you need to capture and try to capture as little of anything else. Local SPAN sends traffic from parts of a single switch to one or more ports on the same switch. Remote SPAN trunks the SPAN traffic to other switches, as the traffic will be sent to an analyzer not connected to the local switch.

Learning Objectives

In this lab exercise, you'll establish a setup that allows you to sniff unicast traffic that you wouldn't ordinarily be able to sniff due to how switches work. By the end of this lab exercise, you'll be able to

- Configure SPAN

- Mirror traffic from SPAN source ports to a SPAN destination port

- Sniff mirrored traffic

Lab Materials and Setup

The materials you'll need for this lab exercise are

- *Mike Meyers' CompTIA Network+ Guide to Managing and Troubleshooting Networks* textbook

- A switch (Layer 2 or multilayer)

- Three PCs

Getting Down to Business

This lab exercise does not continue right where the previous one left off and can be performed with a single Layer 2 or multilayer switch.

Step 1 Connect three PCs to a switch using straight-through cables.

Step 2 Using any IP addressing scheme, assign IP addresses on the same subnet to the three PCs.

Connect a PC to port 1, a PC to port 2, and a PC to port 3.

Make sure the ports you connected them to are in the same VLAN. For this lab exercise, it would be best to start with a factory-reset switch. To clear VLAN information and the startup-config file, see Step 5 in Lab Exercise 11.01.

Step 3   Make sure each PC can ping the other two (make sure the firewalls are disabled).

Step 4   To specify the source port, enter the following command (your interface will vary), which will mirror traffic in both directions (**rx** mirrors just received traffic, **tx** mirrors just transmitted traffic, **both** mirrors received and transmitted traffic):

```
Switch(config)#monitor session 1 source interface GiqabitEthernet 0/1 both
```

Step 5   To specify the destination port, enter the following command (your interface will vary), which will receive traffic that goes in or out of the port specified in the previous step:

```
Switch(config)#monitor session 1 destination interface GigabitEthernet 0/3
```

Step 6   Run Wireshark on the computer connected to port 3.

In Edit | Preferences | Capture, there should be a check in the checkbox next to Capture Packets In Promiscuous Mode by default. If for some reason it's not there, add it.

From the computer connected to port 2, ping the computer connected to port 1.

You should now be able to see all of the traffic going in and out of the computer connected to port 1. You'd be able to see the ARP request anyway, because that's a broadcast. However, now when sniffing on the computer connected to port 3, you'll be able to see the ARP Reply, as well as the ICMP Echo requests and ICMP Echo replies, all of which are unicast and would not normally be sent by the switch to port 3.

Step 7   Execute the following command to see information about the configured SPAN:

```
Switch#show monitor session 1
```

→ Note

A SPAN session can have more than one source and more than one destination.

Lab Analysis

1. Why would you want to use SPAN?

2. Why can't PCs in the same IP subnet but different VLANs communicate?

3. What layer are ports in a multilayer switch in by default?

4. What is an SVI?

5. What's the purpose of a VLAN?

Key Term Quiz

Use the terms in this list to complete the sentences that follow.

access   trunk

multilayer switch   VLAN

SPAN

1. A _____ can be described as a broadcast domain.

2. A switch port that connects to a PC is known as a(n) _____ port.

3. A switch port that connects to another switch is known as a(n) _____ port.

4. The _____ feature allows unicast frames to be sent to a port in addition to the actual destination port.

5. A _____ can have physical ports that operate as switch ports and other ports that operate as router ports.

Chapter 12

IPv6

Lab Exercises

Whether you are a seasoned tech, have been in IT for only a few years, or have just begun your journey toward becoming a networking professional, these are exciting times. IPv6 usage is growing more and more each day.

The CompTIA Network+ exam objectives require a networking professional to be familiar with IPv6 addressing concepts and some of the supporting technologies. The lab exercises in this chapter are designed to give you an opportunity to practice what you have learned about IPv6 from the *Mike Meyers' CompTIA Network+ Guide to Managing and Troubleshooting Networks* textbook, but go much further.

 **60 MINUTES**

Lab Exercise 12.01: IPv6 Facts and Figures

To begin your exploration of IPv6, you'll examine some of the organizations that are involved with it.

Learning Objectives

In this lab exercise, you'll explore various organizations that are responsible for the development, management, and distribution of IPv6. By the end of this lab exercise, you'll be able to

- Describe the purposes and features of the organizations responsible for IPv6 addressing

- List the important dates in the history of IPv6 related to IPv4 address exhaustion

- Research and provide some detail on Request for Comments (RFC) documents associated with IPv6

- Understand how large the IPv6 address space really is

Lab Materials and Setup

The materials you'll need for this lab exercise are

- *Mike Meyers' CompTIA Network+ Guide to Managing and Troubleshooting Networks* textbook

- Internet access

Getting Down to Business

At the very top of the Internet hierarchy is the Internet Corporation for Assigned Names and Numbers (ICANN), which handles the coordination and maintenance of databases of domain names and IP addresses. Just below ICANN is the Internet Assigned Numbers Authority (IANA), which ICANN oversees (IANA is a function of ICANN).

IANA deals with three big pieces of the world of networking (all of which you've seen featured heavily in this book so far):

- **Domain names**   IANA manages the DNS root zone as well as other functions.

- **IP addresses**   IANA coordinates the allocation of IP addresses and autonomous system numbers (ASNs). IANA allocates IP addresses and ASNs to five regional Internet registries (RIRs) that assign IP addresses to ISPs (Internet service providers) and large organizations and ASNs to organizations.

- **Protocols**   IANA maintains protocol registries.

→ Note

Learn more about ICANN at https://www.icann.org/ and about IANA at https://www.iana.org/.

Step 1   Start this exploration of IPv6 with a visit to the following Web sites:

- https://en.wikipedia.org/wiki/IPv4_address_exhaustion

- https://www.computerworld.com/article/2512924/update--icann-assigns-its-last-ipv4-addresses.html

- https://www.iana.org/numbers

- https://ipv4.potaroo.net/

 2a–2b

Step 2   Based on the links in Step 1, answer these questions:

a.   What happened on January 31, 2011?

b.   What happened on February 3, 2011?

Step 3   Why is the term "IPv4 exhaustion" so misunderstood? Compare the use of "exhaustion" in relation to the word "out," as in the phrase "out of IPv4 addresses" in the following Links 1 section to the Links 2 section.

Links 1:

- https://www.zdnet.com/article/its-official-asias-just-run-out-of-ipv4-addresses/

- https://www.engadget.com/2012-09-16-ripe-ncc-handing-out-its-last-block-of-ipv4-addresses.html

- https://arstechnica.com/information-technology/2012/09/europe-officially-runs-out-of-ipv4-addresses/

- https://www.lacnic.net/1532/2/lacnic/no-more-ipv4-addresses-in-latin-america-and-the-caribbean

- https://arstechnica.com/information-technology/2015/07/us-exhausts-new-ipv4-addresses-waitlist-begins/

Links 2:

- https://arstechnica.com/information-technology/2015/09/north-america-is-out-of-ipv4-addresses-for-really-real-this-time/

- https://www.theregister.com/2018/04/18/last_ipv4_address/

- https://www.theregister.com/2019/11/25/ipv4_addresses_gone/

- https://www.ripe.net/publications/news/about-ripe-ncc-and-ripe/the-ripe-ncc-has-run-out-of-ipv4-addresses

- https://www.lacnic.net/4848/2/lacnic/ipv4-exhaustion:-lacnic-has-assigned-the-last-remaining-address-block

Step 4   Why, according to the stats at https://ipv4.potaroo.net/, do each of the five RIRs still have some IPv4 addresses available? Can you get IPv4 addresses from other sources besides an RIR?

Use the following links to help you formulate answers:

- https://www.arin.net/resources/registry/manage/return_revoke/

- https://www.arin.net/resources/guide/ipv4/

- https://www.networkworld.com/article/3191503/mit-selling-8-million-coveted-ipv4-addresses-amazon-a-buyer

- https://www.cfo.com/it-value/2017/07/got-extra-ip-addresses-can-sell/

- https://blog.strom.com/wp/?p=7561

- https://therecord.media/price-of-ipv4-addresses-one-of-the-internets-hottest-commodities-reaches-all-time-high/

Step 5   Fill in the requested information in the following chart. Once again, https://ipv4.potaroo.net/ will be a helpful link.

RIR	Area(s) Covered	Exhaustion Date	Remaining Addresses in RIR Pool (/8s)

Step 6   Fill in the missing information, using Slides 39–42 in this PowerPoint presentation from APNIC: https://www.apnic.net/wp-content/uploads/global-ipv6-summit/assets/apnic-v6-tutorial-distribution.ppt. The standard prefix given to homes, not covered by the PowerPoint presentation, has already been filled in.

Entity	Standard Prefix Length	Provides
RIR	_____	_____ site addresses (networks) Also see https://www.iana.org/assignments/ipv6-unicast-address-assignments/ipv6-unicast-address-assignments.xhtml
ISP	_____	_____ site addresses (networks)
Site (Company)	_____	_____ LANs (networks)
Site (Home)	/56	_____ LANs (networks)
LAN Segment (Network)	_____	_____ addresses per LAN
Device	_____	One IPv6 address

Step 7   Read this blog post that I wrote for ARIN: https://www.arin.net/blog/author/jweissman/.

What are your biggest takeaways from the article?

Step 8 Open RFC 2460, "Internet Protocol, Version 6 (IPv6)," at https://datatracker.ietf.org/doc/html/rfc2460 and record some of the information from the introduction. How many bits long is an IPv6 address compared to an IPv4 address? Click the Obsoletes: 1883 and Obsoleted by: 8200 links for other versions of this RFC.

Step 9 Open RFC 4291, "IP Version 6 Addressing Architecture," at https://datatracker.ietf.org/doc/html/rfc4291. This RFC defines the various addresses available in IPv6, such as unicast addresses, anycast addresses, and multicast addresses. Take a moment and read the Section 2.6 explanation of an *anycast address*. Explain what an anycast address is.

Step 10 Visit the following Web sites. Which stats are the most mind-boggling to you regarding the IPv6 address space?

- http://web.archive.org/web/20141110000741/https://itsnobody.wordpress.com/2012/02/17/how-many-addresses-can-ipv6-hold/

- https://whatis.techtarget.com/feature/IPv6-addresses-how-many-is-that-in-numbers

- https://www.edn.com/ipv6-how-many-ip-addresses-can-dance-on-the-head-of-a-pin/

30 MINUTES

Lab Exercise 12.02: IPv6 Address Compression

As you have learned, the IPv6 address is a 128-bit address displayed as eight groups of four hexadecimal numbers, such as 2001:0470:b8f9:0001:020c:29ff:fe53:45ca. Each group is unofficially known as a hextet, and the eight hextets are separated with colons.

Even though each hexadecimal digit from a to f is not case-sensitive, RFC 5952, "A Recommendation for IPv6 Address Text Representation" (https://datatracker.ietf.org/doc/html/rfc5952), in Section 4.3, states: *The characters "a", "b", "c", "d", "e", and "f" in an IPv6 address MUST be represented in lowercase.*

RFC 5952 (as well as RFC 2373, "IP Version 6 Addressing Architecture" [https://datatracker.ietf.org/doc/html/rfc2373]) also offers two rules to compress IPv6 addresses, making them easier to say, write, read, and configure:

- First, leading 0s in a hextext can be removed (but not trailing 0s, which would make the address different).

  For example, in this address, 2001:**0**db8:**000**f:**00**52:**000**0:**000**0:**000**0:1337, when the leading 0s are removed from hextexts (one from the second, three from the third, two from the fourth, three from the fifth, three from the sixth, and three from the seventh), the address is compressed to this:

  2001:db8:f: 52:0:0:0:1337

- Second, a double colon (::) can stand in place of two or more contiguous hextexts that consist of all 0s. This rule can only be applied once, because otherwise the address would be ambiguous.

  In the compressed address provided earlier, 2001:db8:f: 52:0:0:0:1337, hextexts 5–7 can be compressed with the double colon, and now the address is compressed even further:

  2001:db8:f: 52::1337

If there are more than one contiguous strings of hextexts of all 0s, RFC 5952, in Section 4.2.3, states:

> *When there is an alternative choice in the placement of a "::", the longest run of consecutive 16-bit 0 fields MUST be shortened (i.e., the sequence with three consecutive zero fields is shortened in 2001: 0:0:1:0:0:0:1). When the length of the consecutive 16-bit 0 fields are equal (i.e., 2001:db8:0:0:1:0:0:1), the first sequence of zero bits MUST be shortened. For example, 2001:db8::1:0:0:1 is correct representation.*

Learning Objectives

In this lab exercise, you'll practice converting IPv6 addresses between long-form notation and short-form notation using the shortcuts introduced in the *Mike Meyers' CompTIA Network+ Guide to Managing and Troubleshooting Networks* textbook. By the end of this lab exercise, you'll be able to

- Convert IPv6 addresses from long-form notation to short form-notation
- Convert IPv6 addresses from short-form notation to long-form notation

Lab Materials and Setup

The materials you'll need for this lab exercise are

- *Mike Meyers' CompTIA Network+ Guide to Managing and Troubleshooting Networks* textbook
- Internet access

Getting Down to Business

One of the new clients JSW has taken on is implementing IPv6 exclusively. Jonathan asks you to review and practice the IPv6 address compression rules. As usual, you heartily agree and quickly begin to tackle the problems.

▦ **1a–1e**

Step 1 Using the two rules, convert the following IPv6 addresses from their long-form notation into their short-form notation:

  a. 2001:0000:0000:3210:0800:200c:00cf:1234

  b. fe80:0000:0000:0000:020c:000f:0000:fe53

  c. ff02:0000:0000:0000:0000:0000:0000:0001

  d. 2001:0000:0000:0001:0200:000e:ffc8:0010

  e. fe80:0000:0000:0000:205c:2194.3f57.fd71

▦ **2a–2e**

Step 2 Now using the same two rules, convert the following IPv6 addresses from their short-form notation into their long-form notation:

  a. ::1

  b. fe80::a:0:53

  c. ff02::2

  d. 2001::6:e00:9:ffc8:11

  e. fe80::205c:2194:3f57:fd71

Step 3 Subnetting IPv6 is a lot quicker and easier than subnetting IPv4, shown in Chapter 6.

The first three hextets will be given to an organization by an ISP. Subnet the fourth hextet by simply… counting! That's it!

For example, if given 2001:1337:F00D, count in the fourth hextet:

2001:1337:f00d:0000::/64
2001:1337:f00d:0001::/64
2001:1337:f00d:0002::/64

…

2001:1337:f00d:0009::/64
2001:1337:f00d:000a::/64
2001:1337:f00d:000b::/64

…

2001:1337:f00d:000f::/64
2001:1337:f00d:0010::/64
2001:1337:f00d:0011::/64

This is referred to as the 3-1-4 rule. The first three hextets are given to an organization from an RIR (3), the fourth hextet is where the subnetting occurs (1), and the last four hextets are for the interface ID (4).

60 MINUTES

Lab Exercise 12.03: IPv6 Configuration and Communication

The time has come to send and receive some actual IPv6 traffic! You're going to send and receive traffic using two different types of IPv6 addresses, a unique local address (ULA) and a link-local address.

Learning Objectives

In this lab exercise, you'll again work with the TCP/IP settings on your Windows systems, as well as configure and explore IPv6 address information. By the end of this lab exercise, you'll be able to

- Verify your IPv6 settings

- Configure IPv6 ULAs

- Test and verify IPv6 connectivity with both a ULA and link-local address

Lab Materials and Setup

The materials you'll need for this lab exercise are

- *Mike Meyers' CompTIA Network+ Guide to Managing and Troubleshooting Networks* textbook

- Two Windows 10 systems connected with a switch

- Straight-through cables to connect the Windows 10 systems to the switch

Getting Down to Business

Jonathan comes by the Networking Lab and asks how your IPv6 skills are coming along. He has a concept that he would like you to explore: an IPv6-native network. At the moment, he's not able to free up any of the IPv6-capable routers that would enable you to configure your small network with global unicast addresses. Instead, he wants you to work with a type of address called a ULA.

> ✖ **Cross-Reference**
>
> You can learn more about the different address types by checking out the "IPv6 Basics" section in Chapter 12 of the *Mike Meyers' CompTIA Network+ Guide to Managing and Troubleshooting Networks* textbook.

Step 1 Begin by generating a random ULA. You can accomplish this by navigating to the following Web site, https://simpledns.plus/private-ipv6, and randomly generating a ULA.

✔ **Tech Tip**

> The parameters for the ULA are set forth in RFC 4193 (https://datatracker.ietf.org/doc/html/
> rfc4193), "Unique Local IPv6 Unicast Addresses."

Step 2   Disable Windows Defender Firewall on each Windows 10 system. They will not be connected to the Internet, so there are no worries. However, Chapter 19 has a lab exercise that shows you how to write rules to allow or block certain types of traffic.

Step 3   In the Windows 10 search box, type **sharing**, click Manage Advanced Sharing Settings, click Network And Sharing Center from address bar at the top, click Change Adapter Settings from the right pane, right-click the NIC you're using, select Properties, scroll down until you see Internet Protocol Version 6 (TCP/IPv6), select Internet Protocol Version 6 (TCP/IPv6), and click the Properties button.

Configure each Windows 10 system with an IPv6 ULA address and subnet prefix length (leave the rest blank) in the Properties window shown in Figure 12-1. Make sure to give each system an address on the same link (subnet) as the other

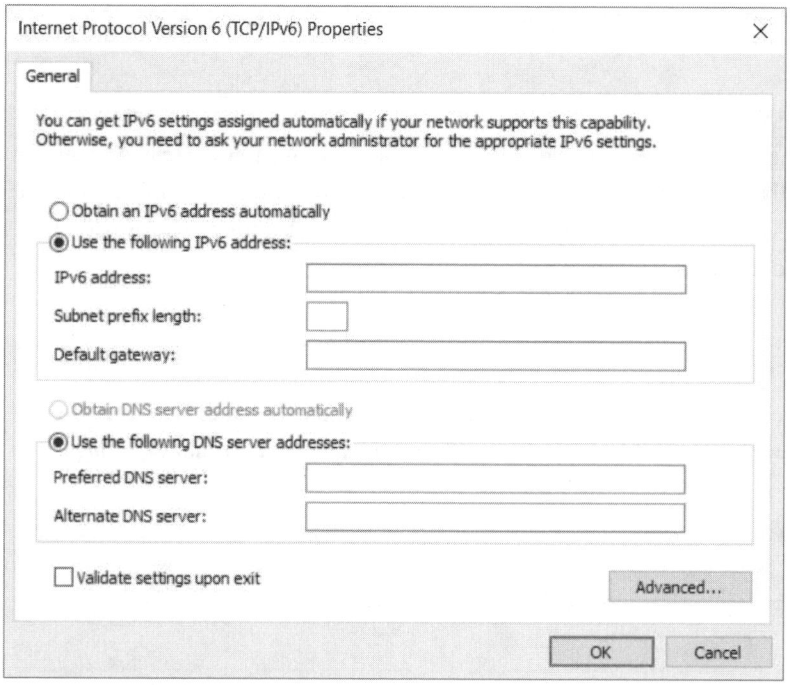

FIGURE 12-1 Windows 10 IPv6 configuration

Step 4   A ULA is a private address in IPv6 used for local communication, like the RFC 1918 addresses (10.0.0.0/8, 172.16-31.0.0/16, 192.168.0-255.0/24) that are used with NAT in IPv4.

✖ **Cross-Reference**

Please refer to the links in Chapter 7 that clearly illustrate that NAT is *not* a security mechanism, although there is a great misconception by some that it is!

The use of NAT with IPv6 is illustrated in this great video, "'Fanboy' series – IPv6 and NATs'": https://youtu.be/v26BAlfWBm8.

There are actually a few flavors of NAT for IPv6, but the main one deals with protocol translation, turning an IPv6 header into an IPv4 header and vice versa (NAT64 along with DNS64), not translating between private inside addresses and a private outside address. NAT66 and NPTv6 actually do the translation between two IPv6 addresses like the NAT most people think of. NAT66 (which is stateful and translates an IPv6 address to another IPv6 address like the NAT for IPv4—NAT44) is described in an expired draft RFC (https://datatracker.ietf.org/doc/html/draft-mrw-behave-nat66-02) and NPTv6 (which is stateless and just translates the leftmost prefix parts of the IPv6 address) is described in RFC 6296 (https://datatracker.ietf.org/doc/html/rfc6296).

All you need to know about NAT and IPv6 is in the Introduction section for RFC 6296:

> *For reasons discussed in [RFC2993] and Section 5, the IETF does not recommend the use of Network Address Translation technology for IPv6.*

In RFC 5902 (https://datatracker.ietf.org/doc/html/rfc5902), Section 2.5, "Simple Security," states:

> *It is commonly perceived that a NAT box provides one level of protection because external hosts cannot directly initiate communication with hosts behind a NAT. However, one should not confuse NAT boxes with firewalls. As discussed in [RFC4864], Section 2.2, the act of translation does not provide security in itself. The stateful filtering function can provide the same level of protection without requiring a translation function. For further discussion, see [RFC4864], Section 4.2.*

Also from RFC 5902, Section 3, "Architectural Considerations of IPv6 NAT," states:

> *It is desirable that IPv6 users and applications be able to reach each other directly without having to worry about address translation boxes between the two ends. IPv6 application developers in general should be able to program based on the assumption of end-to-end reachability (of wanted traffic), without having to address the issue of traversing NAT boxes. For example, referrals and multi-party conversations are straightforward with end-to-end addressing, but vastly complicated in the presence of address translation. Similarly, network administrators should be able to run their networks without the added complexity of NATs, which can bring not only the cost of additional boxes, but also increased difficulties in network monitoring and problem debugging.*

After you have configured both Windows 10 systems, on each system, open a command prompt and execute

```
ipconfig /all
```

to see the ULA on each system.

Step 5   All IPv6 hosts use a link-local address (fe80::/10) for traffic on the same link (the IPv6 term for network). Execute

```
ipconfig /all
```

to see the link-local address on each system.

This is the equivalent of IPv4's APIPA/zeroconf address in the 169.254.0.0/16 block that you never want to have. Link-local addresses in IPv6 are always used for on-link communications! Your default gateway's IPv6 address will be a link-local address. Routers send routing updates to other routers using this type of address.

Step 6   Open up Wireshark, start sniffing, and filter by **icmpv6**. Send a ping from one Windows 10 system to the other's ULA.

Step 7   Now send a ping from one Windows 10 system to the other's link-local address. You'll notice that there is a suffix consisting of a % sign followed by number known as the zone ID. As explained in RFC 4007 (https://datatracker.ietf.org/doc/html/rfc4007), since an IPv6 host can be connected to multiple links with multiple interfaces, each link will have its own link-local address. When sending traffic to each link using a link-local address, it would be ambiguous as to which link should get link-local address traffic. The wired NIC? A second wired NIC? The wireless NIC? A virtual NIC? It's just not clear. The zone ID is used to identify one interface/link from another.

The zone ID is locally significant. Therefore, when pinging out of an interface using a link-local address, add the % sign and the zone ID after the IP address you're pinging.

While Linux systems and macOS always require the zone ID when pinging a link-local address, Windows systems only require it if more than one interface is up.

→ **Note**

The IPv6 unspecified address is just :: (two colons indicating that all 128 bits are zeros). The IPv6 loopback address is ::1. Ping it!

 **60 MINUTES**

Lab Exercise 12.04: IPv6 Neighbor Discovery Protocol (RS, RA)

Neighbor Discovery Protocol (NDP) is run through ICMPv6 (ICMP for IPv6, not the sixth version of ICMP). NDP consists of five elements:

- Router Solicitation (RS; the IPv6 equivalent of a DHCP Discover)

- Router Advertisement (RA; the IPv6 equivalent of a DHCP Offer)

- Neighbor Solicitation (NS; the IPv6 equivalent of an ARP request)

- Neighbor Advertisement (NA; the IPv6 equivalent of an ARP reply)

- Redirect (how routers that are default gateways for PCs let the PCSs know if there is a more optimal router on the network to send traffic to for a specific destination)

This lab exercise will take a look at the first two (RS, RA), while the next lab exercise will take a look at the next two (NS, NA). Redirects will not be covered.

When an IPv6 host has an interface enabled, it sends a router solicitation (RS) to the all-routers multicast address of ff02::2 (more on IPv6 multicast addresses coming up later) in hopes of receiving a router advertisement (RA) in response. (This can either be sent either the all nodes multicast address of ff02::1, or it can be configured to be sent to the link-local unicast address of the host. The host's MAC address is included in the RS as well, so the router has all it needs.) Routers also send unsolicited router advertisements in regular time intervals.

RA messages let hosts know how to go ahead with dynamic addressing and contain a prefix (the IPv6 term for network ID), prefix length (the IPv6 term for subnet mask, which should always be /64 to allow hosts to autoconfigure themselves—coming up later), default gateway, and other information for configuration. A router can also be configured to send IP addresses of DNS servers in an option in an RA.

There are three important flags in the RA:

- **Address Autoconfiguration flag (A flag)**   A 1 (default) instructs a host to create its global unicast address (GUA; the IPv6 term for public IP address) with stateless address autoconfiguration (SLAAC). The RA contains a 64-bit prefix, which will be followed by a 64-bit interface ID generated by the host during the SLAAC process (coming up later).

- **Other Configuration Flag (O flag)**   A 1 instructs a host to get information other than an actual GUA (like DNS server IPv6 addresses and domain name information) from a stateless DHCPv6 (DHCP for IPv6) server.

- **Managed Address Configuration flag (M flag)**   A 1 instructs a host to use a stateful DHCPv6 server for everything, including its GUA and other configuration information, just like an IPv4 host would use a DHCP server. However, the source IPv6 address in the RA becomes the host's default gateway address. DHCPv6 servers never give out default gateway information.

With SLAAC, the host can generate a 64-bit interface ID with either the Extended Unique Identifier-64 (EUI-64) process or a random 64-bit value. Here's the process for EUI-64:

1. Using EUI-64, which was the original method and is still supported by routers but not Windows, macOS, or most distributions of Linux, the host starts off by taking its 48-bit MAC address and splitting it in the middle, with 6 hex digits representing the OUI on one side and 6 hex digits representing the device ID on the other side.

   Let's take 00-03-6b-18-f0-0d and split it in the middle:

   ```
   00-03-6b   18-f0-0d
   ```

2. In the middle, the host puts **fffe**, a special reserved value specifically meaning that the MAC address was used in this process.

   ```
   00-03-6b-ff-fe-18-f0-0d
   ```

3. The seventh bit from the left is known as both the Universally/Locally (U/L) bit and the Local/Global bit. A 0 in this bit position means the Institute of Electrical and Electronics Engineers (IEEE) assigned this address. A 1 means it's locally administered by a company. Looking at what we have so far, again:

   ```
   00-03-6b-ff-fe-18-f0-0d
   ```

   The first two hex digits (00) in binary are 0000000**0** (notice that the seventh bit is in bold).

When you flip this seventh bit, it becomes 0000 00**1**0 (notice again that the seventh bit is in bold). Turning the binary back into hex, since the flipped bit is in the 2s column of the second hex digit, the second hex digit becomes a 2 (again shown in bold):

```
02-03-6b-ff-fe-18-f0-0d
```

From Section 2.5.1 of RFC 2373 (https://datatracker.ietf.org/doc/html/rfc2373):

> The motivation for inverting the "u" bit when forming the interface identifier is to make it easy for system administrators to hand configure local scope identifiers when hardware tokens are not available. This is expected to be case for serial links, tunnel end-points, etc. The alternative would have been for these to be of the form 0200:0:0:1, 0200:0:0:2, etc., instead of the much simpler ::1, ::2, etc.

Now imagine using your laptop on various networks. Your NIC's MAC address, if part of an IPv6 address, can be tracked, aggregated, and correlated on all of the networks you connect to. It will be in log files and network traces. That fear lead to RFC 4941 (https://datatracker.ietf.org/doc/html/rfc4941), "Privacy Extensions for Stateless Address Autoconfiguration in IPv6":

> Any time the same identifier is used in multiple contexts, it becomes possible for that identifier to be used to correlate seemingly unrelated activity. For example, a network sniffer placed strategically on a link across which all traffic to/from a particular host crosses could keep track of which destinations a node communicated with and at what times. Such information can in some cases be used to infer things, such as what hours an employee was active, when someone is at home, etc.

In addition to generating randomized interface IDs, devices will generate temporary addresses to be used as source IPv6 addresses for short periods of time to further aid in privacy. An IPv6 address that does not change will be assigned by the host for incoming connections.

A host can have more than one GUA (on one or more links) in addition to a link-local address for each link. Furthermore, multiple temporary addresses can be in play to allow existing connections to continue while a new temporary address is used for future connections.

Learning Objectives

In this lab exercise, you'll gain experience with IPv6 addresses and RAs. By the end of this lab exercise, you'll be able to

- Identify IPv6 addresses that use EUI-64 notation

- Identify IPv6 addresses that use privacy extensions

- Capture and analyze a router solicitation and router advertisement message

Lab Materials and Setup

The materials you'll need for this lab exercise are

- *Mike Meyers' CompTIA Network+ Guide to Managing and Troubleshooting Networks* textbook

- Windows 10 system with Internet access

Getting Down to Business

Now it's time to bring all those concepts to life with a command prompt and Wireshark!

 1a–1h

Step 1

    a. Open Wireshark and start sniffing with a display filter of **icmpv6**, which will show all ICMPv6 traffic, or **icmpv6.type == 133 || icmpv6.type == 134**, which will only show router solicitations (type 133) and router advertisements (type 134).

        Now, you'll capture a router solicitation and router advertisement message.

    b. In the search box, type **sharing**, click Manage Advanced Sharing Settings, click Network And Sharing Center from the address bar at the top, click Change Adapter Settings from the right pane, right-click the NIC you're using, and select Disable. This will stop any Wireshark capture on that interface.

c. Be very quick for these next two instructions. First, right-click the NIC you're using once again, and select Enable. Second, as fast as you can after selecting Enable, click the blue fin in Wireshark to start capturing.

d. Align the windows next to each other so you can move from one to the next with the mouse easily.

Refer to Figure 12-2 for the following steps.

e. Select the router solicitation in the Packet List pane, and then expand the Internet Control Message Protocol v6 section and notice the link-layer address, which is the MAC address of your interface.

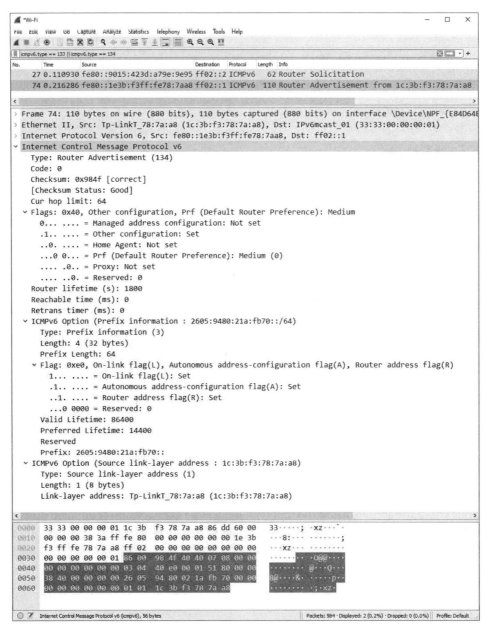

FIGURE 12-2 RS and RA at the Weissman household

f. Select the router advertisement in the Packet List pane, and then expand the Internet Control Message Protocol v6 section and all of the sections inside of it. Then, locate the M and O flags in the ICMPv6 packet's Flags section.

g. In that same section, the Mobile IPv6 Home Agent flag indicates if the router that sent the RA is a Mobile IPv6 home agent. The Router Selection Preferences flag, a 2-bit value, indicates which router to use as a default gateway if multiple RAs are received. (High is 01, Medium is 00, Low is 11, while 10 is a reserved value. In the event of a tie, the host uses the router that sent the first RA that was received.) The Neighbor Discovery Proxy flag is used to determine an upstream proxy interface.

h. Locate the A flag in the Prefix information option's Flag section. In that same section, you'll notice an L flag. The L (On-Link) flag is how a host determines if the destination is on the same link (local communication, indicated by a 1 in this field) or a different link (remote communication, indicated by a 0 in this field), not the way it's done in IPv4 with the two logical AND processes, covered in Chapter 6. Also, in that same section, you'll notice an R (Router Address) flag, which when set with a 1 indicates that the prefix field has a complete IP address assigned to the router that sent the RA.

 2a–2d

 2d

Step 2

a. Open up a command prompt and execute

```
ipconfig /all
```

b. Look at the IPv6 address of your default gateway. Does it have ff:fe in the middle? It most likely will. If so, reverse engineer its MAC address.

For example, this is my default gateway's link-local IPv6 address:

fe80::1e3b:f3ff:fe78:7aa8%26

Notice the ff:fe in the middle.

c. Although it involves IPv4, displaying the ARP cache with

```
arp -a
```

shows me the following entry:

```
Internet Address        Physical Address        Type
192.168.0.1             1c-3b-f3-78-7a-a8       dynamic
```

Notice the last six hex digits of 78-7a-a8, which also happen to be the last six hex digits of my default gateway's IPv6 link-local address.

d. Now, observe the first six hex digits of my default gateway's MAC address: 1c-3b-f3 (see the bolded c). Before the ff:fe in the default gateway's IPv6 link-local address is 1e3b:f3 (see the bolded e). The only difference is that the c has been turned into an e. Why did that happen?

1c in binary is 00011100 (see the bolded seventh bit). 0001 in hex is 1, and 1100 in hex is c (12 in base 10/decimal).

When we flip the seventh bit from a 0 to a 1 to make 00011110, that doesn't affect the first four bits, as they remain 0001, or 1 in hex. However, the last four bits change from 1100 to 1110. 1110 in hex is e (in decimal it's 8 + 4 + 2 = 14).

 120 MINUTES

Lab Exercise 12.05: IPv6 Neighbor Discovery Protocol (NS, NA)

You learned in Chapter 6 how ARP works. In IPv6, there is no broadcast traffic, just unicast, multicast, or anycast. How, then, can hosts get the MAC addresses of the devices they wish to communicate with, having an IP address provided to them directly or through DNS. ARP requests are broadcasts, so that can't be how it's done in IPv6.

The answer is Neighbor Discovery Protocol, which is run through ICMPv6 (ICMP for IPv6, not the sixth version of ICMP), specifically

- Neighbor Solicitation (NS, the IPv6 equivalent of an ARP request)

- Neighbor Advertisement (NA, the IPv6 equivalent of an ARP reply)

Let's say an IPv6 device has to send a packet to **2001:db8:f00d:1::200/64**. That's the destination IPv6 address that will be found in the IPv6 header of the packet. The packet, of course, must be encapsulated inside of a frame, and the source needs the destination's MAC address for the frame.

The source first checks its neighbor cache, the IPv6 equivalent of the IPv4 ARP cache. If the binding is there, it's used, just like the ARP cache is used for IPv4. If it's not, the source sends a Neighbor Solicitation message to the destination's solicited-node multicast address. In this case, it's **ff02::1:ff00:200**.

Let's back up a bit. Each interface's unicast address will always have a corresponding solicited-node multicast address. Like all multicast addresses, it starts off with **ff**. The next hex digit is a 0 for permanent, well-known multicast addresses (IANA assigns these), or a 1 for a multicast address for an organization's needs. The fourth hex digit represents the scope, following this pattern:

- **0 (reserved)**   Don't plan on seeing this one.

- **1 (interface-local scope)**   Don't plan on seeing this one, as it's hard to find a reason for multicasting to yourself aside from troubleshooting and debugging.

- **2 (link-local scope)**   This is the most common one.

- **5 (site-local scope)**   This means it can span routers of an autonomous system.

- **8 (organization-local scope)**   This means it could go through a VPN to another branch of the company.

- **E (global scope)**   Don't plan on seeing this one, as ISPs will not allow a multicast to traverse the backbone of the Internet.

→ **Note**

> To join multicast groups in IPv4, as you learned in Chapter 8, Internet Group Message Protocol (IGMP) is used. To join multicast groups in IPv6, Multicast Listener Discovery (MLD) is used.

OK, we're at ff02, so far.

The prefix for solicited-node multicast addresses is

ff02:0:0:0:0:1:ff00::/104 (or ff02::1:ffxx:xxxx, where x represents hex digits that need to be filled in)

If there are 104 bits given (as indicated by the /104), the other 24 need to be filled in. Here's how it's done. Simply take the last six hex digits (24 bits) of the IPv6 address and put them there! That's it!

In **2001:db8:f00d:1::200/64**, the last six hex digits are 000200, although you don't see all of them. Shortcut notation dealing with leading zeros takes away a zero at the start of the eighth hextet, and the double colon shortcut notation takes away all of the fifth, sixth, and seventh hextets, which are all 0s.

If we start with this

ff02::1:ffxx:xxxx

and fill in the x positions with 000200, we get (notice the bolding for the last six hex digits)

ff02::1:ff**00:0200**

We can remove the leading 0 in the eighth hextet to wind up with

ff02::1:ff00:200

IPv6 multicast addresses have corresponding Ethernet MAC addresses. A multicast MAC address corresponding to an IPv6 address always starts with 33-33, with the rest of the MAC address (the lower 32 bits) corresponding to the lower 32 bits of the IPv6 multicast address. For example:

33-33-00-00-00-01 is the MAC address for ff02::1 (All-devices)

33-33-00-00-00-02 is the MAC address for ff02::2 (All-routers)

→ **Note**

> The reasons for multicast MAC addresses starting with four 3s is written into RFC 7042 (https://datatracker.ietf.org/doc/html/rfc7042) as follows:
>> (Historical note: It was the custom during IPv6 design to use "3" for unknown or example values, and 3333 Coyote Hill Road, Palo Alto, California, is the address of PARC [Palo Alto Research Center, formerly "Xerox PARC"]. Ethernet was originally specified by the Digital Equipment Corporation, Intel Corporation, and Xerox Corporation. The pre-IEEE [802.3] Ethernet protocol has sometimes been known as "DIX" Ethernet from the first letters of the names of these companies.)

We started with **2001:db8:f00d:1::200/64**.

Without shortcut notation, that's 2001:db8:f00d:0001:0000:000:000:0200/64.

We took the last 24 bits (6 hex digits) to make the following solicited-node multicast address (notice the bolding):

ff02:0000:0000:0000:0000:0001:**ff00:0200**

Now let's take the last 32 (8 hex digits) of that address (notice the bolding),

ff02:0000:0000:0000:0000:0001:**ff00:0200**

and put them after 33-33 (notice the bolding):

33-33 **ff-00-02-00**

That is the MAC address placed in the frame, corresponding to the solicited-node multicast address in the packet.

With the use of a Layer 2 multicast address now instead of a broadcast ARP request (which is read in addition to the Ethernet frame by all devices), the NIC can filter NS messages quickly and easily. The IPv6 header and the ICMPv6 packet need not be consulted.

Now, of course, it is possible, although not that likely, to have more than one interface with the same last 6 hex digits. The interface ID is 64 bits long, so these interfaces will differ in their highest 40 bits of the interface ID. If so, these interfaces will have the exact solicited-node multicast address and the exact multicast MAC address. That's not an issue, because inside of the ICMPv6 Neighbor Solicitation message is a Target Address field, and the interface not matching the value in that field will drop the NS at that point.

→ **Note**

> NICs read in Ethernet frames if the destination MAC address is that NIC's unicast address, a solicited-node multicast for a global unicast address, a solicited-node multicast for a link-local address, or any assigned multicast address such as the all nodes address.

Learning Objectives

In this lab exercise, you'll get comfortable with the ARP replacement for IPv6. By the end of this lab exercise, you'll be able to

- Understand the difference between IP address–to–MAC address resolution in IPv4 and IPv6
- Understand how Neighbor Solicitations and Neighbor Advertisements work
- Understand how the neighbor cache and the destination cache work
- Understand IPv6 multicast addresses

- Understand how an IPv6 address is turned into its corresponding solicited-node multicast address

- Understand how an IPv6 solicited-node multicast address is turned into its corresponding MAC address

- Understand how duplicate address detection (DAD) works

- Generate network traffic and analyze all of this with Wireshark and the command prompt

- Understand how the IPv6 header is different than the IPv4 header

Lab Materials and Setup

The materials you'll need for this lab exercise are

- *Mike Meyers' CompTIA Network+ Guide to Managing and Troubleshooting Networks* textbook

- Two Windows 10 systems with Internet access

- Native IPv6 connectivity from your ISP

Getting Down to Business

Just like you did in Chapter 6, you'll be exploring the difference between local communication and remote communication; however, now you'll do it with IPv6. As such, this lab exercise works best if you have a GUA, which will be required to do the remote communication part of this lab exercise. However, if you don't have one, you'll still be able to do the local communication part using the ULA addresses configured earlier.

Step 1   In a command prompt, execute

```
ipconfig /all
```

An IPv6 GUA uses the prefix and prefix length of 2000::/3, which means the first 3 bits (out of 128) need to be 001. The fourth bit of the first hextet could be 0 or 1. If it's a 0 (001**0**), the first hex digit will be a 2 (a 1 in the 2s column). If it's a 1 (001**1**), the first hex digit will be a 3 (a 1 in the 2s column and a 1 in the 1s column). As of now, the only IPv6 GUAs you'll see start with a 2.

If your ISP gives you native IPv6 connectivity, you'll see an IPv6 address that starts with 2 (there are a few exceptions to this—see the Note that follows), as well as one or more addresses listed with the label Temporary IPv6 Address in the output.

→ **Note**

As stated in RFC 3849 (https://datatracker.ietf.org/doc/html/rfc3849), 2001:db8::/32 is reserved to be used in examples in RFCs, books, and documentation. In fact, that's what I've used in this chapter! Also, deprecated tunneling protocols have used 2001::/16 and 2002::/16.

As mentioned earlier in this chapter, temporary addresses are preferred for outgoing connections since they have shorter lifetimes and allow your interface to retain a degree of privacy. The IPv6 address (non-temporary) is used for incoming connections, and it would be problematic if it changed.

Step 2   Open Wireshark and start sniffing with a display filter of **icmpv6.type == 135 || icmpv6.type == 136**, which will only show Neighbor Solicitations (type 135) or Neighbor Advertisements (type 136).

Get the GUA of another device on your link, and ping that address. Stop the capture when the ping completes. Find the corresponding NS and NA messages in Wireshark.

Just like in IPv4, IPv6 local communication is when the source directly communicates with the actual destination, without the need of a default gateway/router.

As you learned in this lab exercise's introduction, fill in the information in the second column of this table with information related to the NS. Enter your answers without looking at the Wireshark capture. Then compare your answers to the Wireshark capture to see if they match.

GUA IPv6 address pinged	
Corresponding solicited-node multicast address	
Corresponding MAC address	

Now look at the NA, and fill in the answer.

Answer in the NA (MAC address of the destination found in the ICMPv6 Option called Target link-layer address)	

Change the display filter in Wireshark to **icmpv6.type == 128 || icmpv6.type == 129,** which will only show ICMPv6 Echo requests or Echo replies. Compare the answer given in the NA to the destination MAC address in the ICMPv6 Echo requests and the source MAC address in the ICMPv6 Echo replies. How do they compare?

If you want to ping the same local device again, clear the neighbor cache with `netsh interface ipv6 delete neighbors` from an administrative command prompt (to be explained later).

→ **Note**

To check if a soon-to-be self-assigned address is already in use on a link, an IPv6 performs duplicate address detection (DAD). This is actually sending an NS to the solicited-node multicast address of the address it's about to assign to itself. If an NA comes back, someone has it! If no NA comes back, it's free to be used.

Step 3   Once again, start sniffing in Wireshark. Use a display filter **icmpv6.type == 135 || icmpv6.type == 136**, which will only show NSs (type 135) or NAs (type 136).

Just as you did for IPv4 remote communication in Chapter 6, make a batch file. Put these commands in:

```
netsh interface ipv6 delete neighbors

ping ipv6.google.com
```

Then, run the batch file from an administrative command prompt. The first command clears the neighbor cache (to be explained later). Find the corresponding NS and NA messages, as well as the Echo requests and Echo replies in Wireshark.

Just like in IPv4, IPv6 remote communication is when the source directly communicates with the default gateway/router, and the default gateway's MAC address will be used as the destination MAC address in the frame in the subsequent outgoing traffic.

As you learned in this lab exercise's introduction, fill in the information in the second column of this table with information related to the NS. Enter your answers without looking at the Wireshark capture. Then compare your answers to the Wireshark capture to see if they match.

IPv6 address of the default gateway	
Corresponding solicited-node multicast address	
Corresponding MAC address	

Now look at the NA, and fill in the answer.

Answer in the NA (MAC address of the default gateway found in the ICMPv6 Option called Target link-layer address)	

Change the display filter in Wireshark to **icmpv6.type == 128 || icmpv6.type == 129**, which will only show ICMPv6 Echo requests or Echo replies. Compare the answer given in the NA to the destination MAC address in the ICMPv6 Echo requests and the source MAC address in the ICMPv6 Echo replies. How do they compare?

 4a–4f

Step 4   An IPv6 host has two caches for every interface: the neighbor cache and the destination cache. The neighbor cache (populated from NAs) is the IPv6 equivalent of the IPv4 ARP cache (populated from ARP replies) and contains a mapping of IPv6 to MAC addresses for recently communicated on-link devices.

Other information contained in the neighbor cache includes the type of device the neighbor is (router or host) and the reachability state. The Reachable state means that this device recently sent a packet. The Stale state means that it's been a while since this device sent a packet (time varies by OS). The Permanent state is for multicast addresses, since as discussed, there is always a Layer 3–to–Layer 2 relationship in multicast addresses.

> **→ Note**
>
> Other states include Delay (re-resolution is pending, the device is waiting for a packet back from other traffic, like TCP), Probe (re-resolution is in progress, the device just sent out an NS for a device that was in cache already), and Incomplete (NS was sent but nothing has come back yet for a device that wasn't in cache).

a.   Resend the local communication ping (just to make sure the entry is there, as it might have been removed since you originally sent the ping).

b.   Open a command prompt as an administrator (needed to delete the neighbor cache, not to display it).

c.   Display the neighbor cache with

```
netsh interface ipv6 show neighbors
```

Find the corresponding entry.

d.   Delete the neighbor cache with

```
netsh interface ipv6 delete neighbors
```

e.   Send the ping again, and once again show the neighbor cache.

f.   You can explore more IPv6 netsh commands by typing

```
netsh interface ipv6
```

which will show more commands.

g.   Now type

```
netsh interface ipv6 show
```

and explore some or all of the commands in the context shown by continuing the command, for example:

```
netsh interface ipv6 show addresses
```

h.   Change the word `addresses` to the other commands shown.

 5a–5d

Step 5   There is no IPv4 equivalent for the IPv6 destination cache, which shows the path maximum transmission unit (PMTU), destination address, and the next-hop address. This destination cache contains entries not only for local connected devices but also devices on other links (networks). For locally connected devices, the next-hop address is the same as the destination address (that's local communication, as shown in Chapter 6). For devices on different links, the next-hop address is the link-local address of the default gateway. IPv6 hosts have a default router list for off-link destinations. The destination cache allows for the caching of off-link addresses with the associated default gateway.

a. Ping some remote hosts that support IPv6. If you've got a GUA, you can ping

- ipv6.google.com

- www.google.com

- www.cisco.com

and more.

b. See if DNS is turning the FQDNs into IPv6 addresses in the command prompt output.

c. Find the corresponding entries in the destination cache, which can be displayed with the following command:

```
netsh interface ipv6 show destinationcache
```

d. To delete the destination cache, execute the following command from a command prompt opened with Run As Administrator selected:

```
netsh interface ipv6 delete destinationcache
```

→ **Note**

As brought out in RFC 6555 (https://datatracker.ietf.org/doc/html/rfc6555), titled "Happy Eyeballs: Success with Dual-Stack Hosts," a dual-stacked host will prefer IPv6, but will fall back to IPv4 if necessary.

 6a–6e

Step 6 Now to put it all together, see if you can capture the following in Wireshark:

a. A device starting with the unspecified address (::) performing DAD for a link-local address (NS)

b. That device sending an RS

c. The router sending an RA

d. That device performing DAD for a GUA

e. That device sending traffic with the GUA

→ **Note**

DAD is mandatory for all unicast addresses (GUAs, link-local addresses) whether the addresses were created through SLAAC, DHCPv6, or even statically configured! There are some exceptions to this behavior, as discussed in in RFC 4429 (https://datatracker.ietf.org/doc/html/rfc4429).

Step 7   Use any IPv4 and IPv6 header in Wireshark to go through the following discussion that compares the IPv4 and IPv6 headers.

Some fields in the IPv6 header have the same name as fields in the IPv4 header:

- The Version field has the same name, but, of course, the value of 6 is there instead of 4.

- The Source Address and Destination Address fields retain their name, but, of course, in the IPv6 header, they are filled with 128 bits, unlike the 32 bits in the IPv4 header.

Some fields in the IPv6 header have been renamed:

- The IPv4 Differentiated Services field has been renamed Traffic Class in the IPv6 header. The functionality remains the same—to classify and manage network traffic by providing quality of service (QoS).

- The IPv4 field TTL has been renamed to the more logical Hop Limit in the IPv6 header. In Chapter 7 you learned about this field, which routers decrement each time a packet is sent out of an interface to prevent routing loops (used by tracert too for troubleshooting, as also shown in Chapter 7).

- The Protocol field has been renamed Next Header. IPv6 uses a fixed-length 40-byte (32 bytes of which are the source and destination addresses) header, which is more efficient than IPv4's variable-length header, although IPv4 options that would raise the minimum 20-byte header (potentially up to the limit of 60 bytes) aren't used today because of security concerns. IPv6 extension headers, used instead of options, include Hop-by-Hop Options, Routing, Fragment, Encapsulating Security Payload (ESP), Authentication Header (AH), Destination Options, Mobility, Host Identity Protocol, and Shim6 Protocol.

Some fields from the IPv4 header do not appear in the IPv6 header in any form:

- The Header Length field is not needed in the IPv6 header because the IPv6 header is a fixed-length header, as mentioned previously.

- The Identification, Flags, and Fragment Offset fields do not appear in the IPv6 header. These fields deal with fragmentation, and unlike IPv4 routers, IPv6 routers don't fragment packets. If a packet exceeds a link's maximum transmission unit (MTU), a router will send an ICMPv6 Packet Too Big error message. Then the source will use a Fragment extension header.

- There is no Header Checksum field in the IPv6 header. There's error checking in the frames at Layer 2 and in TCP segments or UDP datagrams at Layer 4. Therefore, there's really no need to check for errors at Layer 3. However, the UDP checksum, which was optional in IPv4, is now mandatory in IPv6.

- There are no Options in the IPv6 header. As mentioned, extension headers take the place of Options.

- There is no Padding in the IPv6 header. Padding is needed in IPv4 when Options leave the size of a packet on a non-32-bit-boundary. Since there are no Options in IPv6 and also because the size of an IPv6 header is always a fixed-length 40 bytes, there is no need for a Padding field in the IPv6 header.

One field in the IPv6 header has been changed from its counterpart in the IPv4 header:

- The Total Length field in the IPv4 header, which calculated the number of bytes, including Layer 3 and above, has been renamed and changed to the Payload Length field, which just calculates the number of bytes after the main IPv6 header (including extension headers, Layer 4 headers, and upper-layer data). Again, the IPv6 header is fixed-length, and its size will always be 40 bytes.

One brand-new field with no connection to the IPv4 header has been added to the IPv6 header:

- The Flow Label field tags and identifies packets in a single flow or stream.

→ **Note**

You'll also notice in Wireshark that frames encapsulating IPv4 packets have a hex value in the Type field of 0800, while frames encapsulating IPv6 packets have a hex value in the Type field of 86dd.

Lab Analysis

1. Arnel and Steve are studying for the CompTIA Network+ exam. While reading about IPv6, they ask, "What is a link-local address and how can you recognize this address type? How is the IPv6 version different than the IPv4 equivalent?" Explain it to them.

2. Neal and Cain want to know how a system running IPv6 gets a global unicast address. Explain it to them.

3. Stephanie keeps hearing some fellow techs talking about an IPv6 anycast address. Can you help her understand what this is and how it is used?

4. Erica wants you to help her understand some of the different multicast addresses supported by IPv6. What will you tell her?

5. Rachel asks you to explain to her some of the rules for the IPv6 address notation. Break down the format of an IPv6 address for her.

Key Term Quiz

Use the terms in this list to complete the sentences that follow.

interface ID   prefix and prefix length

link   Router Solicitation, Router Advertisement

Neighbor Solicitation and Neighbor
    Advertisement

1. Instead of ARP requests and ARP replies, to get a destination's MAC address, IPv6 hosts use
   _____.

2. The IPv6 equivalent of a DHCP Discover and DHCP Offer is _____.

3. Instead of saying host ID, in IPv6 the term is _____.

4. The term that means network in IPv6 is _____.

5. Instead of saying network ID and subnet mask, in IPv6 the terminology is _____.

Chapter 13

WAN Connectivity

Lab Exercises

In many of the lab exercises you have performed thus far, you have integrated both local area networks (LANs) and wide area networks (WANs) as you worked through the lab exercise steps. Now, you will delve specifically into technologies associated with WAN connectivity and remote connections.

This chapter's lab exercises include configuring and using a VPN for connectivity and confidentiality, configuring and using Remote Desktop Connection to enable the management and administration of a remote system, and lending a helping hand on a remote system using Microsoft Quick Assist.

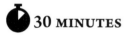 **30 minutes**

Lab Exercise 13.01: VPN

Many of JSW's clients have allowed their employees to join the working from home (WFH) movement ever since the COVID-19 pandemic started to have an effect in March 2020. How will employees working from home access the on-premises resources, though? How will the corporate data be secured as it travels from an employee's house to the organization's infrastructure and back?

Jonathan asks you to use the machines in the Networking Lab to configure and test a virtual private network (VPN) solution for both issues, using the built-in Routing and Remote Access Services (RRAS) role in Windows Server 2019. You will first create the VPN server, and then you will configure the client systems to access that server using VPN.

> ✖ **Cross-Reference**
>
> For additional information on VPN technologies, check out the "Virtual Private Networks" section in Chapter 13 of the *Mike Meyers' CompTIA Network+ Guide to Managing and Troubleshooting Networks* textbook.

Learning Objectives

In this lab exercise, you'll configure a Windows VPN server and a Windows VPN client. By the end of this lab exercise, you'll be able to

- Configure the RRAS VPN on a Windows Server 2019 system
- Implement and test a Windows VPN

Lab Materials and Setup

The materials you'll need for this lab exercise are

- *Mike Meyers' CompTIA Network+ Guide to Managing and Troubleshooting Networks* textbook

- Windows 10 system

- Windows Server 2019 system

- Switch and appropriate cabling

Getting Down to Business

You have really become quite efficient at managing the resources in the Networking Lab and are very skilled at reconfiguring the machines and the network to test different scenarios.

Start this configuration by establishing a connection between the Windows 10 system and the Windows Server 2019 machine. You can use any IP addressing scheme. You can also choose between static addressing and dynamic addressing. Make sure that pings go through in each direction. Remember that the firewall needs to either be off or ICMP needs to be let through. Chapter 19 has a lab exercise that walks you through the latter option, a safer choice, of course.

 1k

Step 1   To configure the RRAS server, complete the following substeps from the Windows Server 2019 machine:

   a.   When you signed into the Windows Server 2019 machine, the Server Manager window should have popped up by default when you got to the desktop. If you closed this window, reopen it by clicking the search box icon or the Start button on the left of the taskbar, typing **server**, and selecting Server Manager.

   b.   In the top-right corner, click Manage and then click Add Roles And Features, and then click the Next > button.

   c.   Click the Next > button through the next couple of screens (Installation Type and Server Selection). The next screen should be the Server Roles selection.

   d.   Select Remote Access and click the Next > button (see Figure 13-1).

   e.   Click the Next > button on this screen (Server Roles) and on the next two screens (Features and Remote Access).

   f.   At the Role Services page, put a check in the checkbox next to DirectAccess And VPN (RAS). Click the Add Features button in the new window that pops up. Then click the Next > button.

   g.   Click the Next > button on the next two screens, Web Server Role (IIS) and Role Services.

   h.   On the Confirmation screen, put a check in the checkbox at the top, next to Restart The Destination Server Automatically If Required, click the Yes button in the new window that pops up, and then click the Install button at the bottom. When the installation succeeds, click the Close button.

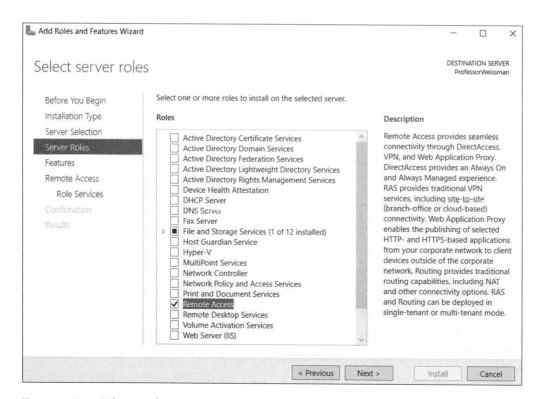

FIGURE 13-1 Selecting the Remote Access role

i.   Click the yellow Notifications triangle at the top of the Server Manager window. In the Post-Deployment Configuration section, click Open The Getting Started Wizard.

j.   In the Configure Remote Access window that pops up, select the Deploy VPN Only option (see Figure 13-2).

k.   In the Routing And Remote Access window that pops up, right-click the server and select Configure And Enable Routing And Remote Access. Click the Next > button on the following screen. On the next screen, select Custom Configuration and click the Next > button. On the following screen, put a check in the checkbox next to VPN Access (see Figure 13-3) and click the Next > button. Then click the Finish button and, finally, click the Start Service button.

Step 2   To create and authorize a user for the VPN, complete the following substeps from the Windows Server 2019 machine:

a.   Click the search box icon or the Start button on the left of the taskbar, type **computer**, and select Computer Management.

b.   Expand Local Users And Groups, select Users, right-click in the middle pane, and select New User….

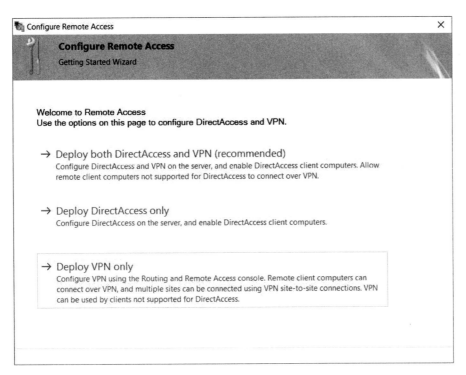

FIGURE 13-2 Selecting the Deploy VPN Only option

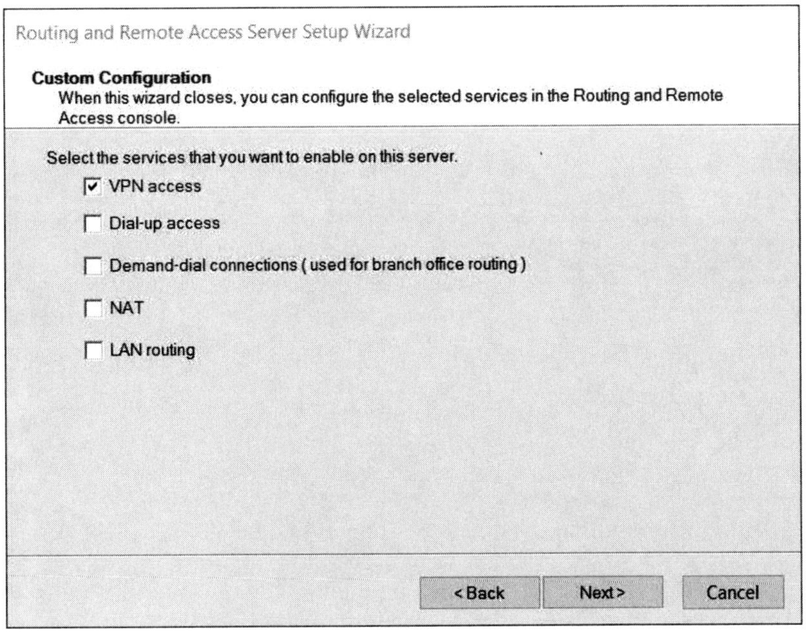

FIGURE 13-3 Enabling VPN access

   c.   Create a new user with a user name (optionally a full name and description as well) and password. Confirm the password in the corresponding textbox and remove the check mark from the User Must Change Password At Next Logon checkbox. Click the Create button and then click the Close button.

   d.   Right-click the user you created and select Properties.

   e.   Click the Dial-in tab (the name could use a refresh). In the Network Access Permission section at the top, put a check in the radio button next to Allow Access. Then click the OK button.

3a–3b, 3f, 3i–3l

Step 3   To send client traffic through the VPN, complete the following substeps:

   a.   From the Windows 10 system, open Wireshark and start sniffing (on either the Ethernet NIC or the Wi-Fi NIC, depending on which one you're using) with a display filter of **icmp**.

   b.   From the Windows 10 system, send a ping to 1.1.1.1 and notice the corresponding ICMP packets in Wireshark.

   c.   From the Windows 10 system, open Network and Sharing Center (click the Start button or in the search box, type **sharing**, select Manage Advanced Sharing Settings, and click Network And Sharing Center in the address bar at the top), and in the Change Your Networking Settings section, select Set Up A New Connection Or Network, which will open the Set Up A Connection Or Network Wizard (see Figure 13-4).

   d.   Select Connect To A Workplace and click the Next button.

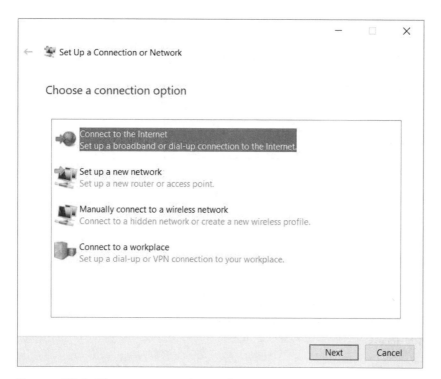

FIGURE 13-4   Choose a connection option

e.   On the next screen, select Use My Internet Connection (VPN).

f.   Enter the IP address of the server, leave all default settings, and click the Create button.

g.   Click Change Adapter Settings in the left pane (you'll be back in the Network and Sharing Center) to open the Network Connections window.

h.   Right-click the VPN Connection icon and select Connect / Disconnect. In the popup in the notification area, click VPN Connection, and then click the Connect button.

i.   Enter the user name and password of the user you created in the previous step and click the Connect button. Under VPN Connection, you should see Connected.

j.   On the Windows 10 system, execute `ipconfig /all` and notice that the system now has another IPv4 address that is on the same network as the physical interface. This new IP address is listed under the PPP Adapter VPN Connection section.

See the following links for explanations of how that address was assigned:

- https://forsenergy.com/en-us/rras/html/27469333-47dc-4036-a371-1c02937a7677.htm

- https://docs.microsoft.com/en-us/windows-server/remote/remote-access/vpn/always-on-vpn/deploy/vpn-deploy-ras

("Configure Remote Access as a VPN Server" section, Step 15)

k.   Now that you are connected to the VPN, from the Windows 10 system, open Wireshark and start sniffing (on either the Ethernet NIC or the Wi-Fi NIC, depending on which one you're using) with a display filter of **icmp**, like before. In addition, sniff in Wireshark on the Windows Server 2019 machine (install Wireshark on it, from https://www.wireshark.org/, if necessary) with a display filter of **icmp** as well.

Send a ping to 1.1.1.1, like before. After the ping completes, stop both Wireshark captures.

This time, you will not see the ICMP packets in Wireshark on the Windows 10 system, but you *will* see them in Wireshark on the Windows Server 2019 machine!

As seen from Wireshark on the Windows Server 2019 machine, the source IP address for the ICMP Echo requests and the destination IP address for the ICMP Echo replies are not the Windows 10 Ethernet or Wi-Fi (depending on which one you're using) NICs. It's the address of the new virtual adapter for the VPN connection.

l.   On the Windows 10 system, in Wireshark, clear the filter. Notice that there is traffic from your Windows 10 system to your Windows Server 2019 machine (displayed in white rows) using Point-to-Point Protocol (PPP) and Generic Routing Encapsulation (GRE). The VPN is using those protocols to tunnel your ICMP to the Windows Server 2019 machine, which decapsulates the ICMPs and sends them out as if you had sent the ping directly from the Windows Server 2019 machine. When the ICMP Echo replies come back, the Windows Server 2019 machine encapsulates them with PPP Comp (Comp stands for compressed) and GRE and then sends it to your machine, which decapsulates the ICMP.

A Point-to-Point Tunneling Protocol (PPTP) tunnel is the default type used in this first of two VPN setups in this lab exercise. It is used here purely for demonstrative purposes, as it is obsolete today and is highly insecure.

PPTP involves establishing a TCP connection, in which the VPN server sends and receives on port 1723. Control information is sent across this connection. The TCP connection initiates and manages a GRE tunnel, which carries PPP traffic, which allows for the tunneling of any protocol that can be transmitted inside PPP, like IP.

Step 4   Redo the entire Step 3, but instead of sending a ping from the client, this time open up a browser and go to www.rit.edu. Instead of sending ICMP through the VPN, this time you're going to send Web traffic through it!

To filter packets to and from the RIT Web server, use the following display filter on the client, which filters by both the RIT Web server's IPv4 and IPv6 addresses (depending on which one your connection will use):

```
ip.addr == 129.21.1.40 || ipv6.addr == 2620:8d:8000:0:aba:ca:daba:217
```

 5e–5f

Step 5   Now, you'll change the PPTP tunnel to an L2TP/IPsec one and create a second VPN connection.

   a.   On the Windows Server 2019 machine, open up Server Manager and click Tools at the top right.

   b.   Selecting Routing And Remote Access.

   c.   Right-click the server and select Properties.

   d.   Click the Security tab.

→ Note

In the IPv4 tab, you'll see where you can specify where to hand out addresses to clients from: DHCP or a static address pool.

---

   e.   Put a check in the checkbox next to Allow Custom IPsec Policy for L2TP/IKEv2 Connection.

   f.   Enter a value in the Preshared Key: textbox.

   g.   Click the OK button in the Properties window.

   h.   Click the OK button in the popup, which instructs you to restart Routing and Remote Access.

   i.   In Server Manager, click Remote Access in the pane on the left.

   j.   In the Services section, right-click the row showing a display name of Routing And Remote Access, and select Restart Services.

📷 **6h–6m, 6r–6s**

Step 6   Now, you'll configure the client to use an Layer 2 Tunneling Protocol (L2TP) tunnel.

L2TP only uses encryption for its own control messages through the use of an optional pre-shared secret, but doesn't offer encryption or confidentiality for the actual data. Instead, it provides a tunnel for Layer 2 (which has the possibility of encryption). The tunnel itself, though, can be passed through a Layer 3 encryption protocol like IPsec. Due to the lack of inherent confidentiality in L2TP, it's often implemented in conjunction with IPsec, and RFC 3193 (https://datatracker.ietf.org/doc/html/rfc3193) standardized this arrangement as L2TP/IPsec.

   a.   Start sniffing in Wireshark on the Windows 10 system.

   b.   Start sniffing in Wireshark on the Windows Server 2019 machine.

   c.   Click the Windows button or in the search box, type **VPN**, and select VPN settings.

   d.   Click Add A VPN Connection.

   e.   For VPN Provider, select Windows (Built-in).

   f.   Type in a name to identify the connection in the Connection Name textbox.

   g.   Enter the IP address of the Windows Server 2019 machine in the Server Name Or Address box.

   h.   For VPN Type, select L2TP/IPsec With Pre-shared Key.

   i.   Enter the pre-shared key in the Pre-shared Key box.

   j.   For Type Of Sign-in Info, select User Name And Password.

   k.   Enter the user name of the account you created on the Windows Server 2019 machine in the User Name (Optional) box.

   l.   Enter the password of the user you created on the Windows Server 2019 machine in the Password (Optional) box.

   m.   Leave the check in the checkbox next to Remember My Sign-in Info.

   n.   Click the Save button.

   o.   In the window you're returned to, click the connection you just created.

   p.   Click the Connect button.

   q.   Stop the Wireshark capture on the Windows 10 system.

   r.   From the capture on the Windows Server 2019 machine, you should see the ICMPs.

   s.   From the capture on the Windows 10 system, identify the two protocols that are used in this L2TP/IPsec VPN connection.

 **30 MINUTES**

Lab Exercise 13.02: Remote Desktop

Most businesses today support users working at remote locations or from home, especially since the COVID-19 pandemic started, and it is not uncommon to manage servers or sign in to client devices from a remote client machine.

There are a number of remote management software solutions that you can use. One of the popular solutions is to enable Remote Desktop on Windows systems. Once a Remote Desktop session is established, you can then fully manage and administer a remote system as if you were sitting in front of the actual computer itself.

Learning Objectives

In this lab exercise, you'll enable Remote Desktop on a Windows server so that you can then administer it remotely. Keep in mind that you can enable Remote Desktop on any Windows system, but the instructions for this lab exercise are specific for Windows 10. By the end of this lab exercise, you'll be able to

- Enable Remote Desktop

- Remotely connect to a system using the Windows Remote Desktop Connection client

Lab Materials and Setup

The materials you'll need for this lab exercise are

- *Mike Meyers' CompTIA Network+ Guide to Managing and Troubleshooting Networks* textbook

- Two Windows 10 systems

- Switch and appropriate cabling

Getting Down to Business

JSW has a number of customers located in remote cities. JSW techs will occasionally travel to the customer site when the customer has a need for server changes. In a discussion with Jonathan, he tells you that the growing trend is to manage servers from the JSW office. He recommends that you explore the features of the Remote Desktop program that is built into Windows and configure a remote session in the JSW Networking Lab.

Start this configuration by establishing a connection between the two Windows 10 systems. You can use any IP addressing scheme. You can also choose between static addressing and dynamic addressing. Make sure that pings go through in each direction. Remember that the firewall needs to either be off or ICMP needs to be let through. Chapter 19 has a lab exercise that walks you through the latter option, which is a safer choice.

Step 1   Sign in with an account that has Administrator privileges on the Windows 10 system you plan to remote into.

Step 2 In the Windows 10 search box, type **This PC**, right-click This PC, and select Properties. In the pane on the left select Remote Desktop (two up from the bottom). Make sure the right pane has the slider in the On position for Enable Remote Desktop. When changing the setting (in either direction), you'll see a confirmation dialog box. Click the Confirm button in that box to complete your selection. Also, notice the instructions and PC name in the How To Connect To This PC section.

Step 3 Click Advanced Settings (above How To Connect To This PC).

Make sure there is no check in the checkbox in the Configure Network Level Authentication section (if you take the check out, click the Proceed Anyway button, as there is no domain controller set up in this lab exercise). Click Why Allow Connections Only With Network Level Authentication, and understand that in a live network deployment, you will have this checkbox checked.

Click the back button (left arrow) at the top of the window.

Step 4 In the User Accounts section, click Select Users That Can Remotely Access This PC. When you give users the capability to use Remote Desktop to connect to the system in this manner, the user accounts are automatically added to a built-in group (which can be seen in the Computer Management window under Local Users And Groups and then Groups) that has the permission to use Remote Desktop to connect to the server called, appropriately enough, Remote Desktop Users.

Click the Add button. Click the Advanced button. Click the Find Now button. A list of accounts will appear in the Search Results section. Double-click the user account you'd like to use and click the OK button. Click the OK button in the Remote Desktop Users window.

✖ Cross-Reference

To create a new user, follow the instructions for Lab Exercise 13.01 Step 2.

Step 5 Now sign in to the other Windows 10 system. You're going to use this system to connect to the first Windows 10 system that you just configured.

In the Windows 10 search box, type **Remote Desktop Connection** and click Remote Desktop Connection.

FIGURE 13-5 Remote Desktop Connection window

This will open the Remote Desktop Connection window. Type the IP address of the first Windows 10 system you configured earlier, and then click Connect. See Figure 13-5.

Step 6 When queried to enter your credentials, enter the user name and password for the machine you are remoting into.

In the window dealing with the authentication and security certificate, click the Yes button.

You'll see the message "Another user is signed in. If you continue, they'll be disconnected. Do you want to sign in anyway?" Click the Yes button.

If you see a Choose Privacy Settings For Your Device screen, make selections as desired and click the Accept button.

Now you can navigate all of the applications and utilities of the target machine as if you were logged on locally.

→ **Note**

If you are signing into an account that's currently signed into on the remote machine (either at the sign-in screen or at the desktop), you'd actually *intercept* that session. For example, you could be at work, using the computer in your office. Then you'd stay signed in to the computer when going home. From home, you could continue working from exactly where you left off as if you went back to the office.

Step 7   Notice that the Remote Desktop Connection window by default fills the entire monitor screen. You can click the Restore Down button in the connection bar at the top, so you can see your local machine again, with the remote machine appearing in a window.

Step 8   Microsoft's proprietary protocol Remote Desktop Protocol (RDP) provides for the graphical user interface that allows connecting to other remote computers over a network connection. RDP servers send and receive on port 3389 using both TCP and UDP. Start sniffing in Wireshark with a display filter of **tcp.port == 3389 || udp.port == 3389** and see the traffic.

Step 9   In typical use, you would click the Start button, select the account you're signed in with, and then click Sign Out to sign out of the target machine and close the Remote Desktop session.

You could also click the Start button, select Power (first icon above the Start button), and select Shut Down to perform a shutdown of the remote machine. This would be useful if you received a notice that the location where your server resides lost power and you would like to shut down the system gracefully, before the UPS battery backup runs out. In fact, go ahead and do that right now.

Lab Exercise 13.03: Microsoft Quick Assist

Remote Desktop is a great solution when you want to take control of a remote machine, but what if you would like to help someone configure settings or troubleshoot a problem when a remote user calls for help? One of the methods you can use is to have the user invite you to "share" control of their system and either do it for them or guide them in the steps required to resolve any issues.

Microsoft offers a great solution, known as Microsoft Quick Assist, which enables a user to invite a technician to connect to a system remotely and then share pointer movement and keystrokes of that system with the tech. This method gives the tech complete access to the remote machine, but at the same time, the user can view and contribute to the session and even pause or stop the session at any point.

Learning Objectives

In this lab exercise, you'll use Microsoft Quick Assist on two Windows 10 systems. By the end of this lab exercise, you'll be able to

- Start a Microsoft Quick Assist session
- Remotely assist a user on a Windows 10 system

Lab Materials and Setup

The materials you'll need for this lab exercise are

- Two Windows 10 systems
- Switch and appropriate cabling

Getting Down to Business

Jonathan has you wrap up your exploration of remote connectivity applications with the configuration, initiation, and use of the Microsoft Quick Assist feature.

Start this configuration by establishing a connection between the two Windows 10 systems. You can use any IP addressing scheme. You can also choose between static addressing and dynamic addressing. Make sure that pings go through in each direction. Remember that either the firewall needs to be off or ICMP needs to be let through. Chapter 19 has a lab exercise that walks you through the latter option, which is a safer choice.

Step 1   Sign in to each Windows 10 system with an administrative account. For the purposes of this lab exercise, consider one machine the office tech machine and the other machine the remote user machine.

Signing in to both machines with an administrative account avoids the User Account Control (UAC) authorization prompt, which needs to be run with the credentials of the local user of the device receiving assistance. This becomes important if a user providing assistance needs an elevated prompt on a remote device and the user receiving assistance does not have administrative credentials. At that point, the user providing assistance will see a black screen with a big pause symbol, while the UAC prompt will appear on the screen of the user receiving assistance. If the user receiving assistance doesn't have an administrative account to provide credentials from, there's nothing that can be done to fix the situation, and the user receiving assistance will have to close the UAC window.

Step 2   On the Windows 10 system that is going to be the office tech machine, click the Start button or in the search box, type **quick**, and select Quick Assist. The Quick Assist window (see Figure 13-6) will appear.

➜ **Note**

Quick Assist replaces an older and similar program, Windows Remote Assistance.

FIGURE 13-6 Quick Assist

Step 3   If you have a Microsoft account, skip this step. Otherwise, create one now.

a.   In the Quick Assist window, click the Assist Another Person button at the bottom. Next to No Account?, click Create One! Then click Get A New Email Address. Enter an account name before the dropdown that allows you to change from the @outlook.com default to @hotmail.com. Click the Next button. Enter a different name if you see the message "Someone already has this email address. Try another name."

b.   Create a password; decide if you want the Information, Tips, And Offers checkbox checked; and click the Next button.

c.   Provide your first name and last name, then click the Next button.

d.   Select your country/region and birthdate (I always use and recommend a fake one) and click the Next button.

e.   A browser window will open. Click the Next button there and follow the prompts to verify you are not a robot. Then click the Done button.

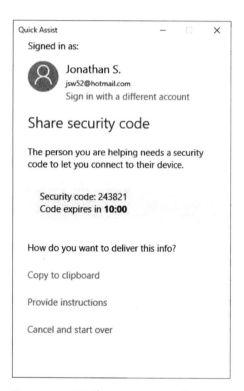

FIGURE 13-7 Share security code

Step 4   Back in the Quick Assist window, once again click the Assist Another Person button. You'll see a security code with a countdown timer that starts at 10 minutes. See Figure 13-7.

Click Provide Instructions and read the information. Then click I Provided The Instructions.

 5a–5j

Step 5   Take control of the remote user machine with the office tech machine.

    a.   On the machine that is serving as the remote user, open Quick Assist. Assuming the office tech gave the remote user the code, enter the code in the Code From Assistant box in the Get Assistance section and click the Share Screen button.

       You'll see "Waiting for helper to set up this session" on the remote user machine and "Connecting" on the office tech machine.

b. On the office tech machine, leave the default Take Full Control radio button selected (the alternative selection, View Screen, allows the office tech just to watch, not control), and click the Continue button. You'll see "Waiting for sharer to grant permission" on the tech machine.

c. On the remote user machine, read the warning and click the Allow button.

Now the office tech has full control of the remote user machine.

See Figure 13-8. On the office tech machine, you'll notice a Quick Assist window, with the remote user machine in the center, including the remote user machine's Quick Assist controls at the top of the desktop. The Administrator controls for the office tech machine appear as icons at the top of the Quick Assist window, just below the title bar.

d. On the remote user machine, in the Quick Assist window, click the Pause button.

Notice that the office tech can't see or do anything now. The office tech's Quick Assist screen is black and a message about what happened is displayed.

e. On the remote user machine, in the Quick Assist window, click the Resume button. The office tech's Quick Assist screen is back to normal now.

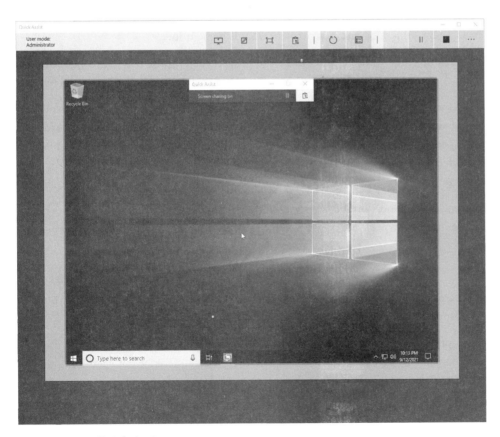

FIGURE 13-8 Quick Assist

f. On the remote user machine, in the Quick Assist window, click the Toggle Instruction Channel button, which is just to the right of the Pause button. Then type a message in the Send textbox and click the Send button.

g. On the office tech machine, in the Quick Assist window, notice the message in the Message Received textbox. On the office tech machine, in the Quick Assist window, type a reply in the Send textbox and click the Send button. Now the office tech and remote user can message each other from their machines.

h. On the office tech machine, from the Quick Assist window, open up an administrative command prompt on the remote user machine and execute the following commands:

ipconfig /all
ping 8.8.4.4
arp -a
arp -d

You are doing some great troubleshooting work for your remote user!

i. On the office tech machine, in the Quick Assist window, click the second button from the left, Annotate. Using the mouse, circle something on the screen. On the remote user machine, you'll see the annotations made. This is handy for an office tech to help a remote user see something on the screen to teach them something and help explain what is being done.

j. On the office tech machine, in the Quick Assist window, you can mouse over the other buttons to reveal their functions, or click the Details ellipsis at the end to display the function of all buttons.

They are, from the left, Select Monitor, Annotate, Fit Screen, Toggle Instruction Channel, Restart, Task Manager (something a tech will likely want to see, although there are multiple ways for the office tech to open it up from the remote user machine), Reconnect (which is grayed out because you are connected), Pause (the office tech can pause the session, too), End (if you click this, the Reconnect button will be active/black and all buttons besides Details will be grayed out), and Details.

On the remote user machine, the Quick Assist window is far less capable, and the way the remote user would end the session is by clicking the X in the upper-right corner of that window.

Lab Analysis

1. Leah heard there are a couple of good reasons for WFH employees to use a VPN. Can you enlighten her on the reasons?

2. Erick needs to provide help to a user. He wants your guidance in determining whether to use Remote Desktop or Microsoft Quick Assist. Can you explain to him the difference between Remote Desktop and Microsoft Quick Assist, and what situation each is used for?

Key Term Quiz

Use the terms in this list to complete the sentences that follow.

Microsoft Quick Assist   VPN

Remote Desktop Protocol (RDP)

1. PPP and GRE are protocols used by default in a Windows implementation of (a) _____.

2. A technician can troubleshoot a remote computer, with the user able to observe and interact at the same time using (a) _____.

3. Port 3389 is used by (a) _____.

Chapter 14

Wireless Networking

Lab Exercises

Wireless networking is the solution to, and the cause of, many network technicians' headaches. Wireless networking has been adopted at a phenomenal rate in all corners of the globe, from small home and office networks to school campuses, local libraries, and large corporate enterprises. You'll also find wireless networking in hotels, airports, cafés, fast-food restaurants, and donut shops. As a networking solution, wireless is an exciting evolution that provides flexibility, scalability, and ever-increasing throughput speeds. On the downside, wireless networks can be finicky to configure, prone to interference, and insecure.

I say "can be" because there are a number of things you, the network tech, can do to overcome the weaknesses of wireless networking to make it a robust, secure, and available solution. The CompTIA Network+ exam expects you to be competent in all aspects of wireless networking.

➔ **Note**

Wi-Fi is actually a specific trademark owned by the Wi-Fi Alliance, an organization that certifies Wi-Fi products in meeting the IEEE's 802.11 wireless standards Contrary to what a lot of people think, Wi-Fi is not a shortened form of Wireless Fidelity. Read more about that here: https://www .scientificamerican.com/article/pogue-what-wifi-stands-for-other-wireless-questions-answered/.

 30 MINUTES

Lab Exercise 14.01: Wireless Standards and Security

Understanding the various specifications, operating ranges, speeds, compatibility issues, security methods, and more enables you to make informed decisions when planning a wireless network rollout.

Learning Objectives

In this lab exercise, you'll explore wireless networking technologies. By the end of this lab exercise, you'll be able to

- Explain the basic facts and figures of each wireless technology and the accepted industry standards that apply to them

- Explain the new naming convention for Wi-Fi standards

- Explain why CSMA/CA is used for wireless networks

- Explain security-related components of Wi-Fi technology

Lab Materials and Setup

The materials you'll need for this lab exercise are

- *Mike Meyers' CompTIA Network+ Guide to Managing and Troubleshooting Networks* textbook

- Internet access

Getting Down to Business

Remember Jonathan's excitement when he was talking about the wireless connectivity that JSW's client is implementing in all of the rest areas along the highways? Well, now it is time to install these sites and make sure that they will function well into the future. Jonathan asks you to research the current offerings in the world of Wi-Fi and make your recommendations on the technologies to use in each of the installments.

Step 1   Your first step is to research the specifications and features of the devices that meet the various Wi-Fi standards. Using the *Mike Meyers' CompTIA Network+ Guide to Managing and Troubleshooting Networks* textbook and the Internet, research and record the specifications for the IEEE 802.11 standards in the following table:

Standard	Frequency	Modulation	Maximum Speed	Maximum Range	Backward Compatibility
802.11					
802.11b					
802.11a					
802.11g					
802.11n					
802.11ac					
802.11ax					

Step 2   Wi-Fi Alliance President and CEO Edgar Figueroa made a major announcement on October 3, 2018:

For nearly two decades, Wi-Fi users have had to sort through technical naming conventions to determine if their devices support the latest Wi-Fi. Wi-Fi Alliance is excited to introduce Wi-Fi 6, and present a new naming scheme to help industry and Wi-Fi users easily understand the Wi-Fi generation supported by their device or connection.

New names were given to previous standards as well.

Fill in the following table with the help of Google:

New Wi-Fi Name	802.11 Standard	Standard's Debut Year
Wi-Fi 1		
Wi-Fi 2		
Wi-Fi 3		
Wi-Fi 4		
Wi-Fi 5		
Wi-Fi 6		

Step 3   Due to the actual architecture of wireless networking, it would be impractical to use carrier sense multiple access with collision detection (CSMA/CD). Wireless networks use carrier sense multiple access with collision avoidance (CSMA/CA). Explain why the CSMA/CD access method wouldn't work with wireless technology, and describe how the CSMA/CA access method functions with the help of Google.

Step 4   Provide an appropriate description for the following components of security associated with Wi-Fi technology:

Security Component	Description
WEP	
WPA	
WPA2	
WPA3	
TKIP-RC4	
CCMP-AES	
SAE	

> ✖ **Cross-Reference**
>
> Many of the wireless security measures may be found in the "Wi-Fi Security"
> section of Chapter 14 in the *Mike Meyers' CompTIA Network+ Guide to Managing and
> Troubleshooting Networks* textbook. Additionally, detailed specifications may be found
> by conducting Internet searches on the named security components.

 **30 MINUTES**

Lab Exercise 14.02: Wireless Network Planning

Now, armed with knowledge of Wi-Fi standards and security, you can look at the requirements for the rest areas. You will want to plan for future growth—including both increased traffic as population and travel continue to expand and performance as technology improves.

Wireless networking is becoming increasingly important to individuals in their homes, as well as businesses that cater to the public. It provides instant connectivity and is the solution to many wired network physical barriers.

Learning Objectives

In this lab exercise, you'll analyze the basic information of how wireless networks function to make recommendations for the implementation of wireless networks in the highway rest areas. By the end of this lab exercise, you'll be able to

- Recommend wireless technology based on application

- Design appropriate wireless models based on usage

- Devise a plan to implement wireless connectivity in highway rest areas

Lab Materials and Setup

The materials you'll need for this lab exercise are

- *Mike Meyers' CompTIA Network+ Guide to Managing and Troubleshooting Networks* textbook

- Internet access

Getting Down to Business

The various rest areas along the most traveled highways have facilities that are fairly standard in size and the number of travelers they support per hour. There is usually one building with a number of restaurants and fast-food eateries around the edges of the space, with a large common area in the center with tables and chairs.

Most of the common areas are wide open with a minimum of obstacles, but they can span hundreds of feet from wall to wall. The general goals for each rest area are as follows:

- The network should be able to support from 20 to 60 devices at one time.

- The network must be secure against unauthorized wireless access, but also allow authorized visitors to join without issues.

- The network should use industry-standard technology that is widely available.

Step 1   Explain the basic hardware and software required to implement wireless networking.

Step 2   Explain the differences between ad hoc and infrastructure modes.

Step 3   Describe at least two methods to implement security on wireless networks. For a public wireless solution, name two security methods that are not practical.

Step 4   Given the typical size of the rest areas, a standard single wireless access point (WAP; also known simply as an access point, AP) probably won't provide enough range to cover the entire space. How can you increase the wireless coverage area?

Step 5   Based on the goals listed for the rest areas, describe the wireless networking solution you plan to implement.

Step 6   Explain how you will connect the wireless network nodes to the existing 1000Base-T network and, ultimately, the Internet.

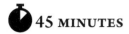 **45 MINUTES**

Lab Exercise 14.03: Wireless Networking Configuration

With only slight variations, installing and configuring wireless network equipment is much like doing so for a wired network. Let's now concentrate on the steps for configuring your wireless network nodes to talk to each other in infrastructure mode.

Learning Objectives

In this lab exercise, you'll configure PCs for wireless networking. By the end of this lab exercise, you'll be able to

- Configure a wireless router for wireless networking in infrastructure mode

- Configure PCs for Wi-Fi wireless networking in infrastructure mode

- Send traffic from the PCs through the wireless router to the Internet

Lab Materials and Setup

The materials you'll need for this lab exercise are

- *Mike Meyers' CompTIA Network+ Guide to Managing and Troubleshooting Networks* textbook

- Internet access

- Two Windows 10 systems equipped with Wi-Fi network adapters

- Wireless router (802.11ac or 802.11ax recommended)

Getting Down to Business

After you've delivered a report of your suggested wireless network implementation to Jonathan, he recommends that you build a prototype of the wireless network in the JSW Networking Lab. If possible, you should try to model the actual usage that will take place in the rest areas. For instance, many of the travelers will have phones, laptops, and tablets. Generally, any of the devices come with integrated wireless network interfaces, so working with various makes and models of wireless network adapters and access points will help prepare you for real-world scenarios.

1b–1d

Step 1   Configuring a wireless network to operate in infrastructure mode requires several steps: clear, configure, and then connect.

  a.   First, plug the wireless router into an electrical outlet. If it's been installed in a network before, you should reset it to factory defaults. That will clear out any sort of configurations, and you'll be able to use the default username and password to configure it. Almost every wireless router has a reset button (some might require a pin to be pushed through a hole) that you hold for a certain length of time to reset it. If you don't have documentation for the wireless router, hold the button for 15 seconds or longer.

  b.   Configuration is done using—you guessed it   a configuration utility supplied by the wireless router manufacturer. The utility is usually browser based, and you can simply open your Web browser, point to the IP address of the default gateway (such as 192.168.1.1), and if there is one by default, enter a password when prompted to access the utility. Some access points require that you install a dedicated configuration utility program. Figure 14-1 shows the configuration utility for a Linksys WAP.

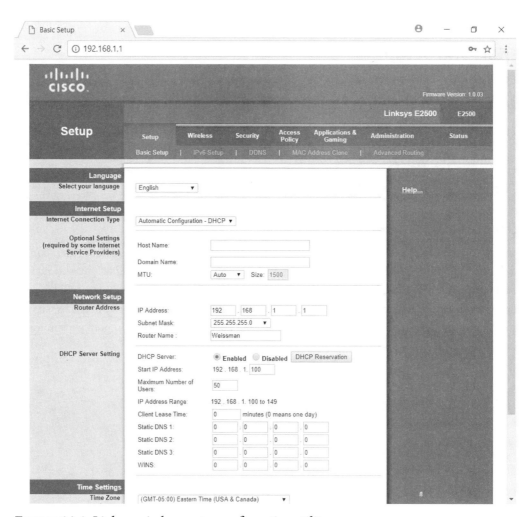

FIGURE 14-1 Linksys wireless router configuration utility

As with the wireless network adapter configuration utility, the wireless router configuration utility may vary in appearance depending on the make and model, but the functions should be practically identical.

    c. Launch your access point configuration utility and configure a unique SSID name, such as TRAVELSTOP.

    d. Verify that DHCP is configured.

➜ **Note**

We are using a SOHO (small office/home office) wireless router, which has a router, firewall, WAP, and more built in and integrated, as opposed to a dedicated WAP. A dedicated WAP often needs to have its IP identified from a custom utility or DHCP server, or it can use a default IP address. You'd connect to that IP address, which may have a Web configuration interface, for configuration and management. With a wireless router, the IP address for configuration and management will be the default gateway's IP address.

Step 2   Connect the WAP to the device provided by your ISP, a cable modem, a DSL modem, Optical Network Terminal (ONT), etc.

 3a–3b

Step 3   To bring the security up to an acceptable level, locate and configure the following settings on your WAP:

    a. Change the default username (if possible) and password for the configuration utility.

    b. Enable WPA2 or WPA3 Personal encryption on the WAP and configure each wireless node with the appropriate passphrase.

 4a–4d

Step 4   Connect clients to the Wi-Fi network using the following steps:

    a. Select the Network icon in the notification area of the taskbar.

    b. Select the Wi-Fi network SSID you configured earlier.

    c. Put a check in the Connect Automatically checkbox.

    d. Click the Connect button.

 **30 MINUTES**

Lab Exercise 14.04: Wireless Network Troubleshooting

The famous science fiction writer Arthur C. Clarke coined one of my favorite sayings when he stated in his third law, "Any sufficiently advanced technology is indistinguishable from magic." Wireless networking isn't quite that advanced, but the results are nonetheless quite impressive—when they work correctly. When they don't work correctly, wireless networks afford network techs some unique opportunities to display their troubleshooting acumen.

Learning Objectives

In this lab exercise, you'll troubleshoot some common wireless networking issues. By the end of this lab exercise, you'll be able to

- Diagnose common wireless networking problems

- Troubleshoot common wireless networking problems

Lab Materials and Setup

The materials you'll need for this lab exercise are

- Two Windows 10 systems equipped with Wi-Fi network adapters

- WAP (802.11ac or 802.11ax recommended)

- Internet access

Getting Down to Business

You have successfully installed and configured the wireless network model to be implemented in the highway rest areas. Jonathan now asks you to demonstrate steps for troubleshooting simple problems.

Step 1   List at least three steps you should take to determine if a loss of wireless connectivity is due to your wireless network adapter's hardware or software configuration.

Step 2   After determining that your wireless network adapter is functioning correctly, how can you find out whether your network node has proper connectivity and signal strength to the wireless network?

Step 3 Name at least three factors that could cause poor signal strength between wireless network nodes.

Step 4 Assuming that a loss of wireless connectivity is not caused by improper hardware or software configuration, excessive distance between wireless network nodes, or environmental factors, what should you check next?

Lab Analysis

1. Christina wants to know which consumer electronics may cause interference with a wireless network using the 2.4 GHz frequency band. What do you tell her?

2. Graham has been doing some research on the frequency bands used by 802.11 devices. He asks you to explain the differences between the 2.4 GHz frequency band and the 5.0 GHz frequency band. Which standards are used in each?

3. Marty is using a dual-band 802.11ac wireless router. He wants to know if you recommend upgrading it to the newer 802.11ax standard and if doing so would require him to replace all client NICs as well. What do you tell him?

4. Juré has been looking over your proposal for the wireless network implementation for the highway rest areas and would like to know why you do not recommend using MAC address filtering as an added security measure. What is your explanation?

5. Therese wants to know what the difference is between 802.11ax and Wi-Fi 6. What do you tell her?

Key Term Quiz

Use the terms in this list to complete the sentences that follow.

Advanced Encryption Standard (AES)   Wi-Fi Protected Access 2 (WPA2)

pre-shared key   Wired Equivalent Privacy (WEP)

RC4

1. The _____ wireless security standard provides a considerable security improvement as compared to the _____ wireless security standard.

2. Configuring client machines with a _____ will allow them to authenticate to a WAP.

3. _____ replaced _____ as the symmetric encryption algorithm for Wi-Fi security protocols.

Chapter 15

Virtualization and Cloud Computing

Lab Exercises

At this point in your studies, you have already worked with virtual environments. You have configured virtual local area networks (VLANs) to organize groups of physical ports on a switch logically, effectively placing the systems connected to those ports into separate broadcast domains/networks. You have also worked with a virtual private network (VPN), which allows you to tunnel traffic through the Internet, sending traffic from a remote network as if you were physically there.

Now you'll be creating and using virtual machines (VMs)! A major trend in client and server systems is to use one physical computer, install a host operating system, and then deploy multiple virtual machines on top of the host OS to meet the needs of the users. The ultimate example of virtualization is the modern data center, where thousands of servers are now hosted on just a few hundred physical machines.

There are various implementations of virtual hardware (NICs, switches, routers, firewalls, etc.) offered by multiple vendors (VMware, Oracle, Citrix, Microsoft, Parallels, and more). These virtualization technologies set up the environment so that you may install and run various operating systems on the same physical hardware simultaneously.

There are many great advantages to virtualization:

- With each VM running on the same hardware, hardware dependency issues are eliminated.

- To make a copy of a VM, simply copy the files and folders that comprise it.

- To move a VM from one machine to the next, simply transfer the files and folders that comprise it. You're going to do this in Lab Exercise 15.05.

- Consolidating servers from many physical machines into VMs reduces the power consumption, carbon footprint, and business expenses (expensive hardware, for example) of data centers. Data centers can even be expanded with VMs on an as-needed basis and contracted when those additional resources are no longer needed.

- Some hypervisors can perform dynamic load balancing, allocating requests to VMs that are not as busy as others, and can even dynamically allocate more resources to VMs that are very busy.

- Instead of hours or days needed to replace or fix a physical machine affected by a disaster, a VM can quickly be provisioned and deployed in minutes by replicating or cloning the affected machine. Reducing downtime is huge for the availability of an organization.

- Installing, updating, and maintaining environments will be more efficient, allowing the IT staff to be more productive.

- A VM can be easily deployed for a developer to test programs and patches in a certain environment.

- Troubleshooting software on various platforms can be done with multiple VMs, which is, of course, much easier than doing it through multiple physical machines running various OSs.

- Security settings can limit malware attacks or software glitches on a VM from affecting other VMs. Furthermore, if one VM suffers a malware attack, an earlier saved copy of that VM can be restored.

In this chapter, after four lab exercises that deal with virtualization, the fifth lab exercise will give you some experience with cloud computing through some of Google's Software as a Service (SaaS) offerings.

 30 MINUTES

Lab Exercise 15.01: Virtualization Technologies

Virtualization takes on many aspects of the physical devices used every day in the computing environment. Organizations may choose to install multiple virtual servers on one physical machine to handle DHCP, DNS, Web services, e-mail services, file sharing, and print services, to name a few.

In this chapter's lab exercises, you will have the opportunity to install and work with one of the most popular virtual machine technologies available today, but this is only one component of virtualization. Before you work with the virtualization, and before you take the CompTIA Network+ certification exam, you will want to explore various technologies associated with virtualization. This lab exercise covers many of them. Time to explore!

Learning Objectives

In this lab exercise, you'll review important virtualization concepts. By the end of this lab exercise, you'll be able to

- Distinguish between different types of hypervisors

- Distinguish between host and virtual machines

- Detail the characteristics of virtual routers, switches, routers, and firewalls

- Distinguish between the various networking configurations a VM can be in

Lab Materials and Setup

The materials you'll need for this lab exercise are

- *Mike Meyers' CompTIA Network+ Guide to Managing and Troubleshooting Networks* textbook

- Internet access

Getting Down to Business

Before you begin your hands-on exploration of virtualization, it is important that you understand the underlying solutions that virtualization technologies provide. Jonathan collects a list of virtual technologies and asks you to use your textbook and the Internet to develop a brief description and summary of the characteristics of each of the technologies.

Step 1   Start by researching hypervisors. What are hypervisors?

Step 2 How are Type 1 hypervisors different from Type 2 hypervisors?

Step 3 What is a host operating system? What is a guest operating system? What's the relationship between hypervisors and host and guest operating systems?

Step 4 How is a guest operating system different from a VM?

Step 5 With the term virtualization, what exactly is being virtualized?

Step 6 A VM can use different networking configurations. The three standard ones in VMware products include bridged (which uses a virtual switch called VMnet0), NAT (which uses a virtual switch called VMnet8), and host-only (which uses a virtual switch called VMnet1). What are the differences between these configurations? Use the following reference to help formulate your answer: https://www.vmware.com/support/ws5/doc/ws_net_configurations_common.html

Step 7 The term *virtual NIC* doesn't just refer to a NIC of a VM. On the host system running a Type 2 hypervisor, virtual NICs (often called virtual host adapters) are present as well. Click the Start button or in the search box, type **Sharing**, click Manage Advanced Sharing Options, click Network And Sharing Center in the address bar at the top, click Change Adapter Settings in the pane on the left, and look at the contents of the Network Connections window. What are the names and functions of the virtual NICs on a host system? For help, use this link (the concept is the same, although the version of the hypervisor is different from the one being used in this chapter): https://docs.vmware.com/en/VMware-Workstation-Pro/16.0/com.vmware.ws.using.doc/GUID-12708023-8126-4E35-A26F-372BAC4475AC.html.

➔ **Note**

> A Type 1 hypervisor, like VMware's ESXi, doesn't have a virtual NIC on the host; instead,
> it manages virtual switches that are connected to physical NICs. More information on ESXi and
> ther components, like vSphere and vCenter, can be found at the following links:
> https://www.nakivo.com/blog/vmware-esxi-vs-vsphere-vs-vcenter-key-differences/
> https://vmiss.net/vsphere-vs-esxi-vs-vcenter/

Step 8   What is a virtual switch, and why isn't there a virtual NIC on the host for bridged networking?

Step 9   pfSense is a FreeBSD-based software distribution of a router and firewall. It can be installed on a physical machine or as a VM (becoming a virtual router/firewall). Visit https://www.pfsense.org/ and list some of your impressions.

 **45 MINUTES**

Lab Exercise 15.02: VMware Workstation Player and Ubuntu

VMware is arguably the leader in large-scale, enterprise-wide virtualization. With scalable products, like vSphere and ESXi, which are fully featured solutions for data centers and cloud providers, to VMware Workstation Player, which is free to individuals exploring virtual solutions for their personal PC, VMware offers solutions at every level.

To get your feet wet with VMware products, you will download the hypervisor, VMware Workstation Player, and install it on a Windows 10 host system. Then you will download, install, and run Ubuntu, a popular Linux distribution, as a guest OS on a VM.

Learning Objectives

In this lab exercise, you'll use VMware Workstation Player to install an Ubuntu guest operating system on a VM on a Windows 10 host system. You will then explore a few of the Ubuntu programs and commands. By the end of this lab exercise, you'll be able to

- Install and configure VMware Workstation Player on a Windows 10 host system
- Install and run Ubuntu as a guest OS on a VM in the VMware Workstation Player hypervisor

Lab Materials and Setup

The materials you'll need for this lab exercise are

- *Mike Meyers' CompTIA Network+ Guide to Managing and Troubleshooting Networks* textbook
- Windows 10 system with Internet access

Getting Down to Business

Jonathan would like you to take advantage of the Networking Lab yet again. This time he wants you to explore virtualization. The Networking Lab offers an excellent environment to work through the idiosyncrasies of virtualization to see how it works before deploying it on production systems.

Step 1 Go to https://wiki.ubuntu.com/Releases to see the past, present, and future of Ubuntu releases. Next, go to https://ubuntu.com/download, configure the tracking settings, and click Ubuntu Desktop. The latest LTS version will be listed. LTS stands for *long-term support*. Click the green Download button to download whatever the current version is at the time you're doing this, which will automatically start the download of the ISO image, which will download to your Downloads folder. Leave it there for now.

Step 2 Navigate to https://www.vmware.com/products/workstation-player.html and click the Download For Free button. With the default selection of the current version, click Go To Downloads in the Product Downloads table. Click the Download Now button in the Windows section, which will start the download for the executable installer, which will download to your Downloads folder.

Step 3 Perform the following tasks to install the hypervisor:

a. Double-click the file starting with VMware-player that is followed by numbers, dashes, and dots (corresponding to version information) and ending with the .exe extension to launch the installer. Click the Yes button on the User Account Control screen. At the Welcome To The VMware Workstation <version number> Player Setup Wizard screen, click the Next button.

b. Put a check in the checkbox to accept the VMware End-User License Agreement and click the Next button.

c. With the default check in the checkbox related to the system PATH, put a check in the checkbox for Enhanced Keyboard Driver and click the Next button.

d. Make your selections on the User Experience Settings screen, and click the Next button.

e. Make your selections on the Shortcuts screen, and click the Next button.

f. On the next screen, click the Install button to start installing.

g. Click the Finish button when the setup wizard completes.

h. Click the Yes button to restart your system. When your machine reboots, continue with the next step.

📷 **4i–4j**

Step 4 Perform the tasks in the following instructions to create a new virtual machine:

a. Double-click the VMware Workstation <version number> Player icon on the Desktop (or in the search box type **VMware** and select VMware Workstation <version number> Player) to launch the application.

b. Use VMware Workstation <version number> Player For Free For Non-Commercial Use is selected by default. Leave this selected and click the Continue button.

c. On the next screen, click the Finish button.

d. At the VMware Workstation <version number> Player screen, click Create A New Virtual Machine. This will launch the New Virtual Machine Wizard.

e. Click the Browse... button to locate and double-click the Ubuntu ISO file you downloaded earlier (it's in the Downloads folder). Then click the Next > button.

f. Now, populate the textboxes for Full Name:, User Name:, Password:, and Confirm:, and click the Next > button.

g. You will now name the virtual machine and choose the location for the virtual machine folder. You may use the defaults or change the name and location. Click the Next > button when done.

h. It's time to specify the disk capacity. The recommended size for Ubuntu is 20 GB. As indicated on the screen, you're not going to be using all 20 GB (or whatever you choose for the size) all at once. The space will be incrementally added to as needed. However, you may choose a smaller disk capacity. In the radio button choice underneath, I recommend changing from the default and selecting Store Virtual Disk As A Single File. With Google Drive (coming up later in this chapter) and other cloud storage technologies, you can copy the single file easily. The message "Splitting the disk makes it easier to move the virtual machine to another computer but may reduce performance with very large disks" seems a little dated for that reason. Throwing large files on a Google Drive is easy, and you don't have to worry about reaching a maximum size for e-mail attachments, for example. You want the performance of a single file over the less efficient multiple files option. Then click the Next > button.

i. Now you are ready to create the virtual machine. Review the displayed virtual machine settings. If you would like to add more RAM allocated to the VM, click the Customize Hardware button, and adjust the value on the right of the screen that appears. Click the Close button to return to the previous screen.

Keep the check in the box next to Power On This Virtual Machine After Creation, and then click the Finish button to begin building the virtual machine. In the Software Updates dialog box, which should pop up right away, click the Download And Install button. VMware Tools is a suite of utilities that enhances the performance of the virtual machine's guest operating system and improves management of the virtual machine. A User Account Control Yes button will need to be clicked shortly thereafter.

→ **Note**

You may see an error message, which can be fixed by enabling virtualization in the BIOS. Read more at https://kb.vmware.com/s/article/1003944 and https://www.howtogeek.com/213795/how-to-enable-intel-vt-x-in-your-computers-bios-or-uefi-firmware/.

j. When the VMware Ubuntu virtual machine boots, you will be prompted for your username and password. After entering your information, you will have a fully functioning installation of Ubuntu as a guest operating system running on a VM through the hypervisor on top of the host operating system, Windows 10, which is running on the hardware of your physical machine.

k. In the Connect Your Online Accounts window, click the Skip button at the top right.

l. On the next screen, click the green Next button at the top right. To use Livepatch, you need to use an Ubuntu One Account.

m. On the next screen, select the radio button for No, Don't Send System Info and click the green Next button at the top right.

n. On the next screen, with the default Location Services selection set to Off, click the green Next button at the top right.

o. On the next screen, You're ready to go!, click the Done button at the top right.

p. If you see a Software Updater dialog box, click the Install Now button.

60 MINUTES

Lab Exercise 15.03: Traffic Between the Host System and the VM

Thus far, you've heard a lot about terms like virtual switch and virtual NIC. You've heard about networking configurations called bridged, NAT, and host-only. You've heard about different types of hypervisors.

Seeing is believing. Talking about host systems and VMs is one thing. Sending traffic between them is something else! Understanding the traffic flow through Wireshark will make the functions of hypervisors crystal clear.

Jonathan is excited, because if you can understand and implement virtualization, JSW can save lots of money in terms of hardware, power, and resources.

Let's get started!

Learning Objectives

In this lab exercise, you'll gain hands-on experience with VMs. By the end of this lab exercise, you'll be able to

- Understand the difference between a physical NIC and a virtual NIC

- Understand the difference between bridged networking and NAT networking

- Send traffic between the host system and VM

Lab Materials and Setup

The materials you'll need for this lab exercise are

- *Mike Meyers' CompTIA Network+ Guide to Managing and Troubleshooting Networks* textbook

- VMware Workstation Player running on the Windows 10 host system from Lab Exercise 15.02

- Ubuntu installed as the guest OS on the VM from Lab Exercise 15.02

Getting Down to Business

On the Windows 10 host system, click the Start button or in the search box and type **sharing**. Click Manage Advanced Sharing Settings, click Network And Sharing Center in the address bar, click Change Adapter Settings on the left, and look at all of your interfaces. Besides your physical interfaces, you now have two new VMware Network Adapters. In bridged networking, the host system and VM are on the same LAN, so no virtual adapter is needed on the host system, since the physical NIC is on the same subnet as the VM.

NAT networking uses a virtual router running NAT between the host system and the VM, which will be on a different network than the host system. However, your host system is already configured for a default gateway on a router that doesn't know about another virtual network behind VMware's NAT router. Therefore, to allow the host system to send traffic to the VM in NAT networking, a virtual NIC—VMware Network Adapter VMnet8—is created for the host system. This virtual adapter has an IP address on the subnet of the VM running NAT networking, which allows the host system to send traffic directly to the VM (and vice versa), without the need of a router (physical or virtual).

Host-only networking, which allows the VM to talk with just the host system, uses the same concept of a virtual NIC on the host system, and this one is called VMware Network Adapter VMnet1. Like in NAT networking, the VM is on a different network than the host system. If the host system wants to communicate with the VM in host-only networking, the host system uses the virtual NIC for host-only networking, because again, the default gateway of the host does not know about the existence of this remote network that the VM is on.

This lab exercise helps you understand these differences by observing traffic patterns in both NAT and bridged networking.

Step 1   Log in to the Ubuntu guest OS on the VM, as explained at the end of Lab Exercise 15.02. From the VMware menu at the top, click Player | Manage | Virtual Machine Settings... and make sure that the Network Adapter is set for NAT. Explore both the Hardware and Options tabs.

Step 2   Click the Show Applications button at the bottom left of the Ubuntu screen, type **Terminal** in the search box, and then click the Terminal icon. Into the Linux shell (known as Bash) that opens, type **ip a**, and then press ENTER. You should see an IP address listed for the ens33 interface (see Figure 15-1).

```
To run a command as administrator (user "root"), use "sudo <command>".
See "man sudo_root" for details.

jonathan@ubuntu:~$ ip a
1: lo: <LOOPBACK,UP,LOWER_UP> mtu 65536 qdisc noqueue state UNKNOWN group default qlen 1000
    link/loopback 00:00:00:00:00:00 brd 00:00:00:00:00:00
    inet 127.0.0.1/8 scope host lo
       valid_lft forever preferred_lft forever
    inet6 ::1/128 scope host
       valid_lft forever preferred_lft forever
2: ens33: <BROADCAST,MULTICAST,UP,LOWER_UP> mtu 1500 qdisc pfifo_fast state UP group default qlen 1000
    link/ether 00:0c:29:f6:47:73 brd ff:ff:ff:ff:ff:ff
    inet 192.168.91.128/24 brd 192.168.91.255 scope global dynamic ens33
       valid_lft 1034sec preferred_lft 1034sec
    inet6 fe80::fba9:f70e:26b9:9ebb/64 scope link
       valid_lft forever preferred_lft forever
jonathan@ubuntu:~$ █
```

Figure 15-1 ens33 configuration

Step 3   Perform the following substeps:

  a.   Type `sudo apt install wireshark`.

  b.   Provide the password to your account.

  c.   Type **Y** and press ENTER.

  d.   Keep the default choice of No by pressing ENTER in the Package Installation screen that pops up.

  e.   Back in the terminal, type `sudo wireshark` and press ENTER.

  f.   Click OK in the dialog box that pops up.

  g.   Double-click ens33 to start capturing on that interface.

  h.   In the filter box, type `icmp` and press ENTER.

  i.   Press CTRL-ALT-T to open a second terminal (an alternative way to open a terminal compared to what you did earlier), as the first terminal is the one running Wireshark in the foreground.

 4a–4b

Step 4

  a.   From the Ubuntu terminal, ping the IP address of your Windows Ethernet or Wi-Fi adapter (whichever one you're currently using). When the ping is successful, press CTRL-C to stop the pings. Linux pings don't stop automatically after four like in Windows.

  b.   Notice the ICMP Echo requests and ICMP Echo replies in Wireshark running on Ubuntu. The source MAC address that was associated with the IP address of the Windows host system in the ICMP Echo requests is *not* the MAC address of the host system (Ethernet or Wi-Fi adapter). Which device is this MAC address associated with? What is that device's IP address? What is the function of that device? Use the commands `ip neighbor` (the equivalent of `arp -a` in Windows) and `ip route` (the equivalent of `route print` or `netstat -r` in Windows) in the Ubuntu terminal to support your answer.

 5a–5b

 5c–5d

Step 5

a. From the Windows command prompt, execute `ipconfig /all` to get both the IP address and MAC address of VMware Network Adapter VMnet8 on the host system.

b. From the Ubuntu terminal, ping the IP address of VMware Network Adapter VMnet8 on the host system.

When the ping is successful, press CTRL-C to stop the pings. Notice the ICMP Echo requests and ICMP Echo replies in Wireshark running on Ubuntu.

c. What are the source IP address and source MAC address seen from the pings? What do they belong to?

d. How are the pings in this step different from the pings from the previous step?

 6a

 6b–6c

Step 6

a. From the Windows command prompt, ping the IP address of the VM. Notice the ICMP Echo request and ICMP Echo replies in Wireshark running on Ubuntu.

b. What IP address was used by the host system in the ICMP Echo requests? What MAC address was associated with that IP address?

c. Why were those IP and MAC addresses used?

 7b–7d

 7b–7d

Step 7

a. With Wireshark running on Ubuntu with a display filter of `icmp`, on the Windows 10 host system open Wireshark and start a capture on the Ethernet or Wi-Fi adapter with a display filter of `icmp`.

b. From the Windows command prompt, ping the IP address of the VM.

You'll see the pings in Wireshark on the VM, but why don't you see *anything* related to these pings in Wireshark on the host system?

   c. From the Ubuntu terminal, ping the IP address of VMware Network Adapter VMnet8.

       You'll see the pings in Wireshark on the VM, but why don't you see *anything* related to these pings in Wireshark on the host system?

   d. From the Ubuntu terminal, ping the IP address of the Ethernet or Wi-Fi adapter on the host system.

       You'll see the pings in Wireshark on the VM, but why don't you see *anything* related to these pings in Wireshark on the host system? The last part of Step 8b might make this clearer.

 8b

8c

Step 8

   a. Stop the Wireshark capture on the host system. Click File | Close and click the Continue Without Saving button. This brings you back to the Welcome To Wireshark screen.

   b. Now start sniffing on VMware Network Adapter VMnet8, with a display filter of **icmp**. Execute the same three pings as in the previous step:

     • From the Windows command prompt, ping the IP address of the VM.

     • From the Ubuntu terminal, ping the IP address of VMware Network Adapter VMnet8.

     • From the Ubuntu terminal, ping the IP address of the Ethernet or Wi-Fi adapter on the host system.

   c. How do the results in Wireshark on Windows 10 differ when sniffing on VMware Network Adapter VMnet8 as opposed to the Wi-Fi or Ethernet adapter? Why is this the case?

 9d–9f

9f

Step 9

   a. Change the Network Adapter settings from NAT networking to bridged networking in VMware Workstation Player by clicking Player | Manage | Virtual Machine Settings | Network Adapter. Click the radio button next to Bridged, and check the checkbox next to Replicate Physical Network Connection State. Click the Configure Adapters button, and make sure that every checkbox is checked. Click OK | OK.

   b. Wait a few seconds for the settings to kick in on the VM. Then in a terminal, type `ip a` and press ENTER to see the new IP address assigned to the virtual machine, which should be an IP address on the same network as the host system.

   c. From the host system, start a capture on the Ethernet or Wi-Fi adapter with a display filter of **icmp**.

   d. From the Windows command prompt, ping the new IP address of the VM.

e. From the Ubuntu terminal, ping the IP address of the host system's physical NIC.

f. In both Steps 9d and 9e, you see the ICMPs through the Ethernet or Wi-Fi adapter! Why are they visible now?

 60 MINUTES

Lab Exercise 15.04: Traffic from the VM to the Internet

When a frame enters a physical NIC, if the destination MAC address is not the NIC's MAC address, a broadcast, or a multicast, the NIC will drop it. Promiscuous mode is a mode for a wired or wireless NIC that causes the NIC to pass all traffic it receives up the network stack on a machine. Now the NIC will accept, capture, and read frames that are unicast addresses other than the NIC's MAC address. Of course, promiscuous mode is not useful on a switched network, because the switch will only send frames to ports associated with destination MAC addresses, as listed in the switch's Media Access Control (MAC) Address Table, also known as Content Addressable Memory (CAM) Table and Source Address Table (SAT).

For a VM running in bridged networking with its own virtual NIC and MAC address, the hypervisor will inject itself through a device driver and force a wired physical NIC to accept a frame with a VM's MAC address so it can be sent to the VM. Even though the destination MAC address is of the virtual NIC for the VM and not the physical NIC of the host system, the physical NIC is able to take the frame in. The virtual bridge will send the traffic to the VM with the listed destination MAC address.

Hypervisors need to tweak that behavior for wireless traffic because some wireless adapters don't support promiscuous mode, and in those cases, the wireless adapter will automatically drop traffic if the destination MAC address is not the MAC address of the physical wireless NIC. All traffic has to use the MAC address of the host system's wireless adapter. The hypervisor needs to change the source MAC address in the Layer 2 header of an outgoing packet to the host's MAC address to make sure the reply will be sent back to the host's MAC address and not the guest's MAC address.

When the hypervisor sees an incoming packet with a destination IP address that belongs to one of the VM's virtual NICs, it replaces the destination MAC address of the host NIC in the Layer 2 header with the VM's virtual NIC's MAC address and sends it on. Layer 2 ARP frames don't have a Layer 3 IP header, so the Target IP Address field is parsed by the hypervisor to know which virtual NIC should get the ARP reply. Hypervisors examine ARP and DHCP traffic so they can learn the IP addresses of virtual machines.

Learning Objectives

In this lab exercise, you'll see the different behaviors hypervisors use for wired and wireless physical NICs. By the end of this lab exercise, you'll be able to

- Send and analyze network traffic from a VM through a physical wired NIC

- Send and analyze network traffic from a VM through a physical wireless NIC

Lab Materials and Setup

The materials you'll need for this lab exercise are

- *Mike Meyers' CompTIA Network+ Guide to Managing and Troubleshooting Networks* textbook

- VMware Workstation Player running on the Windows 10 host system

- Ubuntu installed as the guest OS on the VM from Lab Exercise 15.02

- Both a wired and wireless NIC

Getting Down to Business

If you've been using a laptop and Wi-Fi for these exercises so far, for Step 1, plug a cable into your Ethernet adapter and use a wired Ethernet connection. Then in Step 2, take the cable out and resume using a Wi-Fi connection.

If you've been using a desktop machine to this point, for Step 1 continue as before. For Step 2, if possible, install Ubuntu as a guest OS through VMware Workstation Player on a laptop, and use a Wi-Fi connection (or use a USB wireless NIC on your desktop machine).

If you only have access to one setup (desktop or laptop), explain what you think would happen in the other setup if you were using it in this lab exercise.

Step 1 Log in to the guest OS, as explained at the end of Lab Exercise 15.02. From the VMware menu at the top, click Player | Manage | Virtual Machine Settings and make sure that the Network Adapter is set for bridged networking.

 2a–2b

 2c–2d

Step 2

a. With your host system using its Ethernet adapter, start sniffing with Wireshark using a display filter of **icmp** on both the host system and VM.

b. From the Ubuntu terminal, send a ping to 8.8.8.8.

c. What was the MAC address in the ICMP Echo requests seen through Wireshark on the VM?

d. What was the MAC address in the ICMP Echo requests seen through Wireshark on the host system?

3a–3b

 3c–3d

Step 3

a. With your host system using its Wi-Fi adapter, start sniffing with Wireshark, using a display filter of **icmp** on both the host system and VM.

b. From the Ubuntu terminal, send a ping to 8.8.8.8.

c. What was the MAC address in the ICMP Echo requests seen through Wireshark on the VM?

d. What was the MAC address in the ICMP Echo requests seen through Wireshark on the host system?

 **60 MINUTES**

Lab Exercise 15.05: Cloud Computing with Google Drive

Remember the days of purchasing online or even going to the store to buy Microsoft Office? Remember having to download and install updates? Then, a few years later, your version of Microsoft Office became obsolete, and you needed a new version! Now, with Microsoft Office 365, you use a browser to access the latest and greatest version of the Office suite in the cloud, with security patches applied immediately. Furthermore, you don't have to uninstall the previous version and install the current version. Google Workspace offers a similar set of cloud tools, including

Communication tools	Gmail, Contacts, Calendar, Meet, and Chat
Employee engagement tool	Currents
Storage tool	Google Drive
Content creation tools	Google Docs suite, which includes Google Docs, Google Sheets, Google Slides, Google Drawings, Google Forms, Google Sites, and Google Keep

The Software as a Service (SaaS) model provides access to necessary applications wherever you have an Internet connection, often without needing to carry data with you (the data can be stored in the cloud as well) or regularly update software. At the enterprise level, the subscription model of many SaaS providers makes it easier for organizations to budget software expenses and to keep hundreds or thousands of computers up to date with software for office tasks, messaging, payroll processing, database management, business management, and much more.

In exchange for the flexibility of using public, third-party SaaS, you often have to relinquish strict control of your data. Security might not be crucial when someone uses Google Drive to draft a blog post, but many companies are concerned about sensitive intellectual property or business secrets traveling through untrusted networks and residing on servers they don't control.

Specific examples of SaaS, besides the ones listed previously, include any Web-based e-mail provider, as well as Dropbox, Box, Slack, and Discord. Amazon Web Services and Microsoft Azure have SaaS components. Another example of SaaS is Salesforce, a customer relationship management (CRM) platform that helps with marketing, sales, commerce, and more. Furthermore, SaaS offerings can be client-based or clientless.

SaaS also has a benefit in a data center for much the same reason. For example, with company e-mail, there is no longer a need to maintain the infrastructure to support it. That includes hardware, data center space, cooling, server updates, application updates, and staff to do the previous actions.

Learning Objectives

In this lab exercise, you'll jump into cloud computing. By the end of this lab exercise, you'll be able to

- Use Google Drive to store files

- Use Google Docs, Sheets, Slides, and more

- Use Google Drive to move a VM from one machine to another machine

Lab Materials and Setup

The materials you'll need for this lab exercise are

- *Mike Meyers' CompTIA Network+ Guide to Managing and Troubleshooting Networks* textbook

- Any operating system

- Any browser

- Internet access

Getting Down to Business

You might have carried backups around on floppy disks a very long time ago. More recently, you might have transported files and programs with flash drives. Cloud computing requires you to carry around nothing, as everything is stored in that proverbial cloud.

Step 1 Go to https://drive.google.com and create an account if you don't have one.

Step 2 Click the New button at the top left of the screen. Create and explore each of the following items: Folder, File Upload, Folder Upload, Google Docs, Google Sheets, Google Slides, and Google Forms. If possible, test the ability to access these files and software from any machine with a browser and Internet connection.

Record some of your observations about creating items in Google Drive.

Step 3   Through the More selection, create and explore each of the following items: Google Forms, Google Drawings, Google My Maps, Google Sites, Google Apps Script, Google Jamboard, and Connect More apps. If possible, test the ability to access your newly created items from any machine with a browser and Internet connection.

Record some of your observations.

📷 **4a–4c, 4q**

Step 4   Earlier in the chapter, I mentioned that to move a VM from one machine to the next, you just need to transfer the files and folders that comprise it. Using Google Drive, let's do that now.

> ➡ **Note**
>
> **Google Drive gives you 15 GB for free by default. If you need more storage, you'll have to pay. Check out the following link for more details: https://one.google.com/faq/storage.**

a.   On your Windows 10 host system, in the Documents folder is a Virtual Machines folder. In the Virtual Machines folder will be top-level folders for each VM.

b.   Drag and drop the Ubuntu 64-bit folder to the browser window that has your Google Drive displayed.

c.   From another machine, download the Ubuntu 64-bit folder by right-clicking it and selecting Download. It will download to the Downloads folder as multiple files, including a ZIP with a long filename like Ubuntu 64-bit-20210829T051003Z-001.zip and one or more separate files.

d.   Right-click the ZIP and select Extract All… and in the popup click the Extract button.

e.   There will be a regular folder now that has the same name as the ZIP. In that folder will be a folder called Ubuntu 64-bit. Copy the additional file(s) that were downloaded into the Ubuntu 64-bit folder.

f.   Move the Ubuntu 64-bit folder to the Virtual Machines folder in the Documents folder on that machine.

g.   Download and install VMware Workstation Player on the second machine.

h.   Open up VMware Workstation Player.

i.   Select Open A Virtual Machine.

j.   Browse to Documents | Virtual Machines | Ubuntu 64-Bit.

k. Double-click the .vmx (VMware virtual machine configuration) file.

l. Click Play Virtual Machine.

m. Click the Browse button.

n. Double-click the .vmdk (VMware virtual disk) file.

o. Click the Yes button.

p. If prompted, click the I Moved It button.

q. Your VM should now be booting up from your second machine.

Lab Analysis

1. Tamara wants to know why you might create a VM as a single file instead of as multiple files (through VMware Workstation Player). Can you answer this question for her?

2. Oren asks you if VMware has other products besides VMware Workstation Player. Using https://www.vmware.com/, list different products that VMware offers.

3. Charlie wants to know some pros of virtualization. Can you help?

4. Miles wants to know the pros and cons of Software as a Service. What will you tell him?

Key Term Quiz

Use the terms in this list to complete the sentences that follow.

bridged

Software as a Service (SaaS)

Type 1

Type 2

virtual router/firewall

1. pfSense can be installed as a _____.

2. VMware Workstation Player is a _____ hypervisor.

3. Google Docs, Google Sheets, and Google Slides are all examples of _____.

4. ESXi is a _____ hypervisor.

5. In _____ networking, the host system and VM are on the same LAN.

Chapter 16
Data Centers

Lab Exercises

A data center serves as a home to an organization's mission-critical applications and important data. As you might imagine, servers are a major component of a data center, but so are routers and switches, as well as security components like firewalls, VPN gateways, IDSs, and more. In addition, a data center includes redundant/backup components providing supplies of power, and environmental controls, like air conditioning and fire suppression.

30 MINUTES

Lab Exercise 16.01: Data Center Terminology and Concepts

Jonathan would like you to be confident on the data center terms and technologies you learned about in the *Mike Meyers' CompTIA Network+ Guide to Managing and Troubleshooting Networks* textbook, and asks you to do this lab exercise, as a review.

Learning Objectives

In this lab exercise, you'll solidify your knowledge related to data center terminology. By the end of this lab exercise, you'll be able to

- Identify terminology and concepts related to data centers

Lab Materials and Setup

The materials you'll need for this lab exercise are

- *Mike Meyers' CompTIA Network+ Guide to Managing and Troubleshooting Networks* textbook

- Internet access

Getting Down to Business

If you haven't recently read Chapter 16 of the *Mike Meyers' CompTIA Network+ Guide to Managing and Troubleshooting Networks* textbook, it might be a good idea to review the chapter. Alternatively, jump right in and see what you remember!

Step 1 Using the *Mike Meyers' CompTIA Network+ Guide to Managing and Troubleshooting Networks* textbook or Google, match each data center term with its corresponding definition.

Technologies	Definitions
_____ Tiered architecture	A. Ensures critical systems keep working without interruption or downtime
_____ SAN	B. Enabling a process to work among two or more systems
_____ Top-of-rack switches	C. Movement of data into, out of, and around the data center
_____ Redundancy	D. Dedicated devices that help keep cable runs short and well organized
_____ High availability	E. Access layer, distribution layer, core layer
_____ Load balancing	F. A network that connects individual systems to a centralized bank of mass storage devices, presented over a network as any number of logical disks
_____ Traffic flows	G. Ensures high availability on many levels through the use of additional equipment and connection options

Step 2 Explain the difference between the access layer, the distribution layer, and the core layer.

Step 3 What is north–south traffic?

Step 4 What is east–west traffic?

Step 5 What's the difference between SAN and NAS implementations?

Step 6 What's the difference between an on-premises data center and colocation?

Step 7   What goes into data center documentation?

Step 8   What are some examples of data center network diagrams?

Step 9   How do baseline configurations help in regard to a data center?

Step 10   What's involved in data center assessments?

30 MINUTES

Lab Exercise 16.02: Data Center Research

JSW is a growing company! As such, Jonathan asks you to look into potential data centers to use if the need arises to expand.

Learning Objectives

In this lab exercise, you'll do research on potential data centers. By the end of this lab exercise, you'll be able to

- Understand different offerings of data centers
- Recommend a data center for usage

Lab Materials and Setup

The materials you'll need for this lab exercise are

- *Mike Meyers' CompTIA Network+ Guide to Managing and Troubleshooting Networks* textbook
- Internet access

Getting Down to Business

Fire up a browser and get ready to ask some queries to Google.

Step 1 List five criteria for choosing a data center location/provider.

Step 2 Research three data centers for JSW.

Step 3 Select one and explain your choice.

Lab Analysis

1. Martin and Eva want to know what type of data centers existed in the 1960s and what new type of data centers emerged in the 1990s. Can you help them out?

2. Eli and Maxine want to know what the two choices for implementing a SAN are, and how do they compare? What do you tell them?

Key Term Quiz

Use the terms in this list to complete the sentences that follow.

high availability   redundant

load balancing

1. Data centers are designed to withstand problems through various _____ and backup systems for all critical functions.

2. Using multiple systems to share the work to ensure that a specific resource can be accessed at high-traffic times is _____.

3. Data centers ensure _____ and disaster recovery through proper support for facilities and infrastructure, which means providing proper power, clean cool air for components, and making sure that emergency procedures are in place.

Chapter 17

Integrating Network Devices

Lab Exercises

As machines in plants and factories have become more complex over the years, humans who were operating these machines started to need help from … other machines. The overall system that monitors and controls machines today is called an *industrial control system (ICS)*.

Learning about various ICSs, consisting of various hardware devices and software that monitor and control equipment, is vital, since ICSs are now being networked across the Internet. PLC vs. RTU? DCS vs. PLC? SCADA vs. HMI? DCS vs. SCADA? What's the difference between all of those? Why are they needed? How do they communicate? How are they networked? You'll find out the answers to those questions and much more in this chapter.

The Internet of Things (IoT) encompasses billions of physical devices, things that wouldn't normally be expected to be connected to the Internet and are able to communicate without human interaction. These devices use sensors, software, and many other technological components to send and receive data with other devices, systems, and networks over the Internet.

Learning about vulnerabilities inherent with the convenience of IoT devices is also vital to ensuring the security of systems and networks.

This will be a very eye-opening chapter!

 **60 MINUTES**

Lab Exercise 17.01: Industrial Control Systems

Any industry that makes things, changes things, or moves things is filled with equipment to do the job. From making mousetraps to ice cream, any given industrial plant, power grid, pipeline, or other industry is filled with lots of things that need to be monitored and lots of things that need to be controlled through ICSs.

Things to monitor include

- Temperature
- Power levels
- Fill quantity
- Illumination
- Mass

Things to control include

- Heaters
- Voltage
- Pumps
- Retractable roofs
- Valves

Learning Objectives

In this lab exercise, you'll explore the various concepts that ICS encompasses. By the end of this lab exercise, you'll be able to

- Understand the differences between PLC and RTU
- Understand the differences between DCS and PLC
- Understand the differences between SCADA and HMI
- Understand the differences between DCS and SCADA

Lab Materials and Setup

The materials you'll need for this lab exercise are

- *Mike Meyers' CompTIA Network+ Guide to Managing and Troubleshooting Networks* textbook
- Internet access

Getting Down to Business

If JSW is to become a global force and expand its services, you'll need to understand the following terms and concepts. Jonathan asks you to watch a set of videos to make sure you feel comfortable with ICS terminology. These graphical, animated videos were made by RealPars, an industrial automation company in Rotterdam, Netherlands. What better source to use than a company like that! Their YouTube channel has close to 700,000 subscribers, and their videos have hundreds of thousands of views.

⌨ **1a–1e**

Step 1   Watch the video titled "What Is SCADA?" at https://youtu.be/nlFM1q9QPJw.

    a.   What does SCADA stand for?

    b.   What does SCADA do?

    c.   What components does SCADA include?

    d.   What technologies do modern SCADA systems use, and what does that allow for?

    e.   What other takeaways did you get from this video?

⌨ **2a–2e**

Step 2   Watch the video titled "PLC Basics | Programmable Logic Controller" at https://youtu.be/ PbAGl_mv5XI.

    a.   What did PLCs originally replace?

    b.   What does a PLC consist of?

    c.   What two common connections do applications on desktop/laptop PLCs use to communicate with the PLC?

    d.   What are some things PLC manufacturers haven't agreed on?

    e.   What other takeaways did you get from this video?

⌨ **3a–3e**

Step 3   Watch the video titled "What Is RTU?" at https://youtu.be/Ax1jTp2dl9M.

    a.   What does RTU stand for?

    b.   What is an RTU?

    c.   What device is an RTU compared to, and which one is considered more rugged?

    d.   What are three areas in which an RTU has significant advantages over the device it's compared to?

    e.   What other takeaways did you get from this video?

⌨ **4a–4e**

Step 4   Watch the video titled "What Is DCS? (Distributed Control System)" at https://youtu.be/jXRksET5vNo.

    a.   What is a DCS?

    b.   What was the motivation for the creation of a DCS?

    c.   Why is a DCS more reliable and safety-oriented than a PLC?

    d.   What are some components of a DCS?

    e.   What other takeaways did you get from this video?

   ⌨ **5a–5e**

Step 5   Watch the video titled "What Is an HMI?" at https://youtu.be/kujHQgK352o.

    a.   What does HMI stand for?

    b.   What is an HMI used for?

    c.   What information can be displayed from an HMI?

    d.   What do each indicator and button have to be programmed to?

    e.   What other takeaways did you get from this video?

   ⌨ **6a–6e**

Step 6   Watch the video titled "What Is the Difference Between SCADA and HMI?" at https://youtu.be/xvVCSYt_YsQ.

    a.   Can HMI be part of a SCADA?

    b.   Can SCADA be part of an HMI?

    c.   What can a SCADA be summarized as?

    d.   What can an HMI be summarized as?

    e.   What other takeaways did you get from this video?

   ⌨ **7a–7i**

Step 7   Watch the video titled "What Are the Differences Between DCS and SCADA?" at https://youtu.be/B3YVpgs9RY4.

    a.   Are the roles of SCADA and DCS essentially the same, or are the mechanisms used to handle tasks essentially the same?

    b.   Which has HMIs or computers from different manufacturers?

    c.   Which has graphical interfaces integrated within the system?

    d.   Which has the need for building or importing tags as well as PLCs and RTUs that need programming?

    e.   Which has tagged databases as well as predefined functions that could be customized and deployed for various applications for faster integration?

    f.   Which offers a slight advantage for time-sensitive processes?

    g.   Which offers an advantage of an open communication architecture?

    h.   Which offers an advantage in safety?

    i.   What other takeaways did you get from this video?

 **60 MINUTES**

Lab Exercise 17.02: IoT Vulnerabilities

You've heard about the great convenience that IoT brings homes and businesses, but it's really part of a seesaw. On one side you have security, and on the other side you have convenience. When one side goes up, the other side goes down. Jonathan wants you to review some stories of IoT vulnerabilities in order to understand how to put JSW's best foot forward in the IoT arena.

Learning Objectives

In this lab exercise, you'll analyze stories of IoT vulnerabilities. By the end of this lab exercise, you'll be able to

- Identify ways the exploitation of vulnerabilities could have been prevented

- Make remediation recommendations to minimize similar future occurrences

Lab Materials and Setup

The materials you'll need for this lab exercise are

- *Mike Meyers' CompTIA Network+ Guide to Managing and Troubleshooting Networks* textbook

- Internet access

Getting Down to Business

Explore the following stories and videos.

    For Steps 1–5, identify

    a.   What happened

    b.   Vulnerabilities involved

    c.   Fallout

    d.   What could have prevented the vulnerabilities from being exploited

    e.   Remediation recommendations

For Steps 6–10, explain your thoughts if the theoretical hacks described came to fruition.

⌨

Step 1 4/16/18: Casino Gets Hacked Through Its Internet-Connected Fish Tank Thermometer
https://thehackernews.com/2018/04/iot-hacking-thermometer.html

⌨

Step 2 6/4/18: South Carolina Parents Say Baby Monitor Was Hacked After Camera Lens Moved on Its Own
https://abcnews.go.com/US/south-carolina-parents-baby-monitor-hacked-camera-lens/story?id=55633540

6/5/18: S.C. Mom Says Baby Monitor Was Hacked; Experts Say Many Devices Are Vulnerable
https://www.npr.org/sections/thetwo-way/2018/06/05/617196788/s-c-mom-says-baby-monitor-was-hacked-experts-say-many-devices-are-vulnerable

6/6/18: Another Baby Monitor Camera Hacked
https://www.csoonline.com/article/3279194/another-baby-monitor-camera-hacked.html

⌨

Step 3 12/18/18: Nest Camera Hacker Threatens to Kidnap Baby, Spooks Parents
https://www.nbcnews.com/news/us-news/nest-camera-hacker-threatens-kidnap-baby-spooks-parents-n949251

12/20/18: "I'm in Your Baby's Room": A Hacker Took over a Baby Monitor and Broadcast Threats, Parents Say
https://www.washingtonpost.com/technology/2018/12/20/nest-cam-baby-monitor-hacked-kidnap-threat-came-device-parents-say/

⌨

Step 4 12/13/19: Attackers Terrify Homeowners After Hacking Ring Devices
https://www.bleepingcomputer.com/news/security/attackers-terrify-homeowners-after-hacking-ring-devices/

12/13/19: A Hacker Accessed a Family's Ring Security Camera and Told Their 8-Year-Old Daughter He Was Santa Claus
https://www.abcactionnews.com/news/national/a-hacker-accessed-a-familys-ring-security-camera-and-told-their-8-year-old-daughter-he-was-santa-claus

12/13/19: Terrifying Video of Family's Hacked Ring Camera System
https://abcnews.go.com/GMA/News/video/terrifying-video-familys-hacked-ring-camera-system-67704081

Step 5 **3/9/21: Security Startup Verkada Hack Exposes 150,000 Security Cameras in Tesla Factories, Jails, and More**

https://www.theverge.com/2021/3/9/22322122/verkada-hack-150000-security-cameras-tesla-factory-cloudflare-jails-hospitals

3/10/21: Global Hackers Raid Verkada's Clients' Video Surveillance Data

https://www.securityinfowatch.com/video-surveillance/article/21213804/global-hackers-raid-verkadas-clients-video-surveillance-data

3/15/21: Verkada Breach Demonstrates Danger of Overprivileged Users

https://www.darkreading.com/vulnerabilities-threats/verkada-breach-demonstrates-danger-of-overprivileged-users

Step 6 **8/6/13: How Smart Toilet in Japan Became Prone to Hacking**

https://www.usatoday.com/story/tech/2013/08/06/smart-toilet-hack/2622723/

Step 7 **9/2/16: How Hackers Could Steal Your Cellphone Pictures From Your IoT Crock-Pot**

https://www.vice.com/en/article/wnx7n9/how-hackers-could-steal-your-cellphone-pictures-from-your-iot-crock-pot

Step 8 **2/17/17: German Parents Told to Destroy Cayla Dolls Over Hacking Fears**

https://www.bbc.com/news/world-europe-39002142

Step 9 **2/2/19: "Internet of Things" or "Vulnerability of Everything"? Japan Will Hack Its Own Citizens to Find Out**

https://edition.cnn.com/2019/02/01/asia/japan-hacking-cybersecurity-iot-intl

Step 10 **6/9/21: Amazon Sidewalk Mesh Network Raises Security, Privacy Concerns**

https://www.securityweek.com/amazon-sidewalk-mesh-network-raises-security-privacy-concerns

Lab Analysis

1. Of the ICS concepts discussed in this chapter, which is an ATM (automated teller machine) most like?

2. Which article/story on IoT vulnerabilities was the craziest to you and why?

3. Find an IoT device for sale that should have no business being connected to the Internet. Explain your thought process.

Key Term Quiz

Use the terms in this list to complete the sentences that follow.

DCS   RTU

HMI   SCADA

PLC

1. Software and hardware components providing supervision and control of local and remote plants that examines, collects, and processes data in real time is known as _____.

2. The device that replaced relays and consists of a CPU module and I/O is called _____.

3. A device used to control and monitor machines through an operating panel and monitoring screen (touchscreen or screen with buttons) is called a(n) _____.

4. A microprocessor-based device used to monitor and control field devices connecting to plant control or SCADA systems is called a(n) _____.

5. A system used to coordinate and supervise a full plant of lots of different processes is called a(n) _____.

Chapter 18
Network Operations

Lab Exercises

As far as networks go, risk represents the likelihood that a threat actor will carry out a threat and exploit a vulnerability, which will have security-related consequences to the confidentiality, integrity, and availability of data, resources, and assets. There's no foolproof design to network security. Threat agents include insiders, outsiders, and even Mother Nature. Threat agents need just one mere vulnerability to exploit, but the security team needs to constantly defend against all possible attack vectors. It's not a fair game by any stretch of the imagination!

The more preventive security implementations there are in place from the start, the easier it will be to mitigate a security incident or disaster. Humans are the weakest link in any security implementation. It only takes one user to click a link or to download and run an attachment to undermine everything put into security implementations, including software, hardware, and more. Therefore, any security plan must begin with a solid education plan for employees.

Writing a security policy that will be read by employees, clearly delineating what they can and cannot do, is vital. Making sure users read the policies and making sure that they understand them are vital as well. Furthermore, two important entities need to be in place should an attack happen: disaster recovery and business continuity.

 **30 MINUTES**

Lab Exercise 18.01: AUP

Policies are the cornerstone of an organization's IT security. Policies help define what equipment they use, how they organize data, and what actions people must take to ensure the security of an organization. Policies tell an organization how to handle almost any situation that might arise, such as business continuity and disaster recovery, covered later in this chapter.

A security policy is a document that defines how an organization will protect its IT infrastructure.

The acceptable use policy (AUP) defines what is and what is not acceptable to do with an organization's systems, devices, networks, data, information, resources, assets, and more. It's arguably the most famous of all security policies, as this is one document that pretty much everyone who works for any organization is required to read and sign before they can start working.

Learning Objectives

In this lab exercise, you'll consider an AUP from the administrative side, as opposed to the employee side you might be accustomed to. By the end of this lab exercise, you'll be able to

- Understand required components of an AUP

- Develop required components of an AUP

Lab Materials and Setup

The materials you'll need for this lab exercise are

- *Mike Meyers' CompTIA Network+ Guide to Managing and Troubleshooting Networks* textbook

- Internet access

Getting Down to Business

Assume that you are writing an AUP for your organization. Expand, in multiple paragraphs for each, the following statements in the following steps. You can use your own original thoughts or get some ideas from a sample/template AUP. You can find a great one from the SANS Institute at https://www.sans.org/security-resources/policies (the AUP is the second one down).

Step 1 Expand on this statement in your AUP dealing with ownership: Equipment and any proprietary information stored on the organization's computers are the property of the organization.

Step 2 Expand on this statement in your AUP dealing with network access: Users will only access information they are authorized to access.

Step 3 Expand on this statement in your AUP dealing with privacy/consent to monitoring: Anything users do on the organization's computers is not private. The organization will monitor what is being done on computers at any time.

Step 4 Expand on this statement in your AUP dealing with illegal use: No one may use an organization's computers for anything that breaks a law. This is usually broken down into many subheadings, such as Malware, Hacking, Scanning, Spamming, and so forth.

 **60 MINUTES**

Lab Exercise 18.02: User Education

As mentioned earlier, humans are the weakest link in any security implementation. To mitigate this, training users is a critical piece of managing risk. While a formal course is preferred, it's typically up to the IT department to do what it can to make sure users have an understanding of certain security risks.

Learning Objectives

In this lab exercise, you'll gain experience in user education. By the end of this lab exercise, you'll be able to

- Create a presentation for user training
- Give the presentation to a live audience

Lab Materials and Setup

The materials you'll need for this lab exercise are

- *Mike Meyers' CompTIA Network+ Guide to Managing and Troubleshooting Networks* textbook
- Internet access
- Microsoft PowerPoint or Google Slides
- Computer and projector to give the actual presentation

Getting Down to Business

Using Microsoft PowerPoint or Google Slides, create slides for a formal user education presentation. You'll then deliver the presentation to an audience, which can be your classmates, other students, or even family and friends.

In each of the following steps, make two to three slides dealing with the following concepts.

Step 1   Add slides dealing with security policies: Users need to read, understand, and, when necessary, sign all pertinent security policies. Then, of course, they need to follow everything in the policies.

Step 2   Add slides dealing with passwords: Make sure users understand basic password skills, such as sufficient length and to avoid password reuse.

Step 3   Add slides dealing with social engineering and phishing: Users need to recognize typical social engineering and phishing tactics and how to counter them.

Step 4   Add slides dealing with malware: Teach users to recognize malware attacks and know what to do if they think they have malware on a system.

Step 5   Deliver the presentation to your classmates, other students, or family and friends. Ask for feedback on both content and delivery, and note what they say for this step's submission. Also, submit your presentation file separately.

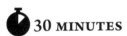 **30 MINUTES**

Lab Exercise 18.03: Disaster Recovery and Business Continuity

Although the terms are sometimes blurred, disaster recovery deals with recovering your primary infrastructure from disaster, and business continuity seeks to keep your business going at alternate locations if the primary location cannot be used. As such, documents known as a business continuity plan (BCP) and a disaster recovery plan (DRP) should be in place, detailing the steps necessary in those cases.

Fault tolerance should not be the end-all of data security. In keeping with the philosophy that the most important part of a network is the data, a comprehensive backup strategy is the point of last defense and should be one of the linchpins of an administrator's network management routines. When RAID arrays fail, when users accidentally delete that critical database, or when malware corrupts a file server, the ability to restore the systems to their most recent state will allow the organization to recover from the disaster gracefully.

Numerous technologies are available to implement quality system backups, especially cloud backups and network attached storage (NAS), to protect the data when disaster strikes. Mission-critical organizations such as world financial institutions, government agencies, and national security operations will even employ entire alternate locations that will have some level of network infrastructure ready to go in case of a complete failure of the primary location.

Data backup technologies, techniques, and strategies are tools that you can apply immediately, from the smallest of organizations to large enterprise networks. Along with preparing for the CompTIA Network+ exam and honing your skills as a network administrator, engineer, or tech, you can also adopt these techniques to keep your precious photos and music safe from disaster!

Learning Objectives

In this lab exercise, you'll explore disaster recovery and business continuity. By the end of this lab exercise, you'll be able to

- Identify members for a disaster recovery team

- Plan backup methods

- Calculate time needed to restore backups

- Understand the differences between hot sites, warm sites, and cold sites

Lab Materials and Setup

The materials you'll need for this lab exercise are

- Internet access

Getting Down to Business

You have almost completed your studies for the Network+ exam! Along the way, you have developed a deep understanding of networking concepts and applied these skills to daily responsibilities in your position as a desktop support specialist. Now a Network Tech, Level 1 position has opened up at JSW, and you would like to apply for the position.

Jonathan is confident of your capabilities, but recommends that you focus on one last area of network management before your interview: disaster recovery and business continuity. He explains that no organization can ever prepare "too much" to avoid the devastating results of a poorly planned backup and recovery strategy.

Step 1   Form a disaster recovery team. Do some research and find out which employees in specific roles might be good choices for membership on this team.

Step 2   Plan your backups. Do some research and decide on a proper plan on backup for your essential and nonessential data.

3c

Step 3 Jonathan puts you on one more important research adventure. He wants you to search the Web for companies that provide disaster recovery and/or business continuity.

a. Select the top three companies and services for disaster recovery.

b. Select the top three companies and services for business continuity.

c. Explain each of your choices and why they are better than others you saw.

Lab Analysis

1. Brandy and Emma have just finished an exhilarating game of *Among Us* when their supervisor steps into their cubicle area and gives them a verbal warning concerning gaming during business hours. She explains to them that there is a company policy that defines what is allowed and what is not allowed in the workplace. After their supervisor leaves, Brandy and Emma ask you what the supervisor was talking about. What do you tell them?

2. Justin and Isaac want to know why everyone around the office talks about social engineering. Tell them why it's of utmost importance.

3. Tracie thinks that disaster recovery kicks in before business continuity. Abe thinks it's the other way around. Who's right, and why? Also, which implementation usually completes first, and why?

Key Term Quiz

Use the terms in this list to complete the sentences that follow.

acceptable use policy (AUP)   disaster recovery

business continuity   user education

1. Restoring access at an organization's primary site depends on the _____ plan.

2. When an organization needs to move to another location, the _____ plan should be consulted.

3. Since humans are the weakest link in any security implementation, a(n) _____ program, which can be in the form of a presentation, can go a long way to minimizing the effects of potential attacks.

4. The _____ defines what can and can't be done on an organization's systems, devices, networks, data, information, resources, assets, and more.

Chapter 19

Protecting Your Network

Lab Exercises

Network protection covers many different security aspects. You have probably already explored various anti-malware programs, especially if you are CompTIA A+ certified. Likewise, the topic of Redundant Array of Inexpensive/Independent Disks (RAID) should be familiar from your prior studies. You have also worked with encryption and VPNs.

Jonathan thinks it's a good idea for you to review common threats to the network and get hands-on experience configuring user accounts with passwords, as well as Windows Defender Firewall.

 30 MINUTES

Lab Exercise 19.01: Common Threats

There are countless threats, malicious or otherwise, that can affect the security of a network and therefore the data contained within. These threats range from the simple but possibly time-consuming loss of data from a hard drive or server crash to the devastating results of data stolen through a mismanaged administrative account or a Trojan horse.

Effective protection of the network and the data requires due diligence on the part of the network administrator when it comes to analyzing these threats and warding them off or planning contingency measures. Employers and the CompTIA Network+ exam expect the network tech to have a working knowledge of the various threats that are waiting to pounce on the unsuspecting network.

Learning Objectives

In this lab exercise, you'll review the common threats you may encounter when working as a network technician. By the end of this lab exercise, you'll be able to

- List and detail the various forms of malware

- Explain the concept of social engineering

- Differentiate between different types of phishing

- Define man-in-the-middle attacks

- Provide the definition of a Denial of Service (DoS) attack

- Identify attacks on wireless connections

- Revisit a breach that you were affected by

- Identify the weakest link in any security implementation

Lab Materials and Setup

The materials you'll need for this lab exercise are

- *Mike Meyers' CompTIA Network+ Guide to Managing and Troubleshooting Networks* textbook

- Internet access

Getting Down to Business

Now that you are progressing well through your studies and are almost ready to take the CompTIA Network+ exam, Jonathan has a request. It has been a while since the department has provided an update to the business managers on the security measures in place to protect the network and corporate data. He asks you to conduct a study of the most common threats affecting networks today, from small home networks to large corporate enterprises, and present a report as part of the team's presentation to management.

Use both the textbook and the Internet for your research. Work through the following steps and further refine your knowledge of threats to the network.

Step 1 Provide an appropriate definition for each of the listed types of malware:

Malware	Definition
Virus	
Worm	
Logic bomb	
Trojan horse	
Rootkit	
Ransomware	

Step 2 Define the method and purpose of social engineering.

Step 3 What is the difference between phishing, spear phishing, and whaling?

Step 4 Provide a scenario depicting a man-in-the-middle attack.

Step 5 Explain the difference between a Denial of Service (DoS) attack and a Distributed Denial of Service (DDoS) attack.

Step 6 Explain the factors that might lead to network intrusion through wireless connections.

Step 7 Describe a cybersecurity attack or data breach that affected you personally.

Step 8 What will always be the weakest link in any security implementation? Why?

 30 MINUTES

Lab Exercise 19.02: User Authentication

One of the most important safeguards against unwanted access to corporate client PCs and servers (and therefore the network) is a strong password. Passwords are the most common form of authentication, which is proving you are who you say you are. Microsoft Windows systems include security policies that allow you to configure various settings that control how a user's password can be formulated.

Your part of the job that includes managing users and security will have you address account passwords, ensuring that only the people who should have access to the particular system they are trying to access actually do have access.

Learning Objectives

In this lab exercise, you'll configure computer security and develop a template for assigning a strong password. By the end of this lab exercise, you'll be able to

- Create a password policy
- Edit account security settings
- Sign in to a system with a valid account and change the password to meet password requirements

Lab Materials and Setup

The materials you'll need for this lab exercise are

- *Mike Meyers' CompTIA Network+ Guide to Managing and Troubleshooting Networks* textbook
- Windows 10 system (Windows 10 Home cannot be used for this lab exercise)

Getting Down to Business

Jonathan has been asked to set up a Group Policy structure for the marketing department of a new client. He invites you to tag along to watch him define and test the user account password policy that he will implement. In preparation, you decide to explore password configuration on a Windows 10 system.

→ **Note**

In a corporate environment, like at JSW and many of their clients, the password policy would be configured for the various departments and all of the users on a global basis. If the corporation is using a Microsoft architecture, the corporate infrastructure will consist of Active Directory domains, organizational units, Group Policy Objects, and more. Typically, the actual configuration of system settings will take place on a Windows Server Domain Controller, using the Group Policy Management Editor (GPME) via the Group Policy Management Console (GPMC). For the purposes of the lab exercise, the exploration and configuration of the password policy can be completely facilitated on a PC running Windows 10.

Step 1 Sign in to the Windows 10 system with an account that has administrative access. Click the Start button or in the Windows search box, type **Local Security Policy**, and click Local Security Policy. In the pane on the left, expand Account Policies and select Password Policy.

→ **Note**

The length of a password is proportional to its strength, as longer passwords are more resistant to brute-force attacks. Keep in mind, however, that two other recommendations of the past, requiring different character sets and requiring periodic password changes, were moved into the "don't" category by the National Institute of Standards and Technology (NIST) in 2017. Requiring different character sets and requiring periodic password changes have actually been proven to be counterproductive, causing users to make small, predictable changes to passwords or to even reuse passwords in multiple locations.

Furthermore, the NIST guidelines now require multi-factor authentication (MFA) when securing personal information that's available online. In addition to something you know, such as a password, other factors of authentication include something you are (biometrics), and something you have, such as a physical token like YubiKey, or a software-based authenticator like Google Authenticator or Duo, but not having a code texted to you (Short Message Service [SMS]), because the underlying SS7 protocol is vulnerable to attacks.

Read about the 2017 NIST password guidelines here: https://www.enzoic.com/surprising-new-password-guidelines-nist/.

Read about the 2020 NIST password guidelines here: https://auth0.com/blog/dont-pass-on-the-new-nist-password-guidelines/.

Step 2   In the Password Policy settings in the right pane (see Figure 19-1), set the following values for the various password policy security settings. As you make these changes, double-click each item and read the information in the Explain tab for further background. These changes are for new users and do not affect existing accounts.

Enforce password history	10
Maximum password age	0 (per the NIST guidelines)
Minimum password age	1
Minimum password length	10
Password must meet complexity requirements	Disabled (per the NIST guidelines)
Store passwords using reversible encryption	Disabled

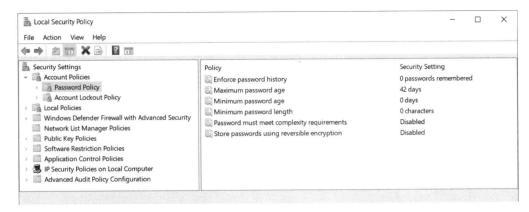

FIGURE 19-1 Configuring the password policy

Step 3 Click the Start button or in the Windows search box, type **Computer Management**, and select Computer Management. This opens the Computer Management Console. Expand Local Users And Groups, and click Users to see all users. Right-click Users or in a blank area of the main pane, and select New User....

In the User Name: textbox enter **DavidBanner**. Leave the Full Name: and Description: textboxes empty. Put in a password of **Hulk** in the Password: and Confirm Password: textboxes, as shown in Figure 19-2. Since that password is less than 10 characters, you'll get an error message, as shown in Figure 19-3.

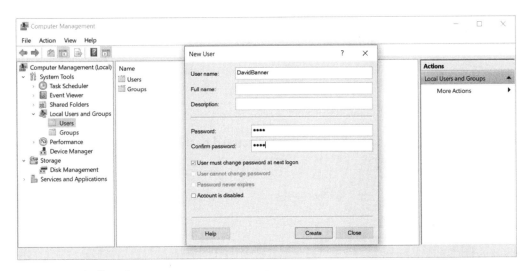

FIGURE 19-2 Creating a new user

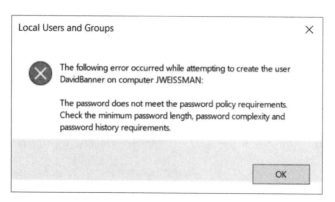

FIGURE 19-3 Local Users And Groups error message

➜ **Note**

Windows uses two words for "user name," although it's one word, username, in many other locations.

Step 4   Now, for the DavidBanner user, assign a password that will be accepted.

A good way to come up with a complex password that's easy to remember is to use the first letter of words from one of your favorite songs. Mixing and matching uppercase letters, lowercase letters, numbers, and symbols is fine if you're able to remember what you did, but as mentioned earlier, not something that should be required per NIST.

Step 5   Sign out and sign in again as DavidBanner. When prompted to change the password, enter the same password and click OK. Why did this fail?

Step 6   Now come up with a new password that will be accepted, based on the changes to the password policy made earlier. Sign in with it.

30 MINUTES

Lab Exercise 19.03: Windows Defender Firewall

Instead of turning off Windows Defender Firewall completely to let pings through, it's a much wiser and safer decision to let certain things, like ICMP, in, while anything else that's unsolicited will still be filtered.

Learning Objectives

In this lab exercise, you'll work with a software firewall. By the end of this lab exercise, you'll be able to

- Understand how software firewalls work

- Create rules to permit or deny traffic

Lab Materials and Setup

The materials you'll need for this lab exercise are

- *Mike Meyers' CompTIA Network+ Guide to Managing and Troubleshooting Networks* textbook

- Windows 10 system and another device that can send pings to the Windows 10 system

Getting Down to Business

Windows Defender Firewall is a host-based (located on an individual computer) firewall and is therefore considered a software firewall. You should always have Windows Defender Firewall enabled. Even if you have a wireless router with a firewall, you'll just end up enhancing the security and providing defense-in-depth.

Step 1   In the Windows search box type **Firewall** and select Windows Defender Firewall (Figure 19-4).

Step 2   Using the Internet, determine if the Windows Defender Firewall is of the Stateful Packet Inspection (SPI) type. Provide a short definition of SPI.

Step 3   In the pane at the left of the Windows Defender Firewall window (opened earlier), click Turn Windows Defender Firewall On Or Off. For each network location (Private network settings and Public network settings), select the radio button next to Turn Off Windows Defender Firewall (Not Recommended). Then, click the OK button. Keep this window open for future steps.

FIGURE 19-4 Windows Defender Firewall

Step 4   Determine what IP address is assigned to the Windows 10 system, and from a different device, ping the Windows 10 system. (Make sure a firewall is not in effect on the other device.) The pings should succeed.

Step 5   In the Windows Defender Firewall window opened earlier, click the Use Recommended Settings button. The red colors will turn green and the x in each shield will turn to a check. Now the firewall is back on.

To revert back to the default firewall configuration, in the pane on the left, click Restore Defaults, then the Restore Defaults button, and then the Yes button. Keep this window open for future steps.

Step 6   From a different device, ping the Windows 10 system. The pings should fail.

Step 7   In the pane at the left of the Windows Defender Firewall window opened earlier, click Advanced Settings. In the left pane of the new window (see Figure 19-5), click Inbound Rules. In the middle pane, there will be four rules called File And Printer Sharing (two Echo Request – ICMPv4-In rules and two Echo

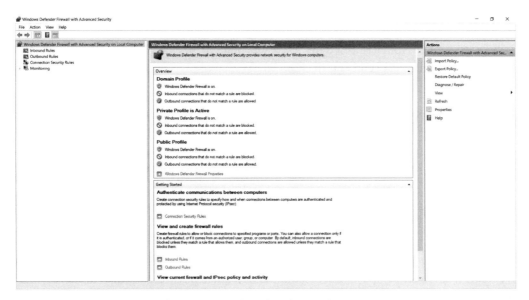

FIGURE 19-5 Windows Defender Firewall with Advanced Security

Request – ICMPv6-In rules; see Figure 19-6). Right click each of them, and select Enable Rule. Two of them deal with ICMP for IPv4 (ICMPv4), and two of them deal with ICMP for IPv6 (ICMPv6). Two of them deal with the Private and Public profiles, and two of them deal with a Domain profile.

Step 8   From a different device, ping the Windows 10 system. The pings should once again succeed.

FIGURE 19-6 Allowing the pings through

Lab Analysis

1. In Lab Exercise 19.03, you performed three separate pings in Steps 4, 6, and 8. Dovid wants to know why each step got those particular results. Can you explain this to him?

2. Chany is working in her cubicle one day when the phone rings. She answers it and is surprised to hear that it is one of the network administrators from the IT department. The caller identifies himself as Yossi and says that he needs to verify Chany's user name and password. Chany hesitates, leans over her cubicle wall, and tells you what's happening. What would you recommend Chany do?

3. Shmuel heard a story about a systems administrator who installed a type of malware that executed a week after he quit. The company hired him back, at double his salary, because they couldn't get anyone to fix the resulting issues and the company couldn't sustain any further downtime. Later, it came out that this systems administrator was behind it all. What type of malware do you tell Shmuel this is?

4. Laivy wants to know why NIST doesn't recommend frequent password changes or the requirements of multiple character sets. Can you explain why?

5. Sruli and Zalmy want to know what a stateful firewall is. What do you say to them?

Key Term Quiz

Use the terms in this list to complete the sentences that follow.

firewall   ransomware

humans   social engineering

longer

1. The locking and encrypting of systems is done with _____.

2. Someone posing as an IT support person and calling a user to get their user name and password is an example of _____.

3. Passwords that are _____ offer the best protection against brute-force attacks.

4. Any device that filters TCP/IP traffic based on IP address or port number, among other things, is, by definition, a _____.

5. The weakest link in any security implementation is/are _____.

Chapter 20

Network Monitoring

Lab Exercises

Setting up a network, establishing connectivity, and sharing resources is not the end of the list of responsibilities for network administrators. You can't just put a network on autopilot. Just like a human body requires monitoring by doctors, dentists, and entities, like scales and mirrors, a network needs to be constantly analyzed, scrutinized, and tweaked to ensure security and efficiency.

What traffic is entering the network? What traffic is leaving the network? How should firewalls that are either too permissive or too restrictive be modified? Is there anything malicious going on inside the network? Without proper monitoring, none of these questions can be answered.

 **20 MINUTES**

Lab Exercise 20.01: SNMP

Simple Network Management Protocol (SNMP) is the de facto network management protocol for TCP/IP networks. Hundreds of systems of different types (servers, routers, switches, etc.) can be monitored through a central point. However, simply using SNMP without understanding the differences in versions can lead to problems because each version adds something new. SNMP has evolved substantially since its initial version.

Learning Objectives

In this lab exercise, you'll research SNMP. By the end of this lab exercise, you'll be able to

- Explain the differences between the different versions on SNMP

Lab Materials and Setup

The materials you'll need for this lab exercise are

- *Mike Meyers' CompTIA Network+ Guide to Managing and Troubleshooting Networks* textbook
- Internet access

Getting Down to Business

Protocols evolve over time for many reasons. Sometimes, they evolve for efficiency purposes. Other times, they evolve for security purposes. Networks and their uses are constantly changing over time. A version of a protocol that was used many years ago might not be robust enough for modern networks today.

Jonathan thinks it would be a good idea for you to take a look at the official RFCs and learn how SNMP has evolved over the years. Open up a browser, and head to http://www.tcpipguide.com/free/t_TCPIPInternetStandardManagementFrameworkandSNMPSta.htm.

Using the RFC numbers in the tables, go to the actual RFC to research further. For example, for RFC 1901, go to https://datatracker.ietf.org/doc/html/rfc1901. Then, change the RFC number at the end of the URL to move to another RFC listed in a table.

Use this technique or other pages from the tcpipguide.com Web site to answer the questions in the following steps.

Step 1   What was the biggest weakness of SNMPv1?

✔ **Hint**

Check out https://datatracker.ietf.org/doc/html/rfc3410.

Step 2   How many different variations of SNMPv2 are there, what are the differences between them, and which one is the one used and referred to?

✔ **Hint**

In addition to the tables at http://www.tcpipguide.com/free/t_TCPIPInternetStandardManagementFrameworkandSNMPSta.htm, check out http://www.tcpipguide.com/free/t_SNMPVersion2SNMPv2MessageFormats.htm.

Step 3   Why should SNMPv3 be the only version used today?

 30 MINUTES

Lab Exercise 20.02: Performance Monitor and Event Viewer

Along with staying on top of the network documentation, technology, and network applications such as e-mail and Internet, it is the responsibility of the network team (often the entry-level network tech) to ensure the continued performance of network components and connectivity. Is the Internet connectivity slowing to a crawl when all of the users are accessing Web sites to complete their tasks? Can upper management use the video conferencing system without experiencing lags in both video and audio data?

Obviously, the initial design of the network must take into account the needs of the users as well as the business application being serviced. If you are designing a system for an organization that expects lots of traffic, the network design should take into account concurrent connections, load balancing, and overall bandwidth. Even small network installations can benefit from careful design and monitoring of the network's performance.

After the initial design is complete, the network tech should establish a baseline of the performance under "normal load," that is, the normal daily use of the network when the business is performing normal operating procedures. The network should then be measured under times of extreme usage to determine bottlenecks, the devices that will hold back the performance when driven to their operating capacities. Is one server being overused? Is the bandwidth enough for the organization when it is in full swing?

Various tools are included with most of the popular operating systems, as well as benchmark test engines from third-party developers. As usual, Microsoft provides many utilities as part of their various operating systems. You are now going to explore two of these tools in Windows 10: Performance Monitor and Event Viewer.

There are other tools, including MRTG, PRTG, Cacti, Nagios, and more (see https://ipcisco.com/network-monitoring/) that use RRDtool (round-robin database tool) to track interfaces, CPU, memory, and more, on routers, switches, and even servers. The RRD tools take readings at periodic intervals (for example, every two minutes), which are reported on an hourly graph. Those times are summarized into a daily graph, and then data from daily graphs are summarized into a monthly graph. This provides you with baseline data and current data to help see where your network systems may be deviating from normal.

Learning Objectives

In this lab exercise, you'll explore Performance Monitor and Event Viewer. By the end of this lab exercise, you'll be able to

- Create a baseline of a system under normal load

- Stress a system and record the change in performance

- Explore the various logs created in Event Viewer

Lab Materials and Setup

The materials you'll need for this lab exercise are

- *Mike Meyers' CompTIA Network+ Guide to Managing and Troubleshooting Networks* textbook

- Windows 10 system

Getting Down to Business

To develop a baseline for the performance of an entire organization, you'll need to monitor and record all of the critical devices during a time of "normal load," or normal operation. Then, during times of increased activity, you can capture additional data on these devices, store the information in log reports, and compare the data captured during normal load to that of the high-stress load. This will help you identify bottlenecks, providing direction on where the next equipment updates are needed.

Jonathan knows the importance of guaranteeing performance to the network users, and that is one of his responsibilities. He recommends that you use the Networking Lab to experiment with the Performance Monitor tool that is included with every version of the Windows operating system.

→ **Note**

> Over the years, Microsoft has called the performance monitoring tool by many names; System Monitor, Performance Monitor, Reliability and Performance Monitor, and just Performance have all seen the light of day. Depending on the version of Windows you are using, there will be slight differences in implementation, but all versions will allow you to create a log of various objects and counters.

Step 1 In the Windows search box, type **perfmon**, right-click Performance Monitor, and select Run As Administrator to open the Performance Monitor utility in Windows 10.

Step 2 Performance Monitor can show and record statistics about almost anything happening inside the computer. Select Performance Monitor under the Monitoring Tools. You can customize the collection of counters by clicking the green + symbol in the main pane or pressing CTRL-N to add a counter (see Figure 20-1).

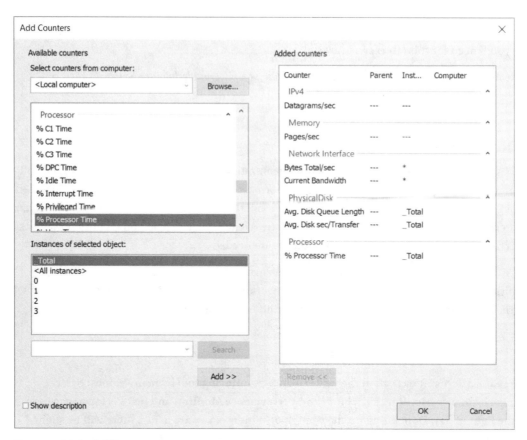

FIGURE 20-1 Adding counters

Using either method, add the following objects and counters (click the down arrow for specific counters for each object):

Object	Instance	Counter
IPv4	N/A	Datagrams/sec
Network Interface	<All Instances>	Bytes Total/sec
		Current Bandwidth
Memory	N/A	Pages/sec
Physical Disk	Total	Avg. Disk Queue Length
		Avg. Disk sec/Transfer
Processor	Total	% Processor Time

Once you have added the counters, you should see a graphic representation of the current usage of each of the objects and counters displayed in Performance Monitor, similar to Figure 20-2. What are some of the values for your system?

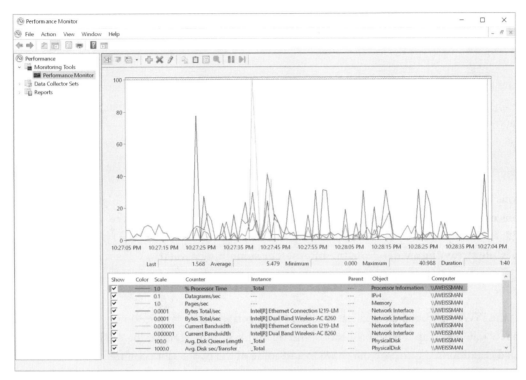

FIGURE 20-2 Performance Monitor

Step 3 Using Performance Monitor to view current transient data is great if you have a specific slowdown that you are trying to diagnose, but if you want to create baselines and peak usage reports, you'll have to create a data collector set. This will be used to collect data over an extended period of time, which you can then use to create reports of network usage.

To use the current objects and counters for your data collector set, right-click Performance Monitor in the left-hand pane and select New | Data Collector Set. Name the data collector set **JSW Baseline** and click Next | Next. When prompted, select Start This Data Collector Set Now and click Finish.

Step 4 Allow the data collector set to run for a few minutes, and then in the Data Collector Sets folder, expand User Defined and right-click JSW Baseline. Select Stop from the drop-down menu. This will create a system monitor log under Reports | User Defined | JSW Baseline | System Monitor. You may have to add some of the objects and counters that you captured, such as the Network Interface: Bytes Total/sec, as they may not appear in the default report. Record some of the average performance data.

Step 5   Create a second data collector set and name it **JSW High Load**. Before you launch the data capture, run the following activities on your system: Go to https://www.youtube.com/Weissman52, and open multiple videos in different tabs. Start streaming from other sites as well.

> ✔ **Tech Tip**
>
> The actions in Step 5 really test your Internet connection and may not produce "high load" conditions on the local devices such as the hard disk drive or NIC. To increase the overall load, you could, for example, set up a network share on another system and download large files across the LAN while streaming a video from the Internet, or something similar.

Now start the JSW High Load data collector set and let it run while the applications are performing their duties. After a few minutes, stop the data collection and open the System Monitor log to view the performance during high-load conditions. Again, you may have to add some of the objects and counters that are not displayed in the default report. Record some of the performance data. How does it compare to the baseline?

Step 6   Event Viewer has been around almost as long as Windows and provides various logs, the most common ones being Application, Security, and System. Further specialized events such as DHCP, DNS, Active Directory, and more, are included with Microsoft Windows Server operating systems.

In the Windows search box type **Event Viewer**, click on Event Viewer, expand the Windows Logs section, and explore some of the Application, Security, and System logs (see Figure 20-3).

Record a few items from your system's information, warnings, errors, and audit failures from each of the three sections.

 **30 MINUTES**

Lab Exercise 20.03: SIEM

Security information and event management (SIEM) represents software products and services that combine security information management (SIM) and security event management (SEM). SIEM technology provides real-time analysis of security alerts generated by network hardware and applications. SIEM is sold as software, appliances, or managed services and is also used to log security data and generate reports for compliance purposes. Jonathan asks you to find a good product that JSW can use.

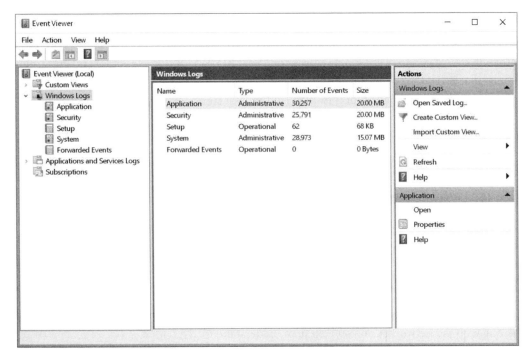

FIGURE 20-3 Event Viewer

Learning Objectives

In this lab exercise, you'll explore various SIEMs. By the end of this lab exercise, you'll be able to

- Understand how SIEM works

- Understand the need for SIEM

- Explore various components of a SIEM product

- Make a recommendation for a specific SIEM product

Lab Materials and Setup

The materials you'll need for this lab exercise are

- *Mike Meyers' CompTIA Network+ Guide to Managing and Troubleshooting Networks* textbook

- Internet access

Getting Down to Business

EventTracker Log Manager is one of many different SIEM solutions. *SC Magazine* named Log Manager the Best Buy product in SIEM for 2014 and awarded it a perfect 5-Star rating in the 2016 UTM-SIEM annual product Group Test review. Therefore, Jonathan wants you to investigate this product, to both understand the concept of SIEM better and possibly make a recommendation for purchase.

Let's not waste any time! Jump right into it.

Step 1   Jonathan instructs you to do a Google search for **"best SIEM"** (with the quotes) and go through some of the results that review the top SIEM products. He asks you to comb through them carefully and take notes so that you can make a recommendation to JSW (in the next step).

Step 2   Explain, in great detail, the top three solutions and capabilities that make the most sense for JSW. Recall that JSW is a mid-sized IT consulting firm with clients of all sizes.

Lab Analysis

1.   Tova and Marc want you to give them a quick explanation of why SNMP is such a valuable protocol. Explain it to them.

2.   Joey and Sara G. want to understand why taking baseline measurements is important, even if nothing is wrong with the network. Can you help them understand this?

3.   Sara E. and Robert have been trying to understand the purpose of SIEM but still have some uncertainty. How would you explain it to make it clear?

Key Term Quiz

Use the terms in this list to complete the sentences that follow.

logs   SIEM

objects   SNMPv3

1.   _____ improves upon its predecessors by adding encryption.

2.   _____ combines information management and security event management.

3.   Event Viewer's _____ can be used to analyze certain types of events that occurred on the network.

4.   Processor, Memory, and Physical Disk are considered _____ in Performance Monitor.

Chapter 21
Network Troubleshooting

Lab Exercises

The skills and processes you'll need to learn and refine to troubleshoot networks are referred to as an "art." The art of troubleshooting can be difficult to master. In order to hone your skills, you need to familiarize yourself with the terms and processes and to practice with the many network troubleshooting tools available, including both hardware and software tools.

 **30 MINUTES**

Lab Exercise 21.01: The Troubleshooting Process

When troubleshooting any problem, it is important to have a plan of attack to develop a solution to that problem. The CompTIA Network+ certification exam objectives set forth a methodology to troubleshoot networking issues and expect you to know these steps to troubleshoot network-related issues. As a network tech, you should not only commit these steps to memory but also work to master the art of troubleshooting, gradually applying simple to complex techniques to arrive at a solution.

The key to troubleshooting is to be mentally prepared when a problem arises. As with any skill, the best way to develop a troubleshooting technique is practice, practice, practice.

Learning Objectives

In this lab exercise, you'll review the troubleshooting process. By the end of this lab exercise, you'll be able to

- Identify the steps of the troubleshooting process

- Describe what each process does

- Develop a number of basic probing questions

Lab Materials and Setup

The materials you'll need for this lab exercise are

- *Mike Meyers' CompTIA Network+ Guide to Managing and Troubleshooting Networks* textbook

- Internet access

Getting Down to Business

You have now been working with Jonathan for a number of months. After watching him troubleshoot network issues, you would like to know how he seems to be able to fix problems fairly quickly. Jonathan explains that it is one thing to know how to use the hardware and software tools, but it is another thing to know when to use them.

He explains that troubleshooting network issues is like learning to play a musical instrument—it is much easier if there is a process to follow, and you must practice as well.

✖ Cross-Reference

Before performing this lab exercise, re-read the section titled "The Troubleshooting Process" in Chapter 21 of the *Mike Meyers' CompTIA Network+ Guide to Managing and Troubleshooting Networks* textbook.

Step 1 The following is a list of the steps to properly troubleshoot a problem. Place a number beside each step to indicate the order in which the steps should be performed.

	Test the theory to determine the cause.
	Document findings, actions, outcomes, and lessons learned.
	Identify the problem.
	Implement the solution or escalate as necessary.
	Establish a theory of probable cause.
	Verify full system functionality and, if applicable, implement preventative measures.
	Establish a plan of action to resolve the problem and identify potential effects.

Step 2 You have been asked by Jonathan to give a brief explanation of each step in the troubleshooting process. Record a brief description of each step.

Step 3 During the "Identify the problem" phase of the troubleshooting process, you'll need to be prepared with some questions that you can ask users to help identify the problem. List five potential questions you could ask a user after they complain about not having Internet access.

✔ Hint

The troubleshooting process and basic questioning techniques are not unique to the IT industry or to networking. If you conduct a Google search, you can augment the basic questions you may find in the textbook. Search for terms like "basic troubleshooting questions."

 30 MINUTES

Lab Exercise 21.02: Hardware Troubleshooting Tools

When troubleshooting network problems, you'll utilize hardware tools to help identify physical issues with the network. The hardware tools will help you identify and correct problems with the physical components of the network, such as network cabling, connectors, and physical connectivity.

Learning Objectives

In this lab exercise, you'll explore information about hardware troubleshooting tools. By the end of this lab exercise, you'll be able to

- Identify the various tools used to work with the physical components of a network

- Contrast the different tools you would use to troubleshoot the physical network and the tools you would use to assemble and repair the physical components of the network

Lab Materials and Setup

The materials you'll need for this lab exercise are

- *Mike Meyers' CompTIA Network+ Guide to Managing and Troubleshooting Networks* textbook

- Internet access

Getting Down to Business

Bonnie, one of the other network techs at JSW, is helping one of her friends outside of work with a small office upgrade. They are upgrading old cabling to Cat 6A and running a piece of fiber-optic cable between two buildings. She invites you to tag along for the experience and recommends that you put together a list of some of the tools you should have on hand and asks you to review the function of each of the tools.

Step 1   In the following mix-and-match exercise, identify the description that corresponds with each hardware tool by recording the correct letter.

Tool	Description
A. Time domain reflectometer (TDR)	_____ Used to capture and analyze network traffic
B. Butt set	_____ Can tell you how much voltage is on the line
C. Protocol analyzer	_____ Removes the insulation from a cable, exposing the conductor
D. Certifier	_____ Can identify where a break in copper cable is

Tool	Description
E. Temperature monitor	_____ Places UTP wires into a 66- or 110-block
F. Multimeter	_____ Can identify if the cable is handling its rated capacity
G. Punchdown tool	_____ Used to firmly connect RJ-45 connectors to Cat cables
H. Cable tester	_____ Can identify where a break in fiber cable is
I. Tone and probe	_____ Can indicate if there is continuity between the two ends of a wire
J. Optical time domain reflectometer (OTDR)	_____ Can tap into a 66- or 110-block to see if a particular line is working
K. Cable stripper	_____ Can help you locate a particular cable
L. Crimping tool	_____ Can be used to monitor and ensure the temperature level

Step 2 Now, conduct a Google search for each of the tools listed and provide the name of one or two popular manufacturers. Make note of whether the tool is primarily an assembly/repair tool or is typically used to verify/troubleshoot connectivity issues.

Tool	Manufacturer/Product	Typical Use
Time domain reflectometer (TDR)		
Butt set		
Protocol analyzer		
Certifier		
Temperature monitor		
Multimeter		
Punchdown tool		
Cable tester		
Tone and probe		
Optical time domain reflectometer (OTDR)		
Cable stripper		
Crimping tool		

 30 MINUTES

Lab Exercise 21.03: Software Troubleshooting Tools

When troubleshooting network problems, you first check the hardware aspects of the network—for example, making sure that everything is connected. After verifying that everything is connected, you then look to the visual indicators, such as the link light on the network card or the "online" light on the printer. What do you do after verifying that everything is physically in place and appears to be working?

The next step is to jump into the operating system and use some of the useful commands that you have learned that allow you to troubleshoot network problems!

Learning Objectives

In this lab exercise, you'll review the different Windows commands that are used to troubleshoot network problems. By the end of this lab exercise, you'll be able to

- Verify your IP addresses
- Verify MAC addresses
- Verify connectivity to other systems
- Verify that DNS is working
- View socket information

Lab Materials and Setup

The materials you'll need for this lab exercise are

- *Mike Meyers' CompTIA Network+ Guide to Managing and Troubleshooting Networks* textbook
- Windows 10 system with Internet access

Getting Down to Business

Crafton calls you over to his desk and appears to be very frustrated. He can't seem to get to a particular Web site and wants you to show him some of the tools he can use to verify network connectivity.

Step 1 Verify that the system has an IP address.

Step 2 Verify that the system is configured with DNS server IP addresses and a default gateway IP address.

Step 3 Verify that the system can communicate with its DNS servers and default gateway.

Step 4 Examine the IP/MAC address bindings the system knows about.

Step 5 Check out the path packets take to www.google.com.

Step 6 Find the IPv4 and IPv6 addresses of www.rit.edu.

Step 7 See all sockets on the system.

 **30 MINUTES**

Lab Exercise 21.04: Vulnerability Scanning

With the heightened need for cybersecurity, maintaining and troubleshooting the various components that can compromise the network's security will continue to be the focus of the skilled network technician. Nmap (Network Mapper) is a wonderful tool that is most known as a port scanner, but it also allows you to create a virtual map of the devices on your network with host names, MAC addresses, IP addresses, OSs, and more.

The Nmap suite of tools also includes Zenmap, a GUI front end for Nmap. It allows you to scan your network, examine the network map, and view some of the detailed information related to the devices on your network, all from a convenient GUI interface. Zenmap is an excellent tool for troubleshooting in addition to vulnerability scanning!

Learning Objectives

In this lab exercise, you'll install and run Nmap – Zenmap. By the end of this lab exercise, you'll be able to

- Run Nmap – Zenmap with different setups
- Compare the output in each case

Lab Materials and Setup

The materials you'll need for this lab exercise are

- *Mike Meyers' CompTIA Network+ Guide to Managing and Troubleshooting Networks* textbook
- Internet access
- Windows 10 system and a few other systems (wired or wireless) running on the same network
- Network switch and cabling if the other systems are using Ethernet

Getting Down to Business

To generate a more realistic scenario, Jonathan recommends that you use the systems and devices in the Networking Lab to construct a simple network consisting of one or two client systems, one or two servers, and a wireless router. You can then run Nmap – Zenmap and use the data to perform a vulnerability assessment and troubleshoot.

Take a few moments, build the small network, and then launch Nmap – Zenmap and commence your exploration!

Step 1   To begin your exploration of your network and the Nmap – Zenmap network mapping tool, you'll first download the installation files from Nmap's Web site.

- **a.**   Go to https://nmap.org/ and click the Download hyperlink on the left.
- **b.**   On the download page, scroll down to the Microsoft Windows binaries section and navigate to the Latest Stable Release Self-Installer, and then click the nmap-7.92-setup.exe hyperlink (current at the time of writing). The Nmap executable installation file will download to your Downloads folder.

Step 2   Use the following instructions to install Nmap – Zenmap:

- **a.**   Launch the Nmap Setup program nmap-7.92-setup.exe.
- **b.**   Click the I Agree button on the License Agreement screen.
- **c.**   Verify that all of the components are checked, and click Next.
- **d.**   Select the destination location (the default location is fine) and click the Install button.

e. At the License Agreement for Npcap 1.55 Setup (current at the time of writing), a separate dialog box will pop up. Click the I Agree button.

f. Click the Install button on the next screen in the Npcap 1.55 Setup screen.

g. When the Npcap installation completes, click the Next > button.

h. On the next screen, click the Finish button.

i. Back in the Nmap Setup wizard, click the Next > button.

j. Keep or remove the checks in the checkboxes for shortcuts and click the Next > button.

k. Click the Finish button.

Step 3 Now launch the Nmap – Zenmap application by double-clicking the icon on the desktop (use the search box if you didn't create shortcuts). In the Target dialog box, type the Network ID of the IP address and an * for the Host ID, such as **192.168.1.***. This will scan all hosts on the 192.168.1.0/24 network. Click the Scan button to begin the process, as shown in Figure 21-1.

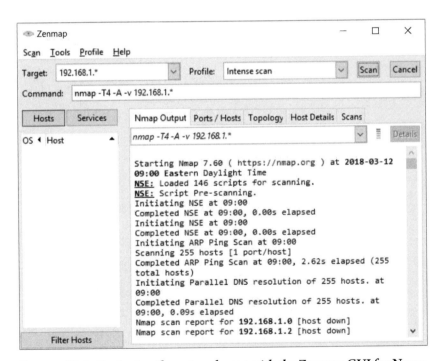

FIGURE 21-1 Beginning the network scan with the Zenmap GUI for Nmap

→ **Note**

You may see a popup that says "Windows Defender Firewall has blocked some features of this app."
If so, click the Allow Access button.

Step 4   After the scan of your network completes, you should have a list of devices (depending on how
many systems you have running) and a large amount of data (scanned addresses, scanned ports, operating
system types, etc.). When the scan completes, click the Topology tab and then click the Fisheye tab. Your
display should look similar to the network map shown in Figure 21-2.

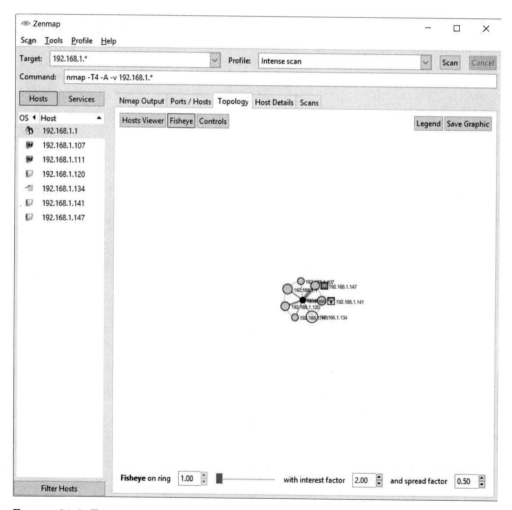

FIGURE 21-2 Zenmap-generated network map

Step 5   Next, select one of the remote Windows systems. This will be the target system. Configure the firewall to block all incoming connections as follows:

    a.   Open Windows Defender Firewall by typing **Firewall** into the search box and selecting Windows Defender Firewall.

    b.   Select Turn Windows Defender Firewall On Or Off from the pane on the left.

    c.   In the Customize Settings screen, confirm that Windows Defender Firewall is turned on for both Private network settings and Public network settings. Put a check in the checkboxes in each section (Private network settings and Public network settings) next to Block All Incoming Connections, Including Those In The List Of Allowed Apps, as shown in Figure 21-3, and click the OK button.

▦ **6c**

Step 6   Now, to scan the specific Windows system you configured in Step 5 (the target system), open Nmap – Zenmap on the system you installed it on, and complete the following steps:

    a.   Enter the IP address for the system that you just configured into the Target dialog box.

    b.   Click the Scan button and let the scan complete.

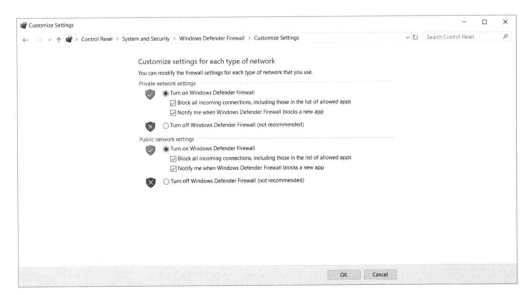

FIGURE 21-3 Windows Defender Firewall

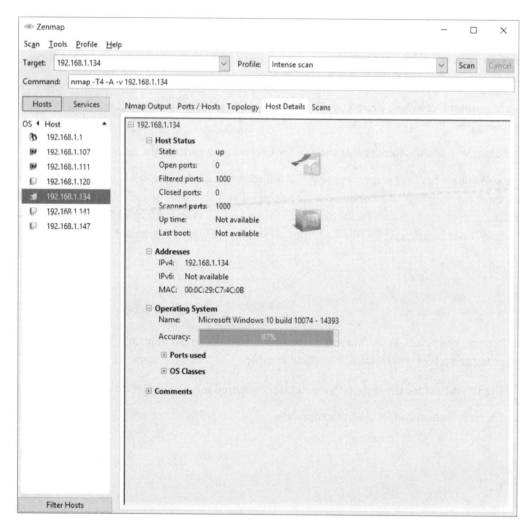

FIGURE 21-4 Zenmap Host details after the scan of a Windows 10 system with Windows Defender Firewall enabled

Select the Host Details tab and note the following information (see Figure 21-4):

Operating System icon	
Open ports	
Filtered ports	
Closed ports	
Security icon	

✔ **Hint**

The Zenmap GUI front end includes a number of icons to indicate which operating system is installed on the system that has been scanned. Zenmap also includes icons that indicate the status of the security of the system, based on the number of open ports. A full list of the icons along with additional information can be found in the *Zenmap GUI Users' Guide* at https://nmap.org/book/zenmap-results.html.

The following list is a simple description of the security icons:

Safe icon: 0–2 open ports

Chest icon: 3–4 open ports

Open Box icon: 5–6 open ports

Swiss Cheese icon: 7–8 open ports

Bomb icon: 9 or more open ports

Step 7 Now, on the target system, back in the Customize Settings screen, in both sections (Private network settings and Public network settings), uncheck the checkboxes for Block All Incoming Connections, Including Those In The List Of Allowed Apps to unfilter some of the ports, and click the OK button. Scan the target system again and note the following information:

Operating System icon	
Open ports	
Filtered ports	
Closed ports	
Security icon	

How do your results compare to those shown in the previous step?

Step 8 Now, on the target system, back in the Customize Settings screen, in both sections (Private network settings and Public network settings), select the radio buttons next to Turn off Windows Defender Firewall

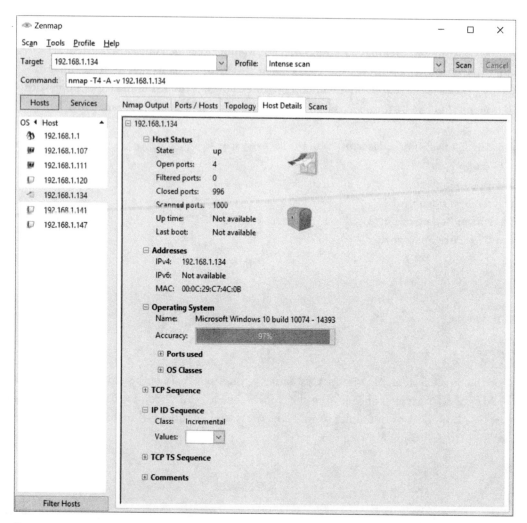

FIGURE 21-5 Zenmap Host details after the scan of a Windows 10 system with Windows Defender Firewall disabled

(not recommended) to completely disable Windows Defender Firewall. Scan the target system again and note the following information (See Figure 21-5):

Operating System icon	
Open ports	
Filtered ports	
Closed ports	
Security icon	

How do your results compare to those shown in the previous two steps?

Lab Analysis

1. Laura has often used a multimeter to check the voltages of a PC's power supply, especially when a component is not working. How can she use a multimeter to help troubleshoot network problems?

2. Emily wants to know the difference in when you'd use `ping` and when you'd use `tracert`. Can you help her out?

3. Tasneem is exploring the `nslookup` utility. She would like to know what it's used for. What would you say?

4. Janet is running a monthly security check on the office network. One of the tools she is using is a port scanner. What is the purpose of a port scanner?

5. Wendy, after studying the steps that CompTIA recommends when troubleshooting networks, wonders if she will actually apply this technique when she is troubleshooting a real problem. Why is it important to know the troubleshooting process?

Key Term Quiz

Use the terms in this list to complete the sentences that follow.

`arp -a`	netstat
certifier	Nmap
`ipconfig /all`	port scanner

1. The _____ command will display your system's MAC address.

2. If you want to analyze a remote system for open ports that may allow for security breaches, you can use _____.

3. The _____ command displays a mapping of two addresses.

4. To see sockets your system is involved in, use the _____ utility.

5. A(n) _____ is responsible for testing a cable to ensure that it can handle its rated capacity.

Index

NUMBERS

A

B

C

D